Dad's A-Level Maths Complex Numbers

The Fantastic Numbers

Andreas Koutras, PhD, FRM

Differential Publishing

Cover Photo by ESA/Hubble & NASA, W. Harris, Acknowledgement: L. Shatz
Photo identifier: 2MASX J03193743+4137580 – Galaxy towards a Cluster of Galaxies

Art. No
ISBN 978-1-7393454-0-2
Edition 1.0

Cover design by AK

Published by Differential Publishing
Printed by Amazon

Contents

To my boys, Philippos and Nikolaos-Petros

Summary
This book is an introduction to the fantastic Complex numbers for high school students (A-Level, International Baccalaureate etc.) who want to have a more formal introduction to the subject. It is aimed at the pupil who wants to dig deeper, or wants to follow a career in Mathematics or Mathematical Physics and as such it is sometimes rather more demanding. The content of the book and the level of exercises can also serve those who prepare for specialised entry exams that many Universities now demand. It also makes a good entry point for those who want to enter into mathematical competitions or simply want to have fun.

The book introduces all the standard topics, starting from how Complex numbers were first discovered, the algebra of Complex numbers to the geometry of the Wessel-Argand plane. Euler's famous identity, the nth-root of unity and complex functions like e^z, $\sin z$ and $\ln z$ as well as topics, like the Matrix representation of Complex numbers and the Riemann stereographic projection are presented. I have included many questions together with hints and answers. Most of these questions make regular appearance in high school exams.

Acknowledgements
I am grateful to the OCR Examination Board for permission to reproduce questions from past examination papers.
I am grateful to Cambridge Assessment Admissions Testing for permission to reproduce questions from past STEP (Sixth Term Examination Paper) examination papers.
I have also included some exam questions from long extinct examination boards like, AEB, UL, JMB, C. I thank them.
Whenever solutions to any exam questions are given, these are not in any way model or official answers for the respective official exams but my own solutions.
I would also like to express my sincere thanks to Dr John O'Connor for allowing me to use biographical information from the School of Mathematics and Statistics, University of St Andrews, website
https://mathshistory.st-andrews.ac.uk/. It is a goldmine of information.
Many of the figures in the book were drawn using GeoGebra.

I am also grateful to Philippos and Nikolaos for many corrections and suggestions. Inevitably, and despite my best efforts, mistakes and typos will be found in the text. If you find them please email them to
TheFantasticNumbers AT gmail.com
together with any suggestions for improvements.

AK

Preface

> Times are bad. Children no longer obey their parents, and everyone is writing a book.
>
> Marcus Tullius Cicero, (106-43 B.C.)

The Pandemic
This book grew out of the Covid pandemic. During the multiple lockdowns home schooling became very important and like many parents, I decided to help my children with their mathematics. I was not completely clueless, as some 30 years ago, one of my first jobs after completing my PhD was teaching A-level mathematics. I was very rusty but I had time and enthusiasm.

Why don't you write a book?
As any parent would testify, teaching your own kids is very hard. After many unsuccessful attempts, I decided that the best way was to write notes in LaTeX and email them. LaTeX is the unsurpassed software for scientific writing. It produces beautifully type-setted equations and beauty is very important in Mathematics. That strategy worked better. It was then that my son suggested of turning the notes into a book. I fancied the idea, but writing a textbook is not easy. It is a bit like people saying "You cook well, why don't you open a restaurant?". Writing a book and especially a mathematics book is not an easy task for seasoned mathematicians. Much harder for a rusty amateur like me. I nevertheless decided to do it and call it Dad's mathematics.

Maths versus Procedural Maths
I surveyed some of the recommended textbooks but found most of them not to my taste. After all, I am rather old fashioned. Many books resemble recipe books. Just a set of rules to be followed. A sort of of HAYNES OWNERS WORKSHOP MANUAL for mathematics. This serves well students that want to pass an exam, but this aim is not equivalent to comprehending the subject. For instance, I always found hard to fathom how one can do derivatives but skip the concept of the limit. Anyway, the intention was not just to write another recipe book for solving problems. There are plenty of those around. I wanted the book to serve both the purpose of passing the exam but also to pass on the mathematical ideas and concepts. I wanted exam success, but more importantly, I wanted the reader to get at least a glimpse of the beauty of mathematics. I hope I have succeeded in that aim.

Mathematics is not easy. It is a hard subject that requires a lot of thinking and huge amount of imagination. But in the past few decades, the trend was for Mathematics to be taught as a secondary subject to the other sciences. Gone are the proofs and the intriguing shapes of Euclidean geometry. Maths is taught and examined using what is known as the "Procedural way".

Pupils are given a recipe on how to solve an equation and afterwards, they are examined on boilerplate questions. They only have to apply the formula correctly with some very simple algebraic manipulation. No wonder many found mathematics boring and without any purpose.
Most, if not all of the exam questions, can now be done by Computer Algebra systems like "MapleSoft" or "Wolfram-Mathematica" or by artificial intelligence algorithms and this makes many pupils think that it is a useless subject. Machines can do it better and faster many say. So, why bother? I heard this argument before, in fact, 40 years ago, when the personal calculator was first introduced. Why bother learning arithmetic when it can be done more accurately with a calculator. Why bother learning long division etc.

The reason for these legitimate questions is because most people think that mathematics is something to do with adding numbers and nothing else. A skill, that like many other skills can be done by computers. That is partially true. Of course there is a practical side to it. However, mathematics is more about patterns and structures. Numbers are just one of the tools to discover these patterns and structures. Another one is geometry as is music.

I decided that the best approach was a mixture of the old school mathematics that emphasizes proof and rigour together with many explanations and examples that illustrate the "why" of the many theorems. Proofs and definitions can sometimes be very dry. One of the many enigmas that students of mathematics have is the "why this or that definition". Many mathematical concepts are introduced by definitions that seem to come out of a rabbit-hat. The truth of course, is that definitions of mathematical objects have a long evolutionary history before they assume the final form in a textbook. I tried, wherever I could, to illuminate that process by adding historical facts about them.

Andreas
London, Apr 2023

To The Student

> Young men should prove theorems, old men should write books.
>
> G. H. Hardy

The book tries to strike a balance between theory and problem solving. By that, I mean that most theorems or propositions are proved rather than stated. I use mathematical notation extensively. It is not only economical but also the proper way to convey mathematical ideas. Mathematical notation and number notation has played and is still playing, a very important role in the development of mathematical ideas. It compacts concepts and makes them easier to understand and work with. This is the language on Mathematics.

··· – – – ··· **Notes**
Scattered throughout the text are DAD'S SOS NOTES. These Save Our Selves notes contain, problem tips, interesting facts about the topic or extensions. Do not pass them. They contain essential info that may prove useful in an exam.

There are many solved exercises of various difficulty. I have tried to give solved examples to the most frequently asked exam questions. Try to do as many as possible if you want to prepare for an exam.

15 Second Questions.
Most exam questions can be classified into two categories. The first category, is the 15 second question and the second, is the 5 minute question. Many exam questions are 15 second questions. Obviously, I do not mean that you will finish the question in 15 seconds. By a 15 second question, I describe questions that once read, it will take you 15 seconds or less, to figure out what needs to be done. These are mostly procedural questions and they aim to test your knowledge of the syllabus not your mathematical prowess. In this category you also have questions that you have seen or solved before. After the initial 15 seconds, it is the execution that takes time. And you will need to be good at this. This is where practice becomes important, to lessen the various trivial errors that we all make. Your aim should be to move, as many as possible of the questions, in the 15 second category. One of the aims of this book is to help you do this.

5 Minute Questions.
There are also the 5 minute questions. These are the kind of questions that after few minutes you still have no clue how to proceed. Most of

these questions have a key that once discovered they fall like ripe fruit. Sometimes, the key is given in the first part of the question. If not, then you may need to try few approaches and use your intuition to decide on the best one. If you get into very messy algebra, this is usually a sign of a dead end. Always look for clues in the actual phrasing of the question. For example, why is there a restriction to positive values only or a variable is non-zero? Perhaps you need to divide by that variable. Why does it say, find the solutions and not the solution? Are there more than one? Did you solve a quadratic and got a $\sqrt{63}$? Check again. Could it be that it is $\sqrt{64} = 8$? Usually, but not always, questions are arranged in such a way so as to give exact numbers.

As many exams test speed as well as knowledge it is very important to have banked enough time in the 15 seconds questions so that you can tackle the 5 minute question with time comfort. That usually is the difference between a good grade and a high grade.

There is no substitute in maths for doing problems. You do not learn (or enjoy) mathematics by reciting theorems or lemmas. The only way is to do as many problems as you can. Your enjoyment would increase massively after a while.

There is a variety of reasons why you picked Mathematics at high school. It may be because it is a prerequisite for studying economics, engineering, computer science or some other subject that needs technical and numerate skills. Or, it may be because you enjoy solving fun puzzles and find mathematics easy or that you are completely intrigued by the mathematical patterns and you wish to explore and discover more of them. Whatever the reason, I hope you will enjoy the trip to the Fantastic Land of the Fantastic Complex numbers and good luck to your exams.

Andreas
London, Apr 2023

Notation

The book uses the following mathematical notation/symbols.

$\Leftrightarrow$	Implies and is Implied
$\Rightarrow$	Implies
$\subset$	Subset of
$\{a, b, c\}$	Set with elements a, b, c
$\vee$	Logical OR
$\wedge$	Logical AND
$\in$	Belongs to a set
$\exists$	There Exists
$\equiv$	Equivalent expressions
$\neq$	Not equal to
$\mathbb{R}$	Set of Real Numbers
$\mathbb{Z}$	Set of Integers
$\mathbb{N}$	Set of Natural Numbers
$\mathbb{Q}$	Set of Rational Numbers
$\mathbb{C}$	Set of Complex Numbers
i	Square root of -1
$\Re(z)$	Real part of a complex number z
$\Im(z)$	Imaginary part of a complex number z
$\arg(z)$	Argument of a complex number z
$\mathrm{Arg}(z)$	Principal argument of a complex number z
z^*	The Complex conjugate of z
$\mathrm{Log}(z)$	Principal logarithm of z
$\square$	Halmos end of proof or answer to a question
$\gcd(m, n)$	Greatest Common Divisor of integers m and n
$\sim$	Similar shapes
$\triangle ABC$	A triangle with vertices A, B and C
$\square ABCD$	A square with vertices A, B, C and D
$\angle MNK$	An angle with the vertex on point N
$\sum_{k=1}^{n} a_k$	Sum of terms a_k. $\sum_{k=1}^{n} a_k = a_1 + a_2 + ... + a_k$
$\prod_{k=1}^{n} a_k$	Product of terms a_k. $\prod_{k=1}^{n} a_k = a_1 a_2 ... a_k$

1. Fantastic numbers

> Imaginary numbers are a fine and wonderful refuge of the divine spirit almost an amphibian between being and non-being.
>
> Leibniz

1.1 Imaginary Numbers

Complex numbers always came with some kind of mystique. The term "imaginary" numbers carries with it many such connotations. Leibniz's[1] quote that they are an *amphibian between being and non-being* is telling. In Greek they are called "fantastic", not because they are fantastic, which they are, but because the word "fantastic" in Greek also means ghostly or non-existent, fictions or constructs of our imagination!

So, what is it about complex numbers that is so out of this world? The short answer is nothing. Complex numbers are as real as the real numbers are, or as real as the natural numbers, the negative numbers or the irrational numbers. At some stage in the history of mathematics, the existence of various numbers was denied. Famously, the irrational numbers like $\sqrt{2}$ completely destroyed the Pythagoreans, who drowned anyone who revealed the secret of their existence.

The negative numbers were thought not to exist because numbers were associated with possession of quantities of objects and you could not possess negative quantity of objects. Negative numbers became accepted with the advent of accounting, when negative numbers were associated with debt, (I owe someone). As for the complex numbers, their existence and usefulness came about in the bitterly fought mathematical contests for solutions to the cubic equation in the 16th century renaissance Italy.

1.2 The Square Root of -1

In most textbooks the square root of -1 is introduced as the solution to the equation $x^2+1=0$. However, this is not how complex numbers where first found. This equation was thought not to have a solution at all. This should not be a surprise. If I asked you to solve $3x=5$, within the natural

[1] Gottfried Wilhelm von Leibniz 1646-1716, was a German mathematician who developed the present day notation for the differential and integral calculus though he never thought of the derivative as a limit.

numbers $\mathbb{N}$, in other words to find a solution that is a natural number, then the equation does not have a solution. Only if I consider the set of rational numbers $\mathbb{Q}$, does $3x = 5$ have a solution.

With complex numbers, it was the solution of the cubic provided by Cardano's[2] formula which showed that square roots of negative numbers not only exist, but are very useful as well. The following example was considered by Rafael Bombelli[3] almost 450 years ago.

It involves the solutions to the cubic equation:

$$x^3 = 15x + 4 \tag{1.1}$$

This innocent looking cubic has three real solutions. They are 4, $-2 \pm \sqrt{3}$ (see Figure 1.1) and they were all known to Bombelli.

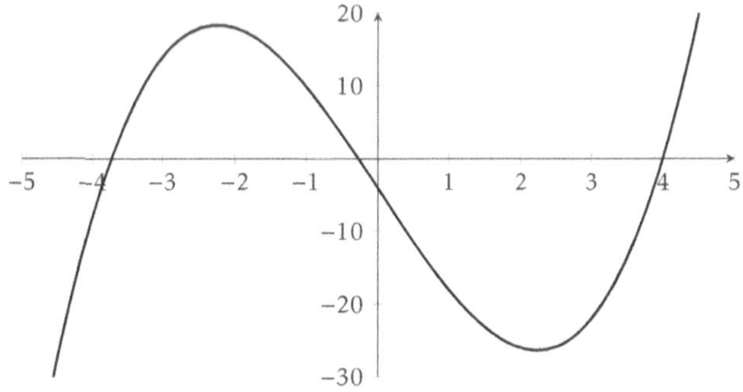

Figure 1.1: The cubic $x^3 = 15x + 4$ has three real solutions. Cardano's formula expresses the solution $x = 4$ with square roots of negative numbers.

On the other hand, applying Cardano's famous formula for the cubic, see Equation (B.10), Bombelli found that the solution $x = 4$ is expressed in terms of square roots of negative numbers!

$$x = \sqrt[3]{2 + \sqrt{-121}} + \sqrt[3]{2 - \sqrt{-121}} \tag{1.2}$$

What is going on? The root is a real number, but is written with the help of some strange or "fantastic" numbers! You can actually verify that this

[2]Girolamo Cardano 1501-1576, was an Italian doctor and mathematician who is famed for his work Ars Magna which was the first Latin treatise devoted solely to algebra. In it he gave the methods of solution of the cubic and quartic equations which he had learnt from Tartaglia.

[3]Rafael Bombelli 1526-1572, was an Italian mathematician who wrote an influential algebra text and made free use of both negative numbers and complex numbers.

solution is $x = 4$. If you place x=4 and cube the relation, then by using the identity $(a+b)^3 = a^3 + b^3 + 3ab(a+b)$ you will get:

$$\begin{aligned}
4^3 &= \left(\sqrt[3]{2+\sqrt{-121}}+\sqrt[3]{2-\sqrt{-121}}\right)^3 = 2+\sqrt{-121}+2-\sqrt{-121}+ \\
&\quad +3\left(\sqrt[3]{2+\sqrt{-121}}\right)\left(\sqrt[3]{2-\sqrt{-121}}\right)\left(\sqrt[3]{2+\sqrt{-121}}+\sqrt[3]{2-\sqrt{-121}}\right) \\
&= 4+\sqrt{-121}-\sqrt{-121}+12\left(\sqrt[3]{2+\sqrt{-121}}\right)\left(\sqrt[3]{2-\sqrt{-121}}\right) \\
&= 4+12\sqrt[3]{(2+\sqrt{-121})(2-\sqrt{-121})} \\
&= 4+12\sqrt[3]{4+2(+\sqrt{-121}-\sqrt{-121})-\sqrt{-121}\sqrt{-121}} \\
&= 4+12\sqrt[3]{4-\sqrt{-121}\sqrt{-121}} = 4+12\sqrt[3]{4-(-121)} = 4+12\sqrt[3]{125} = 64
\end{aligned}$$

The above calculation rests on two assumptions. The first assumption is that you can cancel out terms like $+\sqrt{-121}-\sqrt{-121}$. You can argue that whatever they are, since they have opposite sign it is a reasonable assumption to cancel them out.

The second assumption is that $\sqrt{-121}\sqrt{-121} = -121$. Now, that is a bit strange, but that is exactly what Rafael Bombelli did almost 450 hundred years ago. And by doing this, he not only obtained the correct result, $x = 4$ but more importantly he established the rules of addition and multiplication of complex numbers. We will formalise them in the next section.

This is how complex numbers were recognised and eventually became accepted. Cardano however, though he used them, apparently dismissed them as just pure trickery. For a long time complex numbers were seen as just a conjuring trick and not proper mathematics.

The case of the quadratic equation $x^2+1 = 0$ is, however, very different. Whilst, in the cubic solved by Cardano the end result was a real number and the square roots of negative numbers where seen simply as a trick, this is not the case for $x^2+1 = 0$. If we use the well known formula for the solution of the quadratic we get that

$$x = \pm\frac{\sqrt{-4}}{2} = \pm\sqrt{\frac{-4}{4}} = \pm\sqrt{-1}$$

Factorizing, using these two roots we get

$$(x-\sqrt{-1})(x+\sqrt{-1}) = x^2 + x(\sqrt{-1}-\sqrt{-1}) - (\sqrt{-1}\sqrt{-1}) = x^2+1 = 0$$

In the previous equation one can make Bombelli's assumption, namely, that whatever the $+\sqrt{-1}-\sqrt{-1}$ quantities are, since they have opposite sign they must cancel out. Similarly, if we use the rule $\sqrt{-1}\sqrt{-1}=-1$ for the last term, we get $x^2+1=0$. So the square root of -1 or indeed of any negative number is somewhat special.

> DAD'S SOS NOTE: Note that, one cannot join two square roots so as to make $\sqrt{-1}\sqrt{-1}=\sqrt{(-1)(-1)}=\sqrt{1}=1$. We can only join even roots if the radicants (numbers under the root) are positive. You can still do it if you have odd roots like a cubic but not with even roots (square, quartic etc). ♥

The square root of -1 appeared so often that a special symbol, $i=\sqrt{-1}$, was introduced by Euler[4] in 1777. We can then write any other square root of a negative number using the i-notation. For example, $\sqrt{-5}=\sqrt{-1}\sqrt{5}=i\sqrt{5}$.

> **Definition 1.1:** We denote the square root of -1 by the letter i. We thus have
>
> $$i=\sqrt{-1}\Rightarrow i^2=-1 \tag{1.3}$$

Exercise 1.1: (Powers of i.) Having defined $i=\sqrt{-1}\Rightarrow i^2=-1$ find

(i) i^3, i^4 and i^5

(ii) Finally, prove by induction that $i^{4n}=1$, $i^{4n+1}=i$, $i^{4n+2}=-1$ and $i^{4n+3}=-i$ for $n\in\mathbb{N}$.

Ans: For the powers of i we have $i^3=i^2i=-i$, $i^4=i^2i^2=-1(-1)=1$ and $i^5=i^4i=i$. In order to prove by induction that $i^{4n}=1$ for all $n\in\mathbb{N}$ we need to prove that it holds for $n=1$ (done it earlier) and assuming that it is true for $n=k$, namely $i^{4k}=1$, it also holds for $n=k+1$. Writing $i^{4(k+1)}=i^{4k}i^4=1\cdot1=1$ and therefore the relation holds true for all $n\in\mathbb{N}$. I leave the induction of the other cases as an easy exercise.
We thus have that the only possible set of solutions for the integer powers of i is $\{1,-1,i,-i\}$. We can similarly get the negative integer powers once we observe that $i^{-1}=1/i=i/i^2=-i$. □

[4] Leonhard Euler 1707-1783, was a Swiss mathematician who made enormous contributions to a wide range of mathematics and physics including analytic geometry, trigonometry, geometry, calculus and number theory.

DAD'S SOS NOTE: For any integer power of i the resulting set of solutions is $\{1, -1, i, -i\}$. No other possibilities exist. ♥

Some thoughts to ponder

- Clearly, $i = \sqrt{-1}$ is neither equal to -1 or to 1. So what is it?
- If it is a real number can I place it on the number line, as we have done with the irrational numbers like $\sqrt{2}$?
- Do complex numbers fill some hitherto unknown gaps on the number line?
- Can we built an algebra of complex numbers? By algebra, I mean operations like addition and multiplication and establish rules of how to handle them.
- The ancient Greeks thought of numbers as representing lengths. This is why they had difficulties with negative numbers. Do complex numbers have a similar interpretation? Can we order them like we order lengths? If not, what do we mean by the word "number"?

The answers to these questions would be given in the next few chapters. Starting from how to built an algebra of complex numbers using Bombelli's rules and then moving on how to think of them as "2-dimensional" numbers and represent them on a plane rather than on a line. For a more complete story on the discovery of the $\sqrt{-1}$ see Paul Nahin's book [8].

2. Algebra of Complex numbers

Everything is a number.
Πάντα κατ' αριθμόν γίγνονται.

Pythagoras

2.1 Adding Empirically Complex Numbers

It is clear that numbers involving the square root of negative numbers are a special kind of objects. But Bombelli showed how we can get meaningful results if we apply his rules.

Bombelli's cubic (1.1) strongly suggests how to deal algebraically with the new numbers. First, we separate the numbers into two parts. The first part is our normal Real numbers. The second part is all the expressions that have a $i = \sqrt{-1}$. When adding complex numbers, we add all the Real parts together and we also add all the i-parts together. In terms of the multiplication of two complex numbers, we should follow the normal rules as long as we are careful on how we treat the i and $i^2 = -1$ terms.

This splitting into two parts, a "Real part" and an "Imaginary part" proved extremely useful. By the way, the term "Imaginary" was coined by René Descartes[1] in his famous book La Geometrie. Complex numbers are like a pair of numbers (x, y). The first part x would be the real part and the second part y would be the imaginary part. This is why we sometimes say that complex numbers are 2-dimensional.

2.2 Defining Complex Numbers Axiomatically

Although complex numbers seem to be rather exceptional, when you look closely, they actually satisfy most of the properties of the Real numbers.

Detour to the Real numbers. In the case of the Real numbers, we define two operations, addition and multiplication and list the properties of adding and multiplying two Real numbers.
I know what you are thinking, "this is not how we learnt arithmetic in the school". You are correct. In early school years you learnt how to

[1] René Descartes, 1596-1650 was a French philosopher whose work, La Géométrie [4], includes his application of algebra to geometry from which we now have Cartesian geometry. His work had a great influence on both mathematicians and philosophers.

add and multiply empirically. But now, we need to be more systematic, in order to probe the various mathematical properties. When adding or multiplying real numbers, the order in which we do these operations doesn't matter. In other words, $a + b = b + a$ and $ab = ba$. This property is also known as "commutative". We also have that $a + (b + c) = (a + b) + c$ and $a(bc) = (ab)c$. Namely, the order of the brackets in the operations is immaterial. This property is also known as "associative". We also have a "zero element" (symbolised by "0") for addition, so that $a + 0 = a$ and a "unit element", (symbolised by "1"), for multiplication so that $1 \cdot a = a$ for all non-zero numbers. Moreover, we have the "distributive" property between the operations of multiplication and addition, $a(b + c) = ab + ac$. This property defines how the two operations interact with each other.

Dad's SOS Note: In the early 19th century, arithmetic was a rather empirical subject. By contrast, Euclidean geometry was a matured subject studied for more than 2000 years. And Euclidean geometry was rather exceptional as the whole subject was based on a minimal set of 5 axioms. Many great mathematicians tried to formalise arithmetic in the same way Euclid formalised geometry using the axiomatic approach. Namely, they tried to find the minimum number of axioms that can be used in arithmetic of natural numbers and eventually for Real numbers. The result was the greatest revolution in mathematics since Euclid and the birth of modern mathematics. Real numbers were defined from the rational numbers $\mathbb{Q}$, which in turn were defined from the Integers $\mathbb{Z}$ and the natural numbers $\mathbb{N}$. The various operations and their properties were investigated. We thus have

$$\mathbb{N} \to \mathbb{Z} \to \mathbb{Q} \to \mathbb{R} \to \mathbb{C}$$

or in terms of subsets

$$\mathbb{N} \subset \mathbb{Z} \subset \mathbb{Q} \subset \mathbb{R} \subset \mathbb{C}$$

♥

These properties carry over to the complex numbers. In fact, this should be rather intuitive, since we found them as roots of polynomial equations. It would be very strange to have the Real solution and the complex solutions behaving radically different.

DAD'S SOS NOTE: In this section we introduce the complex numbers using what is called as the "Axiomatic" approach. In other words, we begin by defining what we mean by a complex number and how addition and multiplication is defined. As explained in Section (1.2), this is not how Complex numbers were found or introduced. No one sat down one day and said, "I will now define a new mathematical object, called *complex numbers* and it would have such and such properties". The axiomatic approach came after the complex numbers where found as roots of cubic equations and fit them in the existing framework. In any case, it is all very intuitive and it is important to learn this approach because it systematizes mathematics and it gives a better understanding of the different mathematical structures. ♥

Definition 2.1: A complex number z is composed of two parts, a real part and an imaginary part.

$$z = a + i\,b, \quad a, b \in \mathbb{R} \tag{2.1}$$

The real part of the complex number z is a and the imaginary part is b. Sometimes it is also denoted by

$$\Re(z) = a, \quad \Im(z) = b$$

Be very careful here. The imaginary part of z, is b which is a real number. We leave the i out.

We also define equality of two complex numbers by

Definition 2.2: Two complex numbers $z_1 = a_1 + ib_1$ and $z_2 = a_2 + ib_2$ are equal

$$z_1 = z_2 \Leftrightarrow a_1 + ib_1 = a_2 + ib_2 \Leftrightarrow (a_1 = a_2 \land b_1 = b_2) \tag{2.2}$$

In other words if two complex numbers are equal then their real and imaginary parts are equal. The symbol $\land$ stands for the logical "AND" operation in mathematics, meaning both conditions must be true.

Time now to set the rules of complex algebra as suggested by our examples.

Definition 2.3: We define the addition of two complex numbers $z_1 = a_1 + ib_1$ and $z_2 = a_2 + ib_2$ as

$$z_1 + z_2 = (a_1 + a_2) + i(b_1 + b_2) \tag{2.3}$$

In other words, we are adding the real parts and the imaginary parts of the complex numbers to get a new complex number.

Exercise 2.1: Let $z_1 = 3 + 5i$ and $z_2 = 7 - 3i$. Find $z_1 + z_2$.
Ans: $z_1 + z_2 = 3 + 5i + 7 - 3i = (3 + 7) + i(5 - 3) = 10 + 2i$. □

Definition 2.4: We define the multiplication of two complex number $z_1 = a_1 + ib_1$ and $z_2 = a_2 + ib_2$ as

$$z_1 z_2 = (a_1 a_2 - b_1 b_2) + i(a_1 b_2 + a_2 b_1) \tag{2.4}$$

The rule is nothing more than applying the usual multiplication taking into account that $i^2 = -1$.

Using these definitions we can prove the following properties for any complex numbers regarding addition.

Proposition 2.1: (Addition of Complex numbers) The following properties for addition can be proved easily

Commutative: Addition is commutative, meaning:

$$z_1 + z_2 = z_2 + z_1$$

Associativity: Addition is associative, meaning:

$$z_1 + (z_2 + z_3) = (z_1 + z_2) + z_3$$

Neutral Element: The neutral element for the addition of complex numbers is $0 = 0 + i0$, and obeys $z + 0 = 0 + z = z$

Inverse element: For every complex number $z = a + ib$ there exists a complex number $-z = -a - ib$ such that

$$z + (-z) = 0 + 0i$$

Proof: The proof follows if we substitute $z_1 = x_1 + iy_1$ and $z_2 = x_2 + iy_2$ and follow the definition of addition. For example, $z_1 + z_2 = (x_1 + iy_1) + (x_2 + iy_2) = (x_1 + x_2) + i(y_1 + y_2)$ by definition (2.3) and if we use the commutativity of addition of real numbers it is equal to $(x_2 + x_1) + i(y_2 + y_1)$ which is equal to $z_2 + z_1$. Similarly, for the others. □

Exercise 2.2: Show that if $z_1 = 3+5i$ and $z_2 = 2-4i$ then $z_1 z_2 = 26-2i$:
Ans:

$$z_1 z_2 = (3+5i)(2-4i) = 6 - 12i + 10i - 20i^2 = 6 - 2i - 20(-1) = 26 - 2i$$

□

Exercise 2.3: Prove that the neutral element 0 is unique.
Ans: This is a very important property that, although intuitive, requires proof. We are going to use proof by contradiction. Suppose there was another element $0'$ with the same properties that was different from 0, namely $0 \neq 0'$. Then we would have that $0 + 0' = 0'$ if we treat 0 as the neutral element. On the other hand if we treat $0'$ as the neutral element we have $0 + 0' = 0$. From these two relations we find that $0 = 0'$ which is contrary to our assumption that they are different. Hence, the neutral element for addition is unique. □

Dad's SOS Note: Here we defined addition of two complex numbers. We did not define subtraction as an operation! Instead we defined an "inverse element" sometimes called the "negative element", denoted by $-z$ with the property that when it is added to z we get the Neutral element 0, which we defined earlier.
Can you think why we did not define subtraction instead? Well, lets assume that instead of defining addition we had defined subtraction. Since $a - b \neq b - a$, this operation would not be Commutative and mathematics would be massively more complicated. Also, $a - (b - c) \neq (a - b) - c$, so associativity does not work either. Summarizing, we do not think of Subtraction as a different operation but as addition of an another element, "the negative", with the property that the result is the neutral element which we defined earlier. And you can prove that this inverse element is unique. ♥

DAD'S SOS NOTE: These rules for the addition of complex numbers are also the rules of a commutative group with neutral element 0. Group theory is another beautiful subject. ♥

Similarly, for multiplication we have the following rules.

Proposition 2.2: (Multiplication of Complex numbers) For any complex numbers z_1, z_2, z_3, the following properties are easy to prove

Commutativity: Multiplication is commutative, meaning:

$$z_1 z_2 = z_2 z_1$$

Associativity: Multiplication of complex numbers is associative, meaning:

$$z_1(z_2 z_3) = (z_1 z_2) z_3$$

Neutral Element: The neutral or unit element for complex numbers is $1 = 1 + 0i$!

$$1 \cdot z = z \cdot 1 = z$$

Inverse element: The inverse element for multiplication is the element $1/z$, denoted by z^{-1}, so that $z\frac{1}{z} = 1 = zz^{-1}$. However, as is also the case of real numbers, such an element does not exist for all complex numbers. This is because the zero complex number $0 + 0i$ does not have an inverse.

$$z^{-1} = \frac{a}{a^2 + b^2} - i\frac{b}{a^2 + b^2}, \quad a, b \neq 0$$

Proof: Again the proof of these is done by substituting $z_1 = x_1 + iy_1$ and $z_2 = x_2 + iy_2$ and using the definition of multiplication (2.2). For example,

$$\begin{aligned} z_1 z_2 &= (x_1 x_2 - y_1 y_2) + i(x_1 y_2 + y_1 x_2) \\ &= (x_2 x_1 - y_2 y_1) + i(x_2 y_1 + y_2 x_1) = z_2 z_1 \end{aligned}$$

where we used the commutativity of addition and multiplication of real numbers. □

Finally there is one more property that combines the two operations of addition and multiplication, the distributive property.

Proposition 2.3: (Distributive) The distributive rule for multiplication and addition is

$$z_1(z_2+z_3) = z_1z_2 + z_1z_3$$

You can easily see that the Distributive property also holds from the left. Namely,

$$z_1(z_2+z_3) = z_1z_2 + z_1z_3 = z_2z_1 + z_3z_1 = (z_2+z_3)z_1$$

Proof: The proof is done by substituting $z_1 = x_1 + iy_1$, $z_2 = x_2 + iy_2$ and $z_3 = x_3 + iy_3$. Using the definitions of multiplication (2.2) and addition (2.1) we can verify the distributive property. □

DAD'S SOS NOTE: Again, here we defined multiplication rather than division. The same reasoning with addition holds here. For example, division is not commutative as $z_1 \div z_2 \neq z_2 \div z_1$. Division is just multiplication by the inverse element which gives back the neutral element 1. ♥

Another property of Real numbers, that carries over to the complex number is that if $ab = 0 \Rightarrow (a = 0 \vee b = 0)$ if $a, b \in \mathbb{R}$. The symbol $\vee$ is the logical inclusive "OR" in mathematics, meaning "EITHER" or "BOTH" are true. Namely, at least one or both numbers are zero. For complex numbers the proof is given below.

Proposition 2.4: Show that for any two complex number $z_1, z_2 \in \mathbb{C}$ we have

$$z_1z_2 = 0 \Leftrightarrow (z_1 = 0 \vee z_2 = 0)$$

Proof: If the two numbers were Real then it is an obvious result that one or both of them should be zero. But with complex numbers, this is not obvious. Here, I would give a rather long but very instructive solution. This is a great exercise in being systematic. Let $z_1 = a + bi$ and $z_2 = c + id$ with $a, b, c, d \in \mathbb{R}$. After multiplying and equating real and imaginary parts to zero we have that $ac - bd = 0 \wedge bc + ad = 0$. We now have the following cases

- Assume $c \neq 0$, then we have $a = bd/c$ and after substituting into the second equation we get $bc + bd^2/c = 0 \Rightarrow b(c^2 + d^2) = 0$. The last equation implies that $b = 0$ since we assumed that $c \neq 0$. But if $b = 0$ then $a = 0$ as well. This proves that $z_1 = 0 + 0i$
- Now assume that $c = 0$. We then have $-bd = 0 \Rightarrow (b = 0 \vee d = 0)$. So we again have two cases
  - Case $b = 0$ implies that $ad = 0$. So either $a = 0$ or $d = 0$. If $a = 0$ then since $b = 0$ as well we have that $z_1 = 0 + i0$. If $d = 0$ then since $c = 0$ as well, we have that $z_2 = 0 + i0$.
  - Case $d = 0$, then since $c = 0$ we again have that $z_2 = 0 + i0$.

This proof is going from left to right (remember the question had $\Leftrightarrow$ which means we need to examine both directions). However, the right to left direction is trivial, since if one of z_1 or z_2 is zero the product of $0 + i0$ with anything would give zero. Do not overlook this direction. There was a reason why the question had the if and only if sign rather than the implies sign. It would cost you marks if you ignore it (at least in any serious mathematical exam). □

Using the result of the above proposition we can prove the cancellation law.

Proposition 2.5: (Cancellation law) Prove that if $z \neq 0$ then

$$zz_1 = zz_2 \Rightarrow z_1 = z_2$$

Proof: We can rewrite the equation as $zz_1 - zz_2 = 0 \Rightarrow z(z_1 - z_2) = 0$. Using Proposition (2.4) we conclude that $z = 0 \vee z_1 - z_2 = 0$. Since $z \neq 0$ we must have $z_1 = z_2$. □

So, if addition and multiplication are the same for both the real and the complex numbers, one has the right and the obligation to ask, "*What on earth is different about the complex numbers? What is all the fuss about?*" The answer is that Real numbers have one more property that complex numbers lack. You can order them! And you do this by the following two axioms.

Ordering Axioms Even though it sounds crazy you can get a set of numbers, on which you can define what you mean to add and multiply these numbers, define a "zero" element for addition and an "unit" element for multiplication and still not be able to say if one number is "bigger" than another. Bigger or greater implies ordering. So, you need to have an ordering of these numbers to say which one is "bigger". We are doing this by the following two axioms. We assume that there is a subset P of the real numbers conveniently called the "Positive elements" that satisfy

Axiom 2.1: (Trichotomy) For every element x of the real numbers we have either $x \in P$ or $x = 0$ or $-x \in P$. And the three possibilities are mutually exclusive.

Axiom 2.2: If $x, y \in P$ then $x + y \in P$ and $xy \in P$

These two axioms are enough to define a "total" ordering of the real numbers. "Total" means that all the elements of the set satisfy this ordering.

Definition 2.5: If an element belongs to that set P of positive numbers we write it as

$$x > 0$$

and we define $y > x$ to mean that $y - x$ is in P (namely $y - x > 0$).

Using these axioms you can prove why $(-1)(-1) = 1$ which was always a mystery, at least for me when I was in school. It can be proved that the set of Complex numbers $\mathbb{C}$ cannot have this property and simultaneously be consistent with the definitions of addition and multiplication.

Dad's SOS Note: A set of objects with two operations (call them "Addition" and "Multiplication") that satisfy Propositions (2.1, 2.2 and 2.3) is called a "Field" in Algebra. They are the Axioms of a "Field". You will notice that these rules are also true for Real numbers. So, both the Real numbers $\mathbb{R}$ and $\mathbb{C}$ are "Fields". However, the important difference between the Real numbers $\mathbb{R}$ and the complex numbers $\mathbb{C}$ is that Real numbers obey the ordering Axioms. *Real numbers have order! Complex Do NOT.* ♥

2.3 Complex Conjugate

The following operation, flipping i to $-i$, is called "complex conjugation"

Definition 2.6: The complex "conjugate" of $z = a + ib$ is the complex number $z^* = a - ib$. Complex conjugation is a very important operation. Complex conjugates are usually denoted by a * or a bar over the complex number $\bar{z}$.

Essentially, when we take the conjugate we flip the i to $-i$ in every occurrence in our equation. For example

$$\left(3i + \frac{1}{i} + i^2\right)^* = -3i + \frac{1}{-i} + (-i)^2 = -3i - 1/i + i^2$$

Proposition 2.6: A complex number $z = a + ib$ plus its conjugate is twice the real part

$$z + z^* = 2\mathfrak{Re}(z) = 2a$$

A complex number minus its conjugate is

$$z - z^* = 2i\,\mathfrak{Im}(z) = 2ib$$

Proof: The proof is obvious if we substitute into $z + z^* = (a + ib) + (a - ib) = 2a$ and $z - z^* = (a + ib) - (a - ib) = 2ib$. □

Dad's SOS Note: If a question asks you to prove that a complex number z or an expression is real, then 9 out 10 times the easiest way to do it is to prove that the complex number is equal to its complex conjugate. Namely, it is enough to prove that $z = z^*$, since this would mean that the imaginary part $\mathfrak{Im}(z) = 0$ from the previous property. Do NOT substitute for $z = a + ib$ as this may lead to some very tedious algebra.
If you are asked to prove that a number is purely imaginary, usually the fastest way is to show that $z + z^* = 0$. ♥

Corollary 2.1: A number $z = a + bi$ is real, if and only if, it is equal to its own complex conjugate. Namely if $z = z^*$.
Similarly, a number is purely imaginary if the number plus its conjugate is zero. Namely, if $z + z^* = 2a = 0$.

Complex conjugation obeys the following rules.

Proposition 2.7: The following rules hold for complex conjugation. For any $z_1, z_2 \in \mathbb{C}$ we have

$$(z_1 + z_2)^* = z_1^* + z_2^* \quad (2.5)$$

$$(z_1 z_2)^* = z_1^* z_2^* \quad (2.6)$$

$$(z^n)^* = (z^*)^n, \quad n \in \mathbb{N} \quad (2.7)$$

$$\left(\frac{z_1}{z_2}\right)^* = \frac{z_1^*}{z_2^*}, \quad z_2 \neq 0 \quad (2.8)$$

$$(z^*)^* = z \quad (2.9)$$

The last equation says that if we take the conjugate of a conjugate we get back the complex number.
Proof: To prove that (2.5), $(z_1 + z_2)^* = z_1^* + z_2^*$ we can substitute $z_1 = x_1 + iy_1$ and $z_2 = x_2 + iy_2$ and we get

$$\begin{aligned}(z_1 + z_2)^* &= (x_1 + iy_1 + x_2 + iy_2)^* \\ &= (x_1 - iy_1 + x_2 - iy_2) \\ &= (x_1 - iy_1) + (x_2 - iy_2) \\ &= {z_1}^* + {z_2}^*\end{aligned}$$

and similarly we get (2.6) and (2.8) and (2.9). However, the easiest way to prove (2.7) is by Induction! For $n = 1$ we have $(z)^* = z^*$ by the definition. Assuming that it is true for $n = k$, $(z^k)^* = (z^*)^k$, we have that for $n = k + 1$,

$$\begin{aligned}(z^{k+1})^* &= (z^k z)^* \\ \text{By (2.6)}, \quad &= (z^k)^* (z)^* \\ \text{Using } (z^k)^* = (z^*)^k, \quad &= (z^*)^k z^* = (z^*)^{k+1}\end{aligned}$$

□

The following theorem is an extremely important result.

Theorem 2.1: If a polynomial of degree n, with real coefficients, has a complex number z_1 as a root then the complex conjugate z_1^* is also a root.

Proof: Let $P(x) = a_n x^n + a_{n-1}x^{n-1} + ... + a_1 x + a_0$ be the polynomial with degree n having $a_n \in \mathbb{R}$ and $n \in \mathbb{N}$. If z_1 is a root then we must have

$$P(z_1) = 0 = a_n z_1^n + a_{n-1} z_1^{n-1} + ... + a_1 z_1 + a_0$$

If we take the complex conjugate of this equation and use the Proposition (2.7), we get

$$\begin{aligned} (P(z_1))^* = 0 &= a_n (z_1^n)^* + a_{n-1}\left(z_1^{n-1}\right)^* + ... + a_1 (z_1)^* + a_0 \\ &= a_n (z_1^*)^n + a_{n-1}(z_1^*)^{n-1} + ... + a_1 z_1^* + a_0 \\ &= P(z_1^*) \end{aligned}$$

The last equality, $P(z_1^*) = 0$, proves that z_1^* is also a root of the polynomial. □

Corollary 2.2: If a quadratic equation with real coefficients has complex roots, then they are always complex conjugates of each other.

Proposition 2.8: If a polynomial with real coefficients is of odd degree then it has at least one real root.

Proof: The proof is elementary. If all the roots where complex then the degree of the polynomial would be an even number. Thus, if the order is odd, then at least one root is real.

Graphically, you can see this by placing $x = \pm\infty$ in the polynomial. The dominant term is the highest power in the polynomial which is odd. Hence at $x = +\infty$ the polynomial goes to positive infinity and at $x = -\infty$ the polynomial goes to minus infinity. Since polynomials are continuous functions, their graph must go through zero at least once. Hence there is at least one real root. □

> DAD'S SOS NOTE: Complex roots of polynomials with real coefficients come in pairs!
> This is a very useful property which means that if I know one complex root, I immediately know another one, the conjugate of it! ♥

Exercise 2.4: If $z = 6 - 2i$ is one root of a quadratic polynomial with real coefficients find (i) the other root of the quadratic and (ii) write down the quadratic polynomial.
Ans: Since $z = 6 - 2i$ is a root, we know that the complex conjugate is also a root. Hence $z^* = 6 + 2i$ is the other root. From the Vieta[2] relations for a quadratic we know that the sum of the roots is $\frac{-b}{a}$ and the product of the roots is $\frac{c}{a}$. We thus have $12 = \frac{-b}{a}$ and $zz^* = 6^2 + 2^2 = 40 = \frac{c}{a}$. Hence the quadratic is $P(z) = a(z^2 - 12z + 40)$, with $a \in \mathbb{R}$ an arbitrary constant. Alternative, you can multiply $a[x - (6 - 2i)][x - (6 + 2i)]$ and get the same result after some algebra. □

Exercise 2.5: Given that 2 and $5 + 2i$ are roots of the equation

$$x^3 - 12x^2 + cx + d = 0,\ c, d \in \mathbb{R}$$

(i) write down the other complex root of the equation.

(ii) Find the value of c and the value of d.

Ans: The first part is a simple application of our previous theorem. The other root is $5 - 2i$. Using the Vieta relations you can immediately find d as it is the product of all the roots. Hence $-d = 2(5 - 2i)(5 + 2i) = 58 \Rightarrow d = -58$. You can use the Vieta to find c but since you already have the value of d plugging the value of 2 you will find c. Hence $8 - 48 + 2c - 58 = 0 \Rightarrow c = 49$. □

[2] François Viète 1540-1603 was a French amateur mathematician and astronomer who introduced the first systematic algebraic notation in his book, *In artem analyticam isagoge* [13]. He was also involved in deciphering codes.

2.4 Modulus of a Complex Number

Using the complex conjugate we can also define the modulus or "absolute value" of a complex number z

Definition 2.7: The modulus of a complex number $z = a + ib$ is denoted by $|z|$ and is defined as

$$|z| = \sqrt{zz^*} = \sqrt{a^2 + b^2} \Leftrightarrow |z|^2 = zz^* \tag{2.10}$$

Proposition 2.9: Using definition (2.7) we can prove the following relations for the modulus of a complex number $z = a + ib$

(i) $\mathfrak{Re}(z) \leq |z|$ and $\mathfrak{Im}(z) \leq |z|$. The proof is simple since $\mathfrak{Re}(z) = a \leq \sqrt{a^2 + b^2} = |z|$ and similarly for the imaginary part.

(ii) $|z| = |z^*|$. The proof is simple since they are both equal to $\sqrt{a^2 + b^2}$.

(iii) $|z_1 z_2| = |z_1|\,|z_2|$. The proof is left as Question (2.11).

(iv) The triangle identity

$$|z_1 + z_2| \leq |z_1| + |z_2| \tag{2.11}$$

This is the triangle identity equivalent to $|x + y| \leq |x| + |y|$ for Real numbers. The proof is left as Question (2.11).

(v) $|z - w| \geq |z| - |w|$. The way to prove this is to write $|z| = |z - w + w|$ and use the previous inequality. Namely $|z| = |z - w + w| \leq |z - w| + |w| \Rightarrow |z - w| \geq |z| - |w|$

(vi) $|z - w| \leq |w| - |z|$. The way to prove this is to write $|w| = |z - (z - w)|$ and then $|w| = |z - (z - w)| \leq |z| + |z - w| \Rightarrow |z - w| \geq |w| - |z|$.

(vii) Finally if we combine the previous two results and using the inequality $-A \leq X \leq A \Leftrightarrow |X| \leq A$ with $X = |w| - |z|$ and $A = |z - w|$ we get

$$|z - w| \geq ||w| - |z||$$

Corollary 2.3: The equality sign in the equation (2.11), is satisfied if $z_1 = \lambda z_2, \lambda > 0$

$$|z_1 + z_2| = |z_1| + |z_2| \Rightarrow z_1 = \lambda z_2, \ \lambda > 0$$

The proof of this result is left as an exercise. See Question (2.12). Hint: You can sub for z_1, z_2 and do the algebra.

These inequalities are very useful when asked to find the maximum or the minimum of a number given some condition. The following example makes this more clear.

Exercise 2.6: Find the greatest value $|z|$ if z satisfies $|z - 1 - i| = 2$. Find also, the coordinates of the maximum point.
Ans: In order to find the maximum value of $|z|$ we work as follows. We would make use of the triangle inequalities by writing $|z| = |z - (1 + i) + (1 + i)|$

$$\begin{aligned} |z| &= |z - (1 + i) + (1 + i)| \Rightarrow \\ |z| &\leq |z - (1 + i)| + |1 + i| = 2 + \sqrt{2} \Rightarrow \\ |z| &\leq 2 + \sqrt{2} \end{aligned}$$

When we do the geometric interpretation of complex numbers in the next chapter, you will recognise that z is on a circle with radius 2 and centre the point $1 + i$. The maximum distance would be the distance from the origin, which is $\sqrt{2}$ plus the radius which is 2. Namely when $|z| = 2 + \sqrt{2}$. For the coordinates of the maximum, we know from Corollary (2.3) (with $z_1 = z - (1 + i)$ and $z_2 = 1 + i$), that the maximum occurs when

$$z - (1 + i) = \lambda(1 + i)$$

And since we have that $|z - (1 + i)| = 2$ we get

$$2 = |\lambda|\sqrt{2} \Rightarrow |\lambda| = \sqrt{2}$$

We thus have that the maximum value occurs at $z = 1 + \sqrt{2} + i(1 + \sqrt{2})$. □

A harder example of the application of the inequalities for complex numbers is the following

Exercise 2.7: Show that if $\left|z^3 + \dfrac{1}{z^3}\right| \leq 2$ then $\left|z + \dfrac{1}{z}\right| \leq 2$, for all $z \neq 0$.
Ans: The question involves inequalities, and also cube powers of z. So

we need to form $\left|z^3+\frac{1}{z^3}\right|$ somehow. The only way I can think of, is by raising $(z+1/z)^3$ and see what we get

$$\left(z+\frac{1}{z}\right)^3 = z^3+3\left(z+\frac{1}{z}\right)+\frac{1}{z^3}$$

Now, observe that we have in one equation both (z^3+1/z^3) and $(z+1/z)$. So lets take the modulus of it

$$\left|z+\frac{1}{z}\right|^3 = \left|z^3+\frac{1}{z^3}+3\left(z+\frac{1}{z}\right)\right|$$

Apply Triangle inequality (2.11)

$$\begin{aligned} &\leq \left|z^3+\frac{1}{z^3}\right|+3\left|z+\frac{1}{z}\right| \\ &\leq 2+3\left|z+\frac{1}{z}\right| \end{aligned}$$

The final inequality is

$$\left|z+\frac{1}{z}\right|^3 \leq 2+\left|z+\frac{1}{z}\right|$$

and since we have already used all the assumptions, it must be that this inequality gives the required result. For easiness, lets call $t=\left|z+\frac{1}{z}\right|$. We thus have

$$t^3 \leq 3t+2 \Rightarrow t^3-3t-2 \leq 0$$

We can factorize the cubic in t by noting that $t=2$ is a root. We then get $(t-2)(t-1)^2 \leq 0$. We have now reached our goal. This inequality is only true if $t \leq 2 \Rightarrow \left|z+\frac{1}{z}\right| \leq 2$. Bingo. □

DAD'S SOS NOTE: If a question involves the moduli of complex numbers, like $|z|^2$ then it is advisable to rewrite this as zz^* and do the algebra. The following example is typical.
A *very common mistake* that many students make when they first learn complex numbers, is to assume that $z^2=|z|^2$. This is not the case. $z^2=x^2-y^2+2ixy$ is a complex number, whereas $|z|^2=x^2+y^2$ is the modulus square, a real and positive number. ♥

Exercise 2.8: Prove that for any two complex numbers z_1, z_2 the following relation holds:

$$|z_1 + z_2|^2 + |z_1 - z_2|^2 = 2(|z_1|^2 + |z_2|^2)$$

Ans: Writing the modulus square as the number times its conjugate we get

$$\begin{aligned} |z_1 + z_2|^2 + |z_1 - z_2|^2 &= (z_1 + z_2)(z_1{}^* + z_2{}^*) + (z_1 - z_2)(z_1{}^* - z_2{}^*) \\ &= z_1 z_1{}^* + \cancel{z_1 z_2{}^*} + \cancel{z_2 z_1{}^*} + z_2 z_2{}^* + z_1 z_1{}^* \\ &- \cancel{z_1 z_2{}^*} - \cancel{z_2 z_1{}^*} + z_2 z_2{}^* \\ &= 2 z_1 z_1{}^* + 2 z_2 z_2{}^* \\ &= 2(|z_1|^2 + |z_2|^2) \end{aligned}$$

□

DAD'S SOS NOTE: The previous exercise is known as the parallelogram identity, which states that the sum of the squares of the sides of a parallelogram is equal to the sum of the squares of the diagonals. ♥

The following example comes up in exams in different disguises, geometric and algebraic. This is the algebraic version. We would see the geometrical version of it later (the three complex numbers are vertices of an equilateral triangle!).

Exercise 2.9: If $z_1 + z_2 + z_3 = 0$ and $z_1^2 + z_2^2 + z_3^2 = 0$ show that $|z_1| = |z_2| = |z_3|$.

Ans: Be very careful here z^2 is not the same as $|z|^2$. If we square the given $z_1 + z_2 + z_3 = 0$ we get

$$(z_1 + z_2 + z_3)^2 = \underbrace{z_1^2 + z_2^2 + z_3^2}_{\text{zero}} + 2(z_1 z_2 + z_2 z_3 + z_3 z_1) = 0$$

The last relation is $z_1 z_2 + z_2 z_3 + z_3 z_1 = 0$. If we multiply by z_1 we get

$$z_1^2 z_2 + z_1 z_2 z_3 + z_3 z_1^2 = 0 \Rightarrow z_1^2 \underbrace{(z_2 + z_3)}_{-z_1} = -z_1 z_2 z_3 \Rightarrow z_1^3 = z_1 z_2 z_3$$

If instead of multiplying by z_1 we multiplied by z_2 we would get that $z_2^3 = z_1 z_2 z_3$ and similarly for $z_3^3 = z_1 z_2 z_3$. Hence, $z_1^3 = z_2^3 = z_3^3$ and taking the modulus of this we arrive at $|z_1| = |z_2| = |z_3|$. □

DAD'S SOS NOTE: Many questions give the ratio of two complex numbers $\frac{z_1}{z_2}$ and ask to write them in the standard form $x+iy$. The way to do this is similar to the way we rationalised roots in the denominators of fractions. You simply need to multiply both the top and bottom of the fraction with the complex conjugate of the denominator. In doing so, we get

$$\frac{z_1}{z_2} = \frac{z_1 z_2^*}{z_2 z_2^*} = \frac{z_1 z_2^*}{|z_2|^2}$$

Now the denominator is a real number, the modulus square of z_2.

♥

Exercise 2.10: Express $\frac{1+8i}{2+i}$ in the form $x+iy$

Ans: In order to express the fraction as $x+iy$ you will need to get rid of the complex number that is in the denominator. The way to do this is to multiply top and bottom with the complex conjugate of $2-i$. Hence

$$\frac{1+8i}{2+i} = \frac{(1+8i)(2-i)}{(2+i)(2-i)} = \frac{10+15i}{2^2+1^2} = 2+3i \qquad \square$$

Exercise 2.11: If $z^2-z+1=0$ prove that $z^3=-1$. Hence show that

$$z^{2024} + \frac{1}{z^{2024}} = -1$$

Ans: Since we are given $z^2-z+1=0$ and we are asked to find z^3 the best strategy is to multiply by z to form z^3 (We need to be careful here as we are multiplying by an unknown quantity that could be zero! However, in our case $z \neq 0$, since if it was zero, the given relation would imply $1=0$ which is false). We thus have $z(z^2-z+1)=0 \Rightarrow z^3-z^2+z=0$. Using now the $z^2-z+1=0$ we find that $z^3-(-1)=0 \Rightarrow z^3=-1$.
For the next part, notice that $2024 = 3\times674+2$ and hence $z^{2024}=(z^3)^{674}z^2$. So $z^{2024}=z^2$ and $z^{-2024}=1/z^2$. We thus have

$$z^{2024} + \frac{1}{z^{2024}} = z^2 + \frac{1}{z^2} = \frac{z^4+1}{z^2} = \frac{-z+1}{z^2} = \frac{-z^2}{z^2} = -1 \qquad \square$$

Exercise 2.12: Prove that if the roots of the quadratic equation $x^2+bx+c^2=0$ have the same absolute value r, then the ratio b^2/c^2 is a real number. **(1999 Romanian Math Olympiad)** see [1].

Ans: Let x_1 and x_2 be the roots. It is given that $|x_1| = |x_2|$. From the Vieta relations we know that the sum of the roots is $x_1 + x_2 = -b$ and the product $x_1 x_2 = c^2$. So

$$\frac{b^2}{c^2} = \frac{(x_1 + x_2)^2}{x_1 x_2} = \frac{x_1^2 + x_2^2 + 2x_1 x_2}{x_1 x_2} = \frac{x_1}{x_2} + \frac{x_2}{x_1} + 2$$

Since the roots have equal absolute value r, we must have $x_1 x_1^* = x_2 x_2^* = r^2$. So, we can rewrite

$$\frac{b^2}{c^2} = \frac{x_1}{x_2} + \frac{x_2}{x_1} + 2 = \frac{x_1 x_2^*}{x_2 x_2^*} + \frac{x_2 x_1^*}{x_1 x_1^*} + 2 = \frac{x_1 x_2^*}{r^2} + \frac{x_2 x_1^*}{r^2} + 2$$

Now notice, that the last relation would be real if and only if $x_1 x_2^* + x_2 x_1^*$ is real. But this number is always real since it is equal to its complex conjugate! Hence the ratio b^2/c^2 is a real number. □

Exercise 2.13: Prove that if $|z_1| = |z_2| = 1$ then $A = \dfrac{z_1 + z_2}{1 + z_1 z_2}$, $z_1 z_2 \neq -1$ is a real number.

Ans: The best strategy of proving that a an expression with complex numbers is a real number is to show that it is equal to its complex conjugate. The question gives that $|z_1| = |z_2| = 1$ and this also means that $z_1 z_1^* = z_2 z_2^* = 1$. So taking the complex conjugate of A we have

$$A^* = \frac{z_1^* + z_2^*}{1 + z_1^* z_2^*}$$

$$\text{Using } z_1 z_1^* = 1 = z_2 z_2^*,\ A^* = \frac{\frac{1}{z_1} + \frac{1}{z_2}}{1 + \frac{1}{z_1}\frac{1}{z_2}} = \frac{z_1 + z_2}{1 + z_1 z_2} = A$$

Hence A is a real number since $A = A^*$. □

Exercise 2.14: If $2|z+3| > |z-3|$ show that $|z+5| > 4$

Ans: Since in the given inequality everything is positive we can take the square and use the familiar $|z|^2 = zz^*$ property.

$$\begin{aligned} 4|z+3|^2 > |z-3|^2 \;\Rightarrow\; & 4(z+3)(z^*+3) - (z-3)(z^*-3) > 0 \Rightarrow \\ & 4(zz^* + 3z + 3z^* + 9) - zz^* + 3z + 3z^* - 9 > 0 \Rightarrow \\ & 3(zz^* + 5z + 5z^* + 9) > 0 \Rightarrow \\ & 3(|z+5|^2 - 16) > 0 \end{aligned}$$

And the last inequality proves the required $|z+5| > 4$ □

The next example is absolutely great (I have funny taste).

Exercise 2.15: Let $w = \dfrac{1}{z-a}$ be a complex number and $a \in \mathbb{R}$ a real number. Show that

$$w - w^* = (z - z^*)|w|^2$$

Use this result to show that the equation

$$\frac{1}{z-1} + \frac{1}{z-2} + \frac{1}{z-3} + \frac{1}{z-4} = 5$$

has only real roots.

Ans: The first part of the question is rather straightforward. Forming $w - w^*$ we get

$$w - w^* = \frac{1}{z-a} - \frac{1}{z^*-a} = \frac{z^* - a - z + a}{(z-a)(z^*-a)} = \frac{z^* - z}{|z-a|^2} = (z^* - z)|w|^2$$

Now for the next part we need to use the result of the first part. So we must form $w - w^*$. So lets take the complex conjugate of the equation

$$\frac{1}{z^*-1} + \frac{1}{z^*-2} + \frac{1}{z^*-3} + \frac{1}{z^*-4} = 5$$

and subtract it from the first one to get

$$\left(\frac{1}{z-1} - \frac{1}{z^*-1}\right) + \left(\frac{1}{z-2} - \frac{1}{z^*-2}\right) + \left(\frac{1}{z-3} - \frac{1}{z^*-3}\right) + \left(\frac{1}{z-4} - \frac{1}{z^*-4}\right) = 0$$

The last equation becomes

$$(z - z^*)\left[\frac{1}{|z-1|^2} + \frac{1}{|z-2|^2} + \frac{1}{|z-3|^2} + \frac{1}{|z-4|^2}\right] = 0$$

The expression in the square brackets cannot be zero. We must have $z - z^* = 0$ which means that only real solutions exist. Nice!! □

In the next example, I would show how you can use complex numbers to get the partial fraction decomposition of a rational function that has $x^2 + a^2$ in the denominator.

Exercise 2.16: Find the partial fraction decomposition of

$$\frac{x^2 + 4x - 1}{(x-3)(x^2+1)}$$

Ans: We know that the partial fraction decomposition would be

$$\frac{x^2+4x-1}{(x-3)(x^2+1)} = \frac{A}{x-3} + \frac{Bx+C}{x^2+1}$$

with $A, B, C \in \mathbb{R}$. The A coefficient is very easy to calculate, just set $x = 3$ into $\frac{x^2+4x-1}{(x^2+1)}$ to get that $A = 2$. We can now use $x = i$ in the

$$\frac{x^2+4x-1}{(x-3)} = 2\frac{(x^2+1)}{x-3} + (Bx+C)$$

to get

$$\begin{aligned} \frac{-1+4i-1}{i-3} &= iB+C \Rightarrow \\ -i+1 &= iB+C \end{aligned}$$

Therefore, $B = -1$ and $C = 1$. □

2.5 Square Root of a Complex Number. Algebraic Method

A typical question that arises when you first encounter complex numbers is the following. If the square root of a negative number is a "new" number can we repeat the process? In other words, if I take the square root of an imaginary or complex number do I get something new?
The answer to this is no. We do not get a new kind of number, but another complex number. The following example explains how.
Exercise 2.17: What is the square root of $z = 3 - 4i$?
Ans: Lets assume that the square root is another complex number $x + iy$ with $x, y \in \mathbb{R}$ real numbers. If our assumption is incorrect we would end up with a contradiction. If, on the other hand it is correct, then the square root process gives back another complex number. So,

$$\begin{aligned} \sqrt{3-4i} = x+iy &\Rightarrow 3-4i = (x+iy)^2 = x^2-y^2+2ixy \\ &\Rightarrow 3 = x^2-y^2 \;\wedge\; -4 = 2xy \end{aligned}$$

In the last step we got two equations by equating the real and imaginary parts. Solving, for $y = -2/x$ (x cannot be zero) and substituting back, we get

$$x^2 - \frac{4}{x^2} = 3 \Rightarrow x^4 - 3x^2 - 4 = 0$$

The last quartic equation is easy to solve as it is a bi-quadratic (there is no odd power of x). Using the formula for the quadratic in terms of x^2 we get

$$x^2 = 4 \ \vee \ x^2 = -1$$

As we assumed that x must be real we reject the negative solution and we thus have $x = \pm 2$ and substituting into the y equation we get that $2-i$ and $-2+i$ are the only possible solutions.
Although we assumed that x, y are real numbers the result is not altered if we let x, y to be complex. If we do, then we would get $x = \pm i$ and from the equation for y we get $y = \pm 2i$ and when we substitute back in the z we get the same solutions $i + i(2i) = -2 + i$ and $2 - i$! □

DAD'S SOS NOTE: This method of finding the square root of a complex number is sometimes called the "Algebraic method". Occasionally, they pop up in the exams. Usually, the question asks you to determine the square root using the "Algebraic method". In Chapter 7 we would learn a much more elegant way, to find not just the square root, but any n^{th} root of a complex number. ♥

Generalising:

Proposition 2.10: The square root $z = \sqrt{a+ib}$ is given by

$$\sqrt{a+ib} = \pm\left(\sqrt{\frac{|z|+a}{2}} + i\frac{b}{|b|}\sqrt{\frac{|z|-a}{2}}\right) \tag{2.12}$$

Proof: The proof follows the steps in the example. Let the answer be $(x+iy)$. Then squaring a and comparing real and imaginary parts we get $x^2 - y^2 = a$ and $b = 2xy$. Solving for $y = b/2x$ and substituting we get the bi-quadratic $4x^4 - 4x^2a - b^2 = 0$ whose roots are $x^2 = \dfrac{a+|z|}{2}$ (we discard the minus root since we want x^2 to be real). We can now compute $y^2 = \dfrac{|z|-a}{2}$. The solution for x is $x = \epsilon_1\sqrt{\dfrac{a+|z|}{2}}$ and $y = \epsilon_2\sqrt{\dfrac{|z|-a}{2}}$ where ϵ_1 and ϵ_2 are ± 1. Note that $\epsilon_1^2 = \epsilon_2^2 = 1$ and $\epsilon_1\epsilon_2 = \epsilon_1/\epsilon_2$. Using now the equation $b =$

$2xy = \epsilon_1\epsilon_2|b| \Rightarrow \epsilon_1\epsilon_2 = \frac{b}{|b|}$. The solution is

$$\epsilon_1\sqrt{\frac{a+|z|}{2}} + i\epsilon_2\sqrt{\frac{|z|-a}{2}} = \epsilon_1\left(\sqrt{\frac{a+|z|}{2}} + i\frac{\epsilon_2}{\epsilon_1}\sqrt{\frac{|z|-a}{2}}\right)$$

The last equation can thus be written as

$$\sqrt{a+ib} = \pm\left(\sqrt{\frac{a+|z|}{2}} + i\frac{b}{|b|}\sqrt{\frac{|z|-a}{2}}\right) \qquad \square$$

Dad's SOS Note: It is not a bad idea to memorise this formula for the square root. It is not hard. All you need to remember is to take the modulus of the number and form $a+|z|$ and $a-|z|$. Take half of it and square root each one. And do not forget the sign. ♥

The previous example strongly suggests that taking the square root of a complex number does not generate a new kind of number but another complex number. In other words, the set of complex numbers $\mathbb{C}$ is closed under this operation. We also saw that addition and multiplication are also closed. In fact, the Complex numbers are "The Numbers". It is the largest set of numbers since it includes the Real numbers as a subset.

2.6 Question on Algebra of Complex Numbers

Q 2.1 Find the value of the expression:

(1) $\frac{i+i^2+i^3}{i^3+i^4+i^5}$ (2) $(1+i)^{24}-(1-i)^{24}$ (3) $\frac{1}{i^{13}}+\frac{1}{i^{23}}+\frac{1}{i^{33}}+\frac{1}{i^{43}}$

Q 2.2 Perform the operations

(1) $(5-3i)+(2i-8)$ (2) $(3+2i)(2-i)$ (3) $(4+i)(3+2i)(1-i)$

(4) $\left(\frac{1+i}{1-i}\right)^2$ (5) $\frac{2+3i}{5-i}$ (6) $(2i-1)^2$

Q 2.3 Solve the equations (i) $i(z+z^*)+i(z-z^*)=6i+3$ and (ii) $zz^*+(z+z^*)i-4-2i=0$

Q 2.4 Find the modulus of the following complex numbers

(1) $2+3i$ (2) $2-3i$ (3) $\cos\theta + i\sin\theta$

(4) $\dfrac{\sqrt{3}+i}{-3-4i}$ (5) $-i$ (6) $\dfrac{2+i}{1+2i}$

Q 2.5 If $z = 1+2i$, find, (i) z^3, (ii) $z^2 + z^* + i$, (iii) $\Re(z^2+z)$, (iv) $\Im(z^2)$.

Q 2.6 Solve the system

$$(1+i)z_1 + (1+2i)z_2 = 2+5i$$
$$(3-i)z_1 + (4-2i)z_2 = 2-i$$

Q 2.7 If $|z_1+z_2| = |z_1| = |z_2|$ and $|z_1| \neq 0$ then show that $|z_1 - z_2| = \sqrt{3}|z_1|$. Hint: Divide by $|z_1|$ and set $z_2/z_1 = x+iy$.

Q 2.8 Find the square root of the following complex numbers using the algebraic method.

(1) $3+6i\sqrt{2}$ (2) $21-20i$ (3) $11+60i$

(4) $9+40i$ (5) $-7-24i$ (6) $5-12i$

Q 2.9 Find the value of the expression $A = \sqrt{4+3i\sqrt{20}} + \sqrt{4-3i\sqrt{20}}$.

Q 2.10 Prove by contradiction that the neutral element for multiplication in Proposition (2.2) is unique.

Q 2.11 Prove part (iii) in Proposition (2.9), namely, $|z_1z_2| = |z_1||z_2|$ and the triangle inequality (2.11), $|z_1+z_2| \leq |z_1| + |z_2|$. Hint: Square and use $|z|^2 = zz^*$.

Q 2.12 Show that if z_1, z_2 are non-zero complex numbers and $|z_1+z_2| = |z_1| + |z_2|$ then $z_1 = \lambda z_2$

Q 2.13 Find x and y if (i) $x - iy = \dfrac{1}{5-2\sqrt{6}i}$, (ii) $x+iy = (1+i)^3$

Q 2.14 (i) Use an algebraic method to find the square roots of the complex number $16+30i$. [6]

(ii) Use your answers to part (i) to solve the equation $z^2 - 2z - (15+30i) = 0$, giving your answers in the form $x+iy$. [5]

(OCR FP1 Jun2007)

Q 2.15 (i) Use an algebraic method to find the square roots of the complex number $9+40i$. [6]

(ii) Show that $9+40i$ is a root of the quadratic equation $z^2 - 18z + 1681 = 0$. [1]

(iii) By using the substitution $z = \frac{1}{u^2}$, find the roots of the equation $1681u^4 - 18u^2 + 1 = 0$. Give your answers in the form $x + iy$, where x and y are real. [4]

(OCR FP1 May2016)

Q 2.16 Show that for every complex number z

$$|\mathfrak{Im}(z)| + |\mathfrak{Re}(z)| \leq \sqrt{2}|z|$$

Q 2.17 Show that if $|z_1 - z_2| = |1 - z_1{}^* z_2|$, for two complex numbers $z_1, z_2 \in \mathbb{C}$ then one or both of z_1, z_2 have modulus 1.

Q 2.18 Show that if $A = \frac{z-i}{z+i}$ is purely imaginary ($\mathfrak{Re}(A) = 0$) then $|z| = 1$.

Q 2.19 Show that if $|z_1| = |z_2| = |z_3| = \lambda$, then $|z_1 z_2 + z_2 z_3 + z_3 z_1| = \lambda|z_1 + z_2 + z_3|$

Q 2.20 Given that $|2z - 1| = |z - 2|$ show that $|z| = 1$. Hint:Square the expression.

Q 2.21 Use mathematical induction to prove (i) $(z_1 + z_2 + ... + z_n)^* = z_1{}^* + z_2{}^* + ... + z_n{}^*$ and (ii) $(z_1 z_2 ... z_n)^* = z_1{}^* z_2{}^* ... z_n{}^*$, for all $n \in \mathbb{N}$

Q 2.22 If $S_n = 1 + i + i^2 + ... + i^n$ for $n \in \mathbb{N}$ and $n \geq 1$ show that

$$S_n = \frac{1}{2}(1+i)(1-i^{n+1})$$

Q 2.23 Factorize $x^3 - 1$ and hence find the three roots of the equation $x^3 = 1$

Q 2.24 Factorize $x^3 + 8$ (using the identity $a^3 + b^3 = (a+b)(a^2 - ab + b^2)$) and hence find the three roots of the equation $x^3 + 8 = 0$.

Q 2.25 Prove that $|1 + z_1 z_2{}^*|^2 + |z_1 - z_2|^2 = (1 + |z_1|^2)(1 + |z_2|^2)$

Q 2.26 Find all the complex numbers z such that $|z| = 1$ and $|z^2 + z^{2*}| = 1$.

Q 2.27 Prove that if $z_1 + z_2 + z_3 = 0$ and $|z_1| = |z_2| = |z_3| = 1$ then

$$z_1^2 + z_2^2 + z_3^2 = 0$$

Q 2.28 If z_1 and z_2 are the roots of $z^2 - z + 1 = 0$ show that (i) $z_1^{2024} + z_2^{2024} = -1$ and (ii) $z_1^{2022} + z_2^{2022} = 2$

By considering the cases $n = 6k, 6k+1, 6k+2, 6k+3, 6k+4, 6k+5$ find the possible values of $z_1^n + z_2^n$, $k \in \mathbb{Z}$.

Q 2.29 Show that if $z+\frac{1}{z}$ is real, with $z \neq 0$ then either z is a real number or it is a complex number with $|z|=1$. Hint: set $z=a+bi$

Q 2.30 Show that if $t=\frac{-x+iy}{x+iy}$ then

$$\frac{y^2-x^2}{y^2+x^2}=\frac{1+t^2}{2t}$$

(AEB 632/2 Jun1974p)

Q 2.31 If $|z_1|=|z_2|=...=|z_n|=\lambda$ then show that the expression E below is a real number

$$E=\frac{(z_1+z_2)(z_2+z_3)...(z_{n-1}-z_n)(z_n+z_1)}{z_1z_2...z_n}$$

Hint: $z_1=\lambda^2/z_1{}^*$

Q 2.32 The complex numbers $c_1, c_2, ..., c_n$ lie inside a disc with centre the origin and radius $l>0$. Show that the equation

$$c_1z+c_2z^2\cdots+c_nz^n=k$$

with $k>0$, has a solution if $|z|>\frac{k}{k+l}$.

Q 2.33 One root of the quadratic equation $x^2+px+q=0$, where p and q are real, is the complex number $2-3i$.

(i) Write down the other root. [1]

(ii) Find the values of p and q. [4]

(OCR FP1 Jun2006)

Q 2.34 The equation $z^3+pz^2+40z+q=0$ has a root $3+i$, where p and q are real. Find the values of p and q.

Q 2.35 Given that $z=-2+3i$ is a root of $2z^2+(-1+4i)z+c=0$ find c and the other root of the equation.

Q 2.36 Solve the equation $z^2+z^*=1/4$.

Q 2.37 Solve $z^2+|z|=-2$.

Q 2.38 Show that $\frac{z-|z|}{z+|z|}$ is a purely imaginary number.

Q 2.39 The cubic equation $x^3+ax^2+bx+c=0$, where a, b and c are real, has roots $(3+i)$ and 2.

(i) Write down the other root of the equation. [1]

(ii) Find the values of a, b and c. [6]

(OCR FP1 Jun2008)

Q 2.40 One root of the quadratic equation $x^2 + ax + b = 0$, where a and b are real, is $16 - 30i$.

(i) Write down the other root of the quadratic equation. [1]

(ii) Find the values of a and b. [4]

(iii) Use an algebraic method to solve the quartic equation $y^4 + ay^2 + b = 0$. [7]

(OCR FP1 Jun2011)

Q 2.41 (i) Use the quadratic formula to find the roots of $z^2 - (4+3i)z + 1 + 7i = 0$.
(ii) One root of the equation $z^3 - (5+3i)z^2 + (5+10i)z = 1 + 7i$ is real. Find all three roots of the polynomial. Hint: Since one root is real, separate real and imaginary parts.

Q 2.42 Find the roots of the equation $iz^2 + (1+i)z + 1 = 0$.

Q 2.43 Show that if $\lambda > 0$ then

$$|z_1 + z_2|^2 \leq (1+\lambda)|z_1|^2 + \left(1 + \frac{1}{\lambda}\right)|z_2|^2$$

Hint: Use $|z|^2 = zz^*$ and factorise the resulting expression.

Q 2.44 Find the roots of $z^2 - (3+i)z + 4 + 3i = 0$. Hint: Use the quadratic formula and determine the square root with the algebraic method.

Q 2.45 (i) Write down, in Cartesian form, the roots of the equation $z^4 = 16$. [2]

(ii) Hence solve the equation $w^4 = 16(1-w)^4$, giving your answers in Cartesian form. [5]

(OCR FP3 Jan2010)

Q 2.46 Let a, b, c be complex numbers. Show that if $|b-a|^2 = |b-c|^2 + |a-c|^2$ then the number $w = \dfrac{b-c}{a-c}$ is purely imaginary.

Q 2.47 The equation

$$x^3 + (10-4i)z^2 - (8+46i)z + 108i - 32 = 0$$

has one real root. Using this information determine all three roots.

3. Geometry in the Complex plane

Geometry existed before creation.

Plato

3.1 The Wessel-Argand-Gauss Plane

As I said earlier, complex numbers do not fill any gaps in the real number line. The real number line is fully dense with real numbers. There is no more "space" for anything else. If we want to develop a geometrical intuition for the complex numbers we need to think out of the box or "out of the line" as it happens.

This is exactly what was done by the French mathematician Argand[1] and Norwegian Caspar Wessel[2]. They used the known 2-dimensional Cartesian plane, but instead of a real y-axis, they placed the imaginary part there. In this way, the complex number $z = x + iy$ becomes a pair of coordinates (x, y) in this new complex plane. Every point on the Argand plane corresponds to a complex number and every complex number corresponds to *one and only one point* on the plane, once we fix the origin of our complex plane. In other words, this is a 1-1 mapping. In a completely analogous way to the real Cartesian plane, if we pick a point on this plane to serve as the origin of our axes then any complex number z can also be viewed as a "vector" in the complex plane.

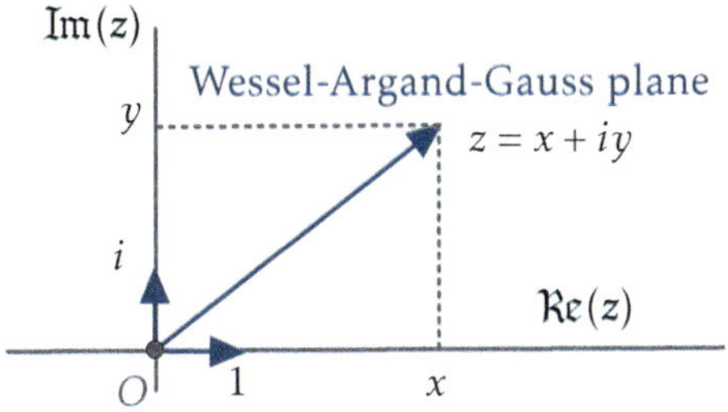

Figure 3.1: The complex plane. The purely imaginary numbers are on a line perpendicular to the horizontal real numbers

[1] Jean Robert Argand 1768-1822, was an amateur Swiss mathematician best known as one of the first to give a geometrical description of the Complex numbers.

[2] Caspar Wessel 1745-1818, was a Norwegian mathematician who invented a geometric way of representing complex numbers which pre-dated Argand.

This new plane, is also known as the Argand plane or the Wessel-Argand plane or Wessel-Argand-Gauss plane, as it was popularized by Gauss[3]. See figure (3.1)

DAD'S SOS NOTE: We know that equations of real numbers are represented as curves or shapes in the Cartesian plane. In a similar way, any algebraic relation between complex numbers corresponds to points and shapes on the Argand plane. This way of representing complex numbers not only helps in solving problems, but also increases our intuition about them. Note however, that this is one of the many possible representations of our relations, not the relation itself, but a very nice and convenient representation nevertheless. ♥

3.2 Length and Argument of Complex Numbers

We now have a new way to visualise, and also to handle, complex numbers as vectors on the Argand plane. We can define the length and the angle a complex number makes with the real axis. If we ignore the i on the y-axis and use the Pythagoras theorem on the vector we find that we can interpret the modulus or absolute value of a complex number that we defined in (2.10) as the length of the vector in the Argand plane.

Definition 3.1: The length or modulus of the z-vector is defined as

$$|z| = \sqrt{zz^*} = \sqrt{x^2 + y^2} \tag{3.1}$$

and the angle that the vector z makes with the x-axis is called the "Argument" of the complex number

$$\arg(z) = \arg(x + iy) = \arctan \frac{y}{x} \tag{3.2}$$

[3]Johann Carl Friedrich Gauss 1777-1855, was a German mathematician who worked in a wide variety of fields in both mathematics and physics incuding number theory, analysis, differential geometry, geodesy, magnetism, astronomy and optics. His work has had an immense influence in many areas. Known as the Prince of Mathematics.

DAD'S SOS NOTE: The angle $\arg(z) = \arctan \frac{y}{x}$ is, however, *Not Unique* as we can add integer numbers of π to it. Remember that for angles the *positive direction Anti-Clockwise.* ♥

As the argument of a complex number could be ambiguous we define the "Principal Argument".

Definition 3.2: The "Principal argument" Arg(z), would is the angle that is in the interval $(-\pi, \pi]$. We usually denote it with an upper case Arg instead of arg. So

$$-\pi < \operatorname{Arg}(z) \leq \pi$$

DAD'S SOS NOTE: I know that the "Principal Argument" versus the "Argument" can be confusing. In order to avoid making mistakes if you are asked to find the Principal Argument of a complex number draw the Argand diagram and remember

(i) Always mark on which quadrant your complex number lies in order to avoid mistakes.

(ii) Angles are positive if they are measured ANTI-CLOCKWISE.

(iii) If you use a calculator to compute the arctan, remember that it gives you the answer in the trigonometric principal value. In other words, your calculator will give you an answer in the range $(-\pi/2, \pi/2)$.

(iv) Then the principal argument is $\arctan \frac{y}{x} + k\pi$ with $k = -1, 0, 1$, see Figure (3.2)

$$\operatorname{Arg}(z) = \begin{cases} k = 0 & \text{IF } z, \text{ IN THE 1ST OR 4TH QUADRANT} \\ k = -1 & \text{IF } z, \text{ IN THE 3RD QUADRANT} \\ k = 1 & \text{IF } z, \text{ IN THE 2ND QUADRANT} \end{cases}$$

♥

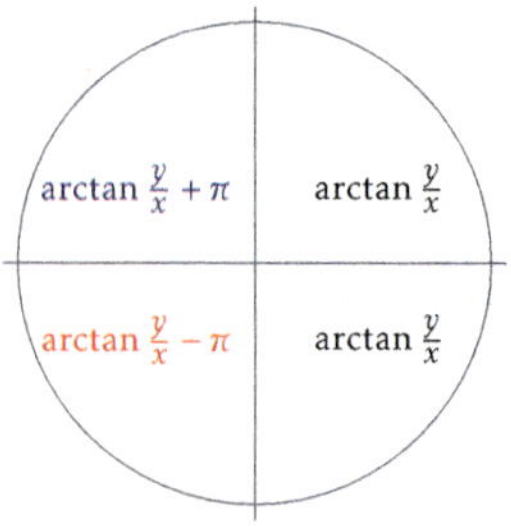

Figure 3.2: Once you find the angle with your calculator, you can find the principal argument Arg(z) by adding π if z is in the 2nd quadrant, subtracting π if it is in the 3rd quadrant, or leaving it unchanged if z is in the 1st or 4th quadrant.

The next exercise should clear any confusion....(hopefully)

Exercise 3.1: Find the modulus and principal argument of (i) $z_1 = 3 + 4i$, (ii)$z_2 = -40 - 9i$, (iii) $z_3 = -6 + 6i$.

Ans: For (i) we have that the modulus is $|z| = \sqrt{3^2 + 4^2} = 5$ and that $\arg(z) = \arctan(4/3)$. This number is in the first quadrant of the complex plane and your calculator would evaluate this to $\arg(z) = 53.1°$.

For (ii) the modulus is $|z| = \sqrt{40^2 + 9^2} = 41$ and $\arctan(9/40) = 0.22rad = 12.7°$. However, the number is in the third quadrant and hence the principal argument is $-\pi + 0.22 = -2.9$ or $-180 + 12.7 = -167.3°$.

For (iii) we have $|z| = \sqrt{36 + 36} = 6\sqrt{2}$ and $\arctan(-1) = -\pi/4 = -45°$. This number is in the second quadrant so the argument is $\mathrm{Arg}(z) = \pi - \pi/4 = 135°$. See Figure (3.3). □

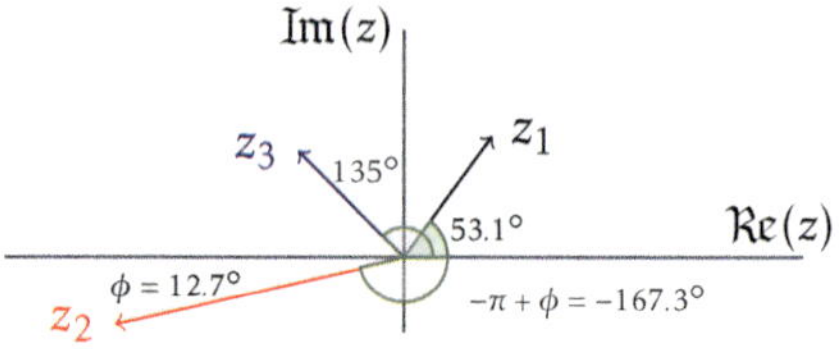

Figure 3.3

Proposition 3.1: The complex conjugate of any complex number is the reflection of that number with respect to the real axis.

Proof: This is because the operation of conjugation flips the i to $-i$ and hence complex conjugate numbers are mirrored along the x-axis. See figure (3.4). □

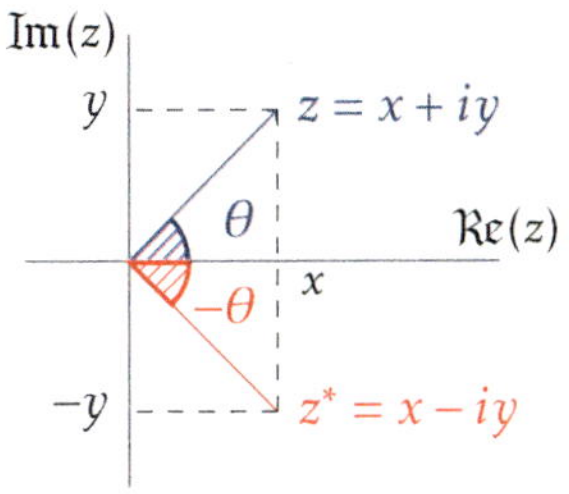

Figure 3.4: Complex conjugation reflects complex numbers with respect to the Real axis.

3.3 Polar Form of Complex Numbers

Now that we have the picture of a complex number as a vector, we can employ all the trigonometric machinery that we know. If we write the modulus of the complex number $|z| = \sqrt{x^2 + y^2} = r$ and $\theta = \arg(z)$ then the x-component of the complex vector is $x = r\cos\theta$ and the y-component is $y = r\sin\theta$. We can thus write

Definition 3.3: (Polar form) The complex number $z = x + iy$ can be written in terms of the modulus $r = |z|$ and its argument $\theta = \arg(z) = \arctan y/x$ as

$$z = r(\cos\theta + i\sin\theta) \tag{3.3}$$

Proposition 3.2: Two complex numbers $z_1 = r_1(\cos\theta_1 + i\sin\theta_1)$ and $z_2 = r_2(\cos\theta_2 + i\sin\theta_2)$ are equal if their moduli are equal and their arguments differ by multiples of 2π

$$z_1 = z_2 \Rightarrow (r_1 = r_2 \wedge \theta_1 - \theta_2 = 2k\pi), \quad k \in \mathbb{Z}$$

Proof: By comparing real and imaginary parts we get $r_1\cos\theta_1 = r_2\cos\theta_2$ and $r_1\sin\theta_1 = r_2\sin\theta_2$. Squaring these two relations and adding them gives

$$r_1^2(\cos^2\theta_1 + \sin^2\theta_1) = r_2^2(\cos^2\theta_2 + \sin^2\theta_2) \Rightarrow r_1^2 = r_2^2 \Rightarrow r_1 = r_2$$

Next we see that $\cos\theta_1 = \cos\theta_2$ and $\sin\theta_1 = \sin\theta_2$ and these two imply that the angles differ by a multiple of 2π. □

DAD'S SOS NOTE: Many questions either ask, or require, you to switch between the polar form of a complex number and the $z = x + iy$ form. To get from the polar form to the $z = x + iy$ it is fairly straightforward. All you need to do is to write that $x = r\cos\theta$ and $y = r\sin\theta$ and you are done. This is easily done as long as you remember the sine and cosine of the standard angles. If not, then you would lose time. Memorise the sine and cosine of the standard angles. It is necessary. ♥

Exercise 3.2: Write $z = 2(\cos\pi/3 + i\sin\pi/3)$ in the $x + iy$ form where $x, y \in \mathbb{R}$.

Ans: The cosine of $\pi/3$ is $1/2$ and the sine is $\sqrt{3}/2$. Hence $z = 1+i\sqrt{3}$. □

DAD'S SOS NOTE: If however, you need to get the polar form from the $z = x + iy$ form, then you need to do the following steps.

(i) Find the modulus $r = \sqrt{x^2 + y^2} \geq 0$ of the complex number. Remember no i's here. It is a positive number.

(ii) Now, factor out the modulus and write the number as

$$z = r\left(\frac{x}{\sqrt{x^2+y^2}} + i\frac{y}{\sqrt{x^2+y^2}}\right)$$

(iii) Identify if the $\frac{x}{\sqrt{x^2+y^2}}$ is the cosine of a known angle θ (see p. 188). If not, then use your calculator and remember the steps to determine the argument we listed before. Done! ♥

Notation: A point P on the Argand plane has a position vector $\overrightarrow{OP}$. The point P represents the complex number $z = x+iy$ and sometimes we write that $\overrightarrow{OP} = z$. This is an abuse of notation, since one is a number and the other a vector object, but is used extensively. As long as no confusion arises I guess it is ok. Also, in many texts, the complex numbers are written as the pair (x, y), a notation introduced by W.R.Hamilton[4]. This is correct, however we would not use this notation as it is rather tedious. ☺

[4] W.R.Hamilton 1805-1865, was an Irish astronomer and mathematician who discovered the quaternions.

Exercise 3.3: If $z = 1 - i$ find its polar form.
Ans: You first need to find the modulus of z using Eq. (3.1), $|z| = \sqrt{2}$. Next, you factor out the modulus and write

$$z = \sqrt{2}\left(\frac{1}{\sqrt{2}} - i\frac{1}{\sqrt{2}}\right) = \sqrt{2}\left(\frac{\sqrt{2}}{2} - i\frac{\sqrt{2}}{2}\right)$$

If you don't recognise the argument as one of the standard angles, use your calculator to compute arctan(−1). You will get $-\pi/4$. Remember to check on which quadrant it resides. In this case, it is on the 4th quadrant, so the Principal argument is indeed $-\pi/4$. You are done. Write the number as $z = \sqrt{2}(\cos\pi/4 - i\sin\pi/4)$ and verify if you can that you have done it correctly. □

DAD'S SOS NOTE: Earlier on, I said that in order to prove that a complex number is real it is enough to show that it is equal to its complex conjugate. Another way, is to show that the argument of the complex number is a zero, or a multiple of π. The proof of this is obvious, since in polar form, the imaginary part is $r\sin\theta$, and if θ is an integral multiple of π then the imaginary part is zero. So, $\arg(z) = k\pi \Rightarrow \mathfrak{Im}(z) = 0$.
Similarly, a complex number is purely imaginary if the argument is an odd multiple of $\pi/2$, namely $\arg(z) = (2k+1)\pi/2 \Rightarrow \mathfrak{Re}(z) = 0$ $(k \in \mathbb{Z})$ and hence the number is purely imaginary. The following relations would be used extensively when we need to prove that a number is real or purely imaginary.

$$\mathfrak{Im}(z) = 0 \Leftrightarrow \arg(z) = k\pi \quad \Leftrightarrow z \text{ IS REAL}$$

$$\mathfrak{Re}(z) = 0 \Leftrightarrow \arg(z) = (2k+1)\frac{\pi}{2}, \quad \Leftrightarrow z \text{ IS IMAGINARY}$$

with $k \in \mathbb{Z}$. ♥

3.4 Questions on Polar form

Q 3.1 Find the distance of the complex number

$$z = \left(\frac{-1 + i\sqrt{63}}{8}\right)^{2024}$$

from the origin.

Q 3.2 Given that $z = 6 + 3i$. Find the modulus $|z|$ and the $\text{Arg}(z)$. Furthermore, if $\text{Arg}(\mu + 5i + z) = \pi/4$ find the value of $\mu \in \mathbb{R}$.

Q 3.3 Place the following complex numbers in polar form and find the principal argument.

(1) $z = 2 + 2\sqrt{3}i$	(2) $z = \sqrt{6} - i\sqrt{2}$	(3) $z = -1 + i$
(4) $z = 1 - i$	(5) $(i + i)(1 + i\sqrt{3})$	(6) $\dfrac{2}{1 + i\sqrt{3}}$

Q 3.4 If $z = \cos\theta + i\sin\theta$ use the half angle transformation $t = \tan\dfrac{\theta}{2}$ to show that

$$z = \frac{1 + it}{1 - it}$$

for $\theta \neq \pi$. You can use that $\cos\theta = \dfrac{1 - t^2}{1 + t^2}$ and $\sin\theta = \dfrac{2t}{1 + t^2}$.

Q 3.5 Show that for a non-zero complex number z we have $\text{Arg}(z + z^*) = 0$ if $\mathfrak{Re}(z) > 0$. What if $\mathfrak{Re}(z) < 0$?

Q 3.6 Show that if $|z| = 1$ then

$$\mathfrak{Re}\left(\frac{1}{1 - z}\right) = \frac{1}{2}$$

Hint: Use $z = \cos\theta + i\sin\theta$

Q 3.7 If $z_1 = 7 + 6i$ and $z_2 = 1 - 3i$, find the modulus $|z_1 - 2z_2|$ and its principal argument $\text{Arg}(z_1 - 2z_2)$.

Q 3.8 Let $z_1 = a/(1 + i)$ and $z_2 = b/(1 + 2i)$, $a, b \in \mathbb{R}$. Find a, b if $z_1 + z_2 = 1$. Find the distance between the two points z_1 and z_2 in the Argand diagram.

Q 3.9 Factorise $P(z) = z^3 - 8$. Hence, find the three roots of $P(z) = 0$ and plot them on an Argand diagram.

3.5 Geometric Meaning of Complex Operations

The Argand diagram enables us to view complex numbers as a points on the complex plane or as a position vectors of these points. The difference with the usual Cartesian plane is that this time the vector represents a complex number. The concepts of "Free" and "Bound" or position vectors carry over to the complex plane unaltered. Addition of vectors on the complex plane is also the same, as is multiplication by a real number. We just do the same geometric operations forgetting for the time being that the y-axis has the imaginary i as a unit of measurement.

Proposition 3.3: We can add and subtract complex vectors in exactly the same way we do it for vectors in the real plane.

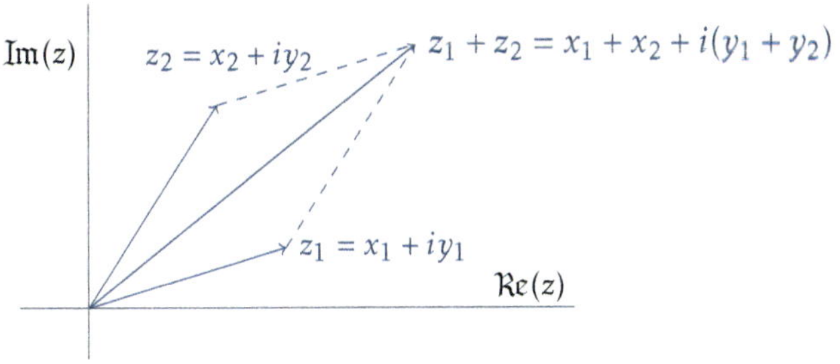

DAD'S SOS NOTE: The vector approach on the complex plane is more than just a coincidence. The rules of addition of complex numbers together with the operation of multiplication by a real number make the set of complex numbers a Vector Space in the algebraic sense. All the usual rules of adding vectors, like Chasle's law and trigonometry work here too. For example, the sine and cosine laws we used in plane geometry also work here. ♥

Corollary 3.1: The length of the "Free" P_1P_2 vector between two points $P_1(z_1)$ and $P_2(z_2)$ is $|OP_2 - OP_1| = |z_2 - z_1|$. This is the same as with the vectors on the Cartesian plane.

Proposition 3.4: The triangle inequalities we proved earlier in Proposition (2.9) now take a geometrical meaning as the sides of a triangle formed by the vectors representing these complex numbers. So, the sum of the lengths of two sides in a triangle is always greater than the third side....

$$|z_1 + z_2| \le |z_1| + |z_2|, \quad |z_1 - z_2| \le |z_1| + |z_2|, \quad |z_1 - z_2| \ge \big||z_1| - |z_2|\big|$$

Adding two complex numbers is equivalent to adding two vectors exactly in the same way we did with the real vectors. But how about multiplication or division? What is the geometric representation of these two operations? Multiplication of a complex number by a real number $\lambda \in \mathbb{R}$ is easy. We just get a new complex vector with modulus increased by $|\lambda|$ times. The direction of the new vector would depend on the sign of λ. So this is the same as with vectors on the real Cartesian plane.

But multiplication of two complex numbers is different. With real numbers, if we multiply a number, say 3, by another number, say 4, we just move along the number line 3 times 4 units, or 4 times 3 units. Similarly, with division, the geometric meaning of it, is just dividing a line segment.

With complex numbers, being "2-dimensional" the geometrical meaning is more interesting. If we use the polar form of two complex numbers we have

$$\begin{aligned} z_1 z_2 &= r_1 r_2 (\cos\theta_1 + i\sin\theta_1)(\cos\theta_2 + i\sin\theta_2) \\ &= r_1 r_2 \left[\cos\theta_1 \cos\theta_2 - \sin\theta_1 \sin\theta_2 + i(\cos\theta_1 \sin\theta_2 + \sin\theta_1 \cos\theta_2)\right] \\ &= r_1 r_2 \left[\cos(\theta_1 + \theta_2) + i\sin(\theta_1 + \theta_2)\right] \end{aligned}$$

This result is remarkable. Multiplying two complex numbers, results in a complex number which extends to $r_1 r_2$ but also rotates! If z_1, z_2 were real then the result of the multiplication would be the $r_1 r_2$. But now we have an added dimension. The multiplication of complex numbers results in a rotation of the original complex vector as well as a magnification.

Proposition 3.5: Multiplying two complex numbers z_1 and z_2 is the same as multiplying their moduli and adding their arguments. See Figure (3.5). We thus get a new complex number z that has

$$\begin{aligned} |z| &= |z_1 z_2| = |z_1|\,|z_2| \\ \arg(z) &= \arg(z_1 z_2) = \arg(z_1) + \arg(z_2) \end{aligned}$$

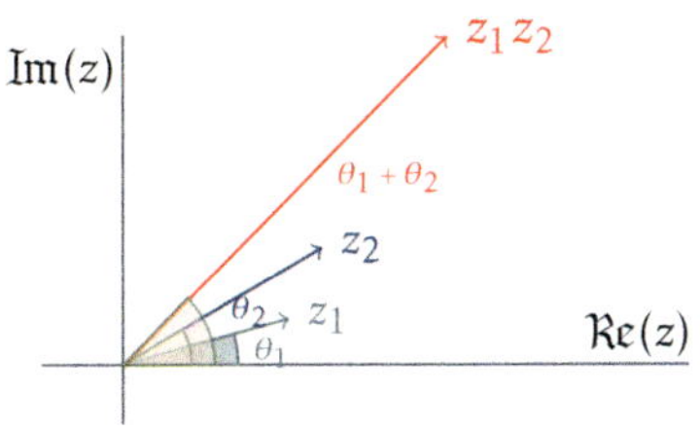

Figure 3.5: Multiplying z_1 with z_2 gives a new complex vector which is at an angle θ_1 away from the z_2 vector. So its argument is $\theta_1 + \theta_2$ and its modulus is the product $|z_1||z_2|$.

DAD'S SOS NOTE: Be very careful here. If you multiply two complex numbers in polar form you multiply the moduli and add the arguments. However, when adding the argument you may fall out of the range $(-\pi, \pi]$ and hence it would not be the principal argument. ♥

Another interesting type of questions is to use the product of complex numbers to obtain the arctan.

Exercise 3.4: Show that

$$\frac{\pi}{4} = \arctan\frac{1}{2} + \arctan\frac{1}{3}$$

by considering the product $(2+i)(3+i)$.

Ans: If you multiply the complex numbers you get $(2+i)(3+i) = 5+5i$. Now, we know that the argument of the product of two complex numbers is the sum of the arguments. We thus have

$$\arg[(2+i)(3+i)] = \arg(2+i) + \arg(3+i) = \arg(5+5i)$$

From which it follows that

$$\arctan\frac{1}{2} + \arctan\frac{1}{3} = \arctan 1 = \frac{\pi}{4} \qquad \square$$

DAD'S SOS NOTE: This is by far the best way to obtain these kind of identities with arctan. Complex numbers make our mathematical lives so much more fun. You can see a generalisation of this formula in Question (3.26). ♥

The following result is very useful in types of questions that involve arctan

Exercise 3.5: If $\arg(z) = \arctan\left(\frac{y}{x}\right)$, show that $\arg(z^2) = 2\arctan\left(\frac{y}{x}\right)$. Show by induction that

$$\arg(z^n) = n\arctan\left(\frac{y}{x}\right) = n\arg(z)$$

Ans: Since $\arg(z^2) = \arg(z \cdot z) = \arg(z) + \arg(z) = 2\arg(z)$. Now for the induction part, the $n = 1$ is obvious. Assume that the relation is true for $n = k$, namely $\arg(z^k) = k\arctan\left(\frac{y}{x}\right) = k\arg(z)$. For $n = k+1$, we have

$$\begin{aligned}\arg(z^{k+1}) = \arg(z^k z) = \arg(z^k) + \arg(z) &= k\arctan\frac{y}{x} + \arctan\frac{y}{x} \\ = (k+1)\arctan\frac{y}{x} &= (k+1)\arg(z)\end{aligned}$$

Thus, the relation is true for all $n \in \mathbb{N}$. □

Proposition 3.6: Dividing two complex numbers z_1 and z_2 is the same as dividing their moduli and subtracting their arguments. See figure (3.6). We thus get a new complex number z that has

$$\begin{aligned}|z| &= \left|\frac{z_1}{z_2}\right| = \frac{|z_1|}{|z_2|} \\ \arg(z) &= \arg\left(\frac{z_1}{z_2}\right) = \arg(z_1) - \arg(z_2)\end{aligned}$$

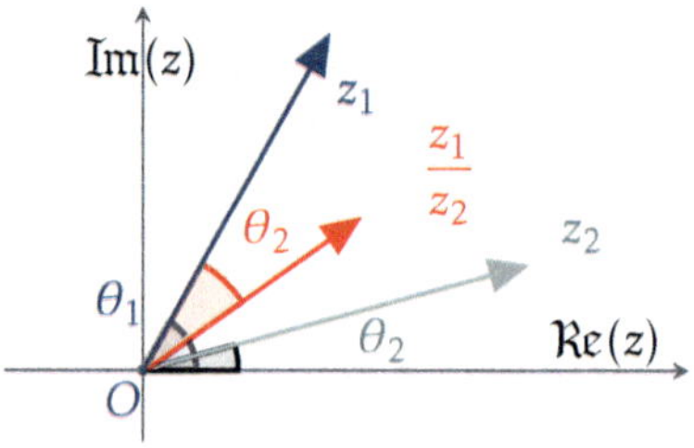

Figure 3.6: Dividing z_1 by z_2 gives a new complex vector which is rotated from z_1 towards z_2 by an angle θ_2. Hence the resulting vector has angle $\theta_1 - \theta_2$ which is the in-between angle of the two vectors. The modulus of the new vector is just $|z_1|/|z_2|$.

The way to view division is as follows

- Rotate the denominator (z_2 in our case) anticlockwise, until it falls on z_1.
- The angle is then the argument of the new complex number, while its modulus is $\frac{|z_1|}{|z_2|}$.
- This angle of course is the in-between angle of the two vectors but it could be positive or negative depending on the angle orientation.

You must be very careful, as angles have orientation. In Figure (3.6), the angle is positive. If we swap the vectors in the diagram, then the vector z_2 would rotate anticlockwise by $2\pi - (\theta_2 - \theta_1)$.

DAD'S SOS NOTE: You can also view the division by a complex number z as a CLOCKWISE rotation of the plane by the argument of z. This way of viewing division is very important when we want to rotate points around. The new $z' = 1$ is now the unit point on the real axis, whereas every other point w is now $\frac{w}{z}$. ♥

The following exercise illustrates the point.

Exercise 3.6: Let AB be a segment with endpoints $A(a)$ and $B(b)$ and $Z(z)$ a point on the complex plane. Show that the reflection of the point $Z(z)$ with respect to the segment AB is the point $W(w)$

$$w = \frac{z^* - a^*}{b^* - a^*}(b - a) + a$$

Ans: In order to find the reflection with respect to AB we are going first to translate the segment so that the point A is at the origin.

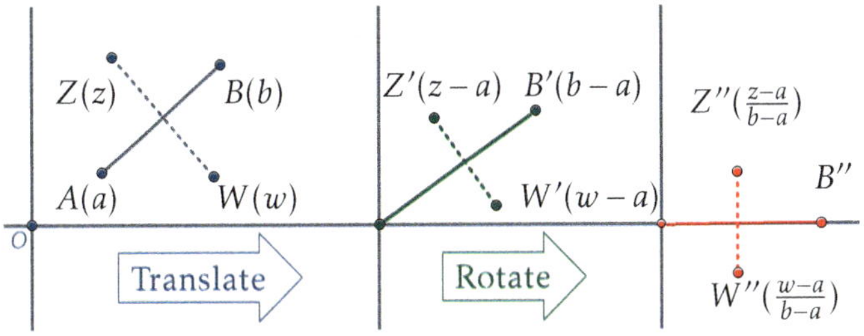

Figure 3.7: First translate by a, then rotate by $b - a$.

This means that $Z(z) \to Z'(z-a)$ and $W(w) \to W'(w-a)$ and of course the point $B(b) \to B'(b-a)$. If we now divide by $b-a$ we are rotating all the points clockwise. See Figure (3.7). The points now move to $B'(b-a) \to B''(1)$, $Z'(z-a) \to Z''(\frac{z-a}{b-a})$ and $W' \to W''(\frac{w-a}{b-a})$. However, the reflection of Z'' is now the complex conjugate. So point $W''(w'')$ has $w'' = \frac{z^*-a^*}{b^*-a^*}$. We now need to reverse the transformations to find the point W. So, we rotate anticlockwise by $b-a$, which means multiplying by $b-a$ and then add a to get back to our original position. Hence, $w = w''(b-a)+a$ and this is

$$w = \frac{z^* - a^*}{b^* - a^*}(b-a) + a \qquad \square$$

This is a very powerful technique.

The following proposition is really important. It comes up in many advanced questions. It is about the angle of two vectors on the Argand plane.

Proposition 3.7: The points Q, P_1 and P_2 represent the complex numbers z, z_1 and z_2 respectively. Then the angle between the two free vectors on the complex plane $\overrightarrow{QP_1}$ and $\overrightarrow{QP_2}$ with corresponding complex numbers $z_1 - z$ and $z_2 - z$, see figure (3.8), is given by

$$\arg \frac{z_1 - z}{z_2 - z} = \phi \tag{3.4}$$

Proof: If I rotate the vector $\overrightarrow{QP_2}$ anticlockwise until it falls onto $\overrightarrow{QP_1}$ then the angle ϕ is the argument of $\arg \frac{z_1 - z}{z_2 - z}$. See figure (3.8) Note that, if I swap the vectors then the angle would be $-\phi$, as I am now going anticlockwise a full circle minus ϕ. $\square$

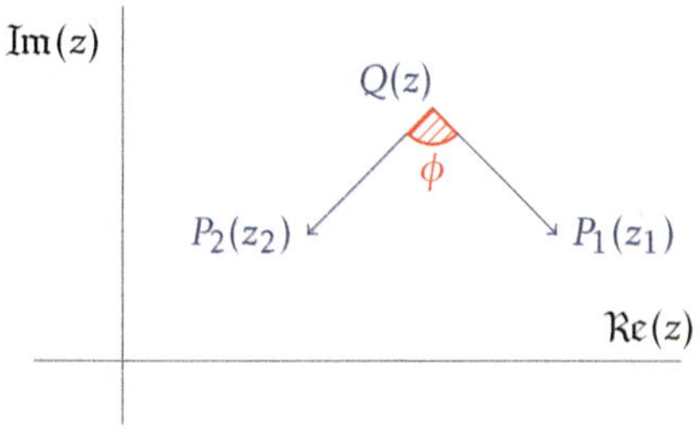

Figure 3.8: ϕ is the argument of the ratio $\frac{z_1 - z}{z_2 - z}$.

DAD'S SOS NOTE: Spend few minutes to understand these diagrams for multiplication and division and the angle of two complex vectors. Do not pass them. They will prove very useful in developing an intuition and also in solving geometrical problems. For example, you can view multiplication by a real positive number κ as multiplication by $\kappa(\cos 2\pi + i\sin 2\pi)$ (or by $\kappa e^{2\pi i}$ when we learn the Euler representation). Similarly, multiplication by a negative number is a rotation by π, since $\cos\pi + i\sin\pi = -1$ (or $e^{i\pi} = -1$). So, to get negative real numbers just rotate the positive ones by π.
If, on the other hand, you want to rotate anti-clockwise by 90 degrees a vector in the complex plane, all you need to do is to multiply by $i = \cos\pi/2 + i\sin\pi/2$ (or by $i = e^{i\pi/2}$). ♥

Exercise 3.7: Find the principal argument of the complex number $z = \dfrac{-1}{1+\sqrt{3}i}$.

Ans: The question asks for the argument only. We could of course bring it in the normal $x + iy$ form by multiplying the denominator by its complex conjugate and then working out the argument. If we do this we will find

$$z = \frac{-1 + i\sqrt{3}}{4} = \frac{1}{2}\left(\cos\frac{2\pi}{3} + i\sin\frac{2\pi}{3}\right)$$

Another way, is to see z as a quotient of two complex numbers and take their difference. The numerator is -1, and hence the argument is π (negative real number). The denominator is $1 + i\sqrt{3} = 2(1/2 + i\sqrt{3}/2)$ which is equal to $2(\cos\pi/3 + i\sin\pi/3)$ and its argument is $\pi/3$. Subtracting them we get $\pi - \pi/3 = 2\pi/3$. This is a principal argument since it falls in the range $(-\pi, \pi]$ so there is nothing more to do. □

Corollary 3.2: If the argument of a complex number $\arg(z) = \phi$ then the argument of its complex conjugate is $\arg(z^*) = -\phi$. This is because the complex conjugate, geometrically is the reflection with respect to the real axis.

Cosine Law. We can prove the cosine law for triangles using complex numbers and the proof is in my opinion very elegant.

Proposition 3.8: (Cosine Law) Let z_1 and z_2 be the two sides of the triangle and let θ_1 and θ_2 be their respective arguments. See Figure (3.9). Prove the cosine law

$$|z_1 - z_2|^2 = |z_1|^2 + |z_2|^2 - 2|z_1||z_2|\cos\theta$$

Proof: The third side is $z_1 - z_2$ and the angle between the z_1 and z_2 is $\theta = \theta_2 - \theta_1$. The length square is then given by

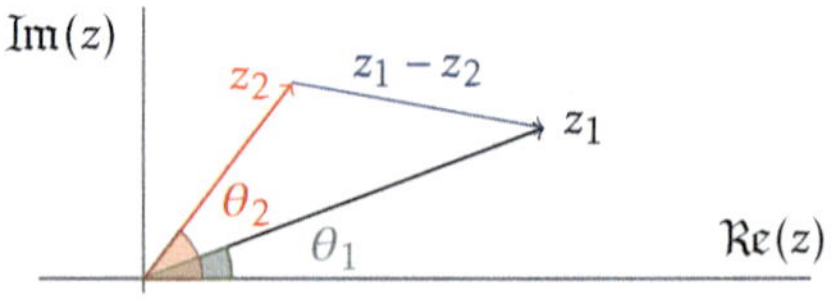

Figure 3.9: The cosine law on the complex Argand plane.

$$\begin{aligned}
|z_1 - z_2|^2 &= (z_1 - z_2)(z_1^* - z_2^*) \\
&= |z_1|^2 + |z_2|^2 - (z_1 z_2^* + z_2 z_1^*) \\
&= |z_1|^2 + |z_2|^2 - 2\Re(z_2 z_1^*) \\
&= |z_1|^2 + |z_2|^2 - 2|z_1^*||z_2|\cos(\arg(z_2) + \arg(z_1{}^*)) \\
&= |z_1|^2 + |z_2|^2 - 2|z_1||z_2|\cos(\theta_2 - \theta_1) \\
&= |z_1|^2 + |z_2|^2 - 2|z_1||z_2|\cos\theta
\end{aligned}$$ □

3.6 Equation of a Line

A line on the Argand plane can also be represented using complex numbers. The following proposition shows how.

Proposition 3.9: The equation of a straight line on the complex plane is given by

$$Az + A^* z^* + B = 0, \text{ where } A \in \mathbb{C} \text{ and } B \in \mathbb{R} \tag{3.5}$$

Proof: You can prove this equation for the line on the complex plane in many ways. Perhaps the easiest way is to start from the equation of the line $ax + by + c = 0$ and substitute for $x = (z + z^*)/2$

and $y = (z - z^*)/(2i)$. If you do this you will get

$$(a - ib)z + (a + ib)z^* + 2c = 0$$

and by renaming the coefficients $A = a - ib$ and $B = 2c$ we get the required equation.
Note that, the coefficients of the z and z^* must be complex conjugates of each other and the constant term must be real. □

We can use the above proposition to find the slope of the line.

Exercise 3.8: The slope m of the line $ax + by + c = 0$, with equation $Az + A^*z^* + B = 0$ is given by

$$m = i\frac{A + A^*}{A - A^*}$$

Ans: The slope of the line in Cartesian coordinates is $m = -\frac{a}{b}$. But $A + A^* = 2a$ and $A - A^* = -2ib$ hence dividing we get

$$m = i\frac{A + A^*}{A - A^*}$$ □

You can also find the condition for two lines in the complex plane are parallel.

Exercise 3.9: Show that two lines, $\epsilon_1 : A_1 z + {A_1}^* z^* + B_1 = 0$ and $\epsilon_2 : A_2 z + {A_2}^* z^* + B_2 = 0$ are parallel if

$$\frac{{A_1}^*}{A_1} = \frac{{A_2}^*}{A_2}$$

Ans: For the two lines to be parallel we must have that they have the same slope. Hence

$$m = i\frac{A_1 + {A_1}^*}{A_1 - {A_1}^*} = i\frac{A_2 + {A_2}^*}{A_2 - {A_2}^*}$$

Cross multiplying and simplifying we get the required result. □

3.7 Collinearity of Three Points

If you want to show that three points represented by complex numbers on the Argand plane lie on the same line then the following theorem is very handy.

Theorem 3.1: Three points z, z_1 and z_2 are collinear if any of the following conditions hold true:

(i) Three points are collinear if $\left(\dfrac{z-z_1}{z-z_2}\right)$ is a real number and hence it must be equal to its conjugate.

$$\frac{z-z_1}{z-z_2} = \frac{z^* - {z_1}^*}{z^* - {z_2}^*}$$

(ii) Condition (i) can also be written in determinant form as

$$\begin{vmatrix} 1 & z & z^* \\ 1 & z_1 & z_1^* \\ 1 & z_2 & z_2^* \end{vmatrix} = 0$$

This determinant is the equivalent to the one used for the collinearity of three points in the Cartesian plane.

(iii) The argument of

$$\arg \frac{z-z_1}{z-z_2} = n\pi, \text{ WHERE } n \in \mathbb{Z} \qquad (3.6)$$

In terms of the principal argument it must be 0 or π.

(iv) If $z = (1-t)z_1 + tz_2$, where $t \in \mathbb{R}$ is a real number.

Proof: I will prove (i) with an intuitive geometric argument.

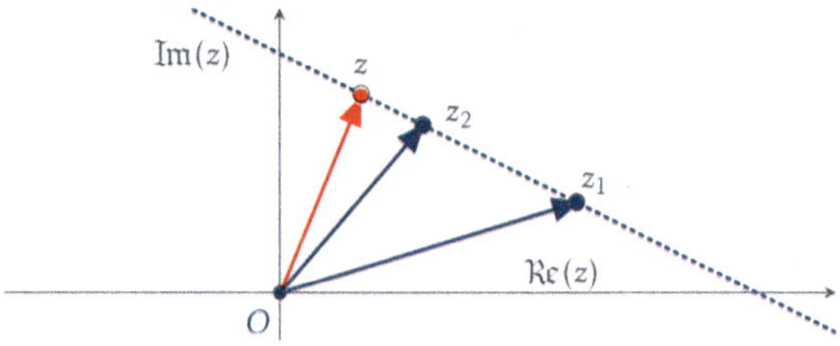

From the figure we see that for z to be on the line joining z_1 and z_2 we must have $(z-z_2) = \lambda(z-z_1)$ where λ is a real parameter. Hence $\dfrac{z-z_1}{z_2-z} = \lambda$ and since λ is real, it is equal to its complex conjugate.

Thus we must have:

$$\frac{z - z_1}{z_2 - z} = \frac{z_1^* - z^*}{z_2^* - z^*} \tag{3.7}$$

To prove (ii), just note that in the determinant we can subtract row 1 from rows 2 and 3 without altering the value of the determinant. We can now evaluate the determinant along the first column to get:

$$\begin{vmatrix} 1 & z & z^* \\ 1 & z_1 & z_1^* \\ 1 & z_2 & z_2^* \end{vmatrix} = \begin{vmatrix} 1 & z & z^* \\ 0 & z_1 - z & z_1^* - z^* \\ 0 & z_2 - z & z_2^* - z^* \end{vmatrix} = (z_1 - z)(z_2^* - z^*) - (z_1^* - z^*)(z_2 - z)$$

And using Eq (3.7) we get the required zero.

To prove (iii), note that if the $\left(\frac{z - z_1}{z_2 - z}\right)$ is a real number then its argument must be a multiple of π in order for the imaginary part to be zero.

Finally, for (iv) we can rewrite $\left(\frac{z - z_1}{z_2 - z}\right) = \lambda$ as

$$z = -\frac{\lambda}{1 - \lambda} z_1 + \frac{1}{1 - \lambda} z_2$$

If we now re-parametrise using $t = 1/(1 - \lambda)$ we get

$$z = (1 - t)z_1 + tz_2$$

□

Exercise 3.10: Show that three points z_1, z_2 and z_3 are collinear if and only if there exists real numbers k, l and m, not all zero, such that $kz_1 + lz_2 + mz_3 = 0$ and $k + l + m = 0$.

Ans: We are going to use the fact that three points are collinear if

$$\frac{z_3 - z_1}{z_3 - z_2} = \lambda \in \mathbb{R}$$

In fact, you can pick any combination of z's as long as there is a common point in both the numerator and denominator. Doing the algebra we find that this is equivalent to

$$(1 - \lambda)z_3 + \lambda z_2 - z_1 = 0$$

The coefficients are $k = -1$, $l = \lambda$ and $m = 1 - \lambda$ and $k + l + m = 0$.

The questions says "if and only if". So we must prove the converse statement to fully answer the question. Assume that $k \neq 0$, then solving for z_1

we have

$$z_1 = -\frac{l}{k}z_2 - \frac{m}{k}z_3$$

Substituting into the ratio $\dfrac{z_3 - z_1}{z_3 - z_2}$ and after some algebra (taking into account $k + l + m = 0$) we end up with

$$\frac{z_3 - z_1}{z_3 - z_2} = 1 - k - l = 1 + m$$

Which is a real number and hence the points are collinear. □

Exercise 3.11: (i) The distinct points A, Q and C lie on a straight line in the Argand diagram, and represent the distinct complex numbers a, q and c, respectively. Show that $\dfrac{(q-a)}{(c-a)}$ is real and hence that

$$(c-a)(q^* - a^*) = (c^* - a^*)(q - a)$$

Given that $aa^* = cc^* = 1$, show further that

$$q + acq^* = a + c$$

(ii) The distinct points A, B, C and D lie, in anticlockwise order, on the circle of unit radius with centre at the origin (so that, for example, $aa^* = 1$). The lines AC and BD meet at Q. Show that

$$(ac - bd)q^* = (a + c) - (b + d)$$

where b and d are complex numbers represented by the points B and D respectively, and show further that

$$(ac - bd)(q + q^*) = (a - b)(1 + cd) + (c - d)(1 + ab)$$

(iii) The lines AB and CD meet at P, which represents the complex number p. Given that p is real, show that $p(1 + ab) = a + b$. Given further that $ac - bd \neq 0$, show that $p(q + q^*) = 2$. **(STEP III 2018)**

Ans:

(i) The first part is a simple application of Theorem (3.1). As this is not part of the regular syllabus the question asks you to prove it. For the next part just use the fact that $aa^* = cc^* = 1$ in the previous relation. Notice that the required answer does not have a^* or c^* so just substitute $a^* = 1/a$ and $c^* = 1/c$ to get

$$(c-a)(q^*-a^*) = (c^*-a^*)(q-a) \Rightarrow$$
$$(c-a)\left(q^*-\frac{1}{a}\right) = \left(\frac{1}{c}-\frac{1}{a}\right)(q-a) \Rightarrow$$
$$aq^*-1 = \frac{a-q}{c} \Rightarrow acq^*+q = a+c$$ □

(ii) The question gives you that the points AQC are collinear and also the BQD are collinear. Hence, you can aply the result of the previous part to to get

$$acq^*+q = a+c$$
$$bdq^*+q = b+d$$
$$\text{Subtracting } (ac-bd)q^* = a+c-(b+d)$$ □

For the last part, take the complex conjugate of the previous part, namely $(a^*c^*-b^*d^*)q = a^*+c^*-(b^*+d^*)$ use again the $a^* = 1/a$ and $c^* = 1/c$ and after some algebra you will get the result

$$(a^*c^*-b^*d^*)q = a^*+c^*-(b^*+d^*) \Rightarrow$$
$$\left(\frac{1}{ac}-\frac{1}{bd}\right)q = \frac{a+c}{ac}-\frac{b+d}{bd} \Rightarrow$$
$$(ac-bd)q = (b+d)ac-(a+c)bd$$ □

Now you can add the two equations

$$(ac-bd)(q+q^*) = abc+adc-abd-cbd+a+c-b-d \Rightarrow$$
$$(ac-bd)(q+q^*) = (a-b)(1+cd)+(c-d)(1+ab)$$ □

(iii) Finally, you know that the points PBA are collinear. Therefore, apply the result of part (i) by changing $c \to b$ and $q \to p$ to get $p+abp^* = a+b$, and since p is said to be real we have $p = p^*$ and therefore $p(1+ab) = a+b$.
Similarly, the points PCD are also collinear and by applying again the results of (i) we get $p(1+cd) = c+d$. Substituting these two into the result of part (ii) we get

$$(ac-bd)(q+q^*) = (a-b)\frac{c+d}{p}+(c-d)\frac{a+b}{p} \Rightarrow$$
$$(ac-bd)(q+q^*)p = ac+ad-bc-bd+ac+cb-ad-bd \Rightarrow$$
$$(ac-bd)(q+q^*)p = 2(ac-bd) \Rightarrow (q+q^*)p = 2, \text{ Since } ac-bd \neq 0$$ □

Exercise 3.12: Let AB be a chord on a unit circle. The complex representations of the points A and B are a and b respectively. Show that the equation of the line of the chord is $z = a + b - abz^*$.
Ans: Let z be an arbitrary point on the line. Then $\frac{z-a}{b-a} = \frac{z^*-a^*}{b^*-a^*}$. Since points A and B are on a unit circle we have $aa^* = bb^* = 1$ and

$$\frac{z-a}{b-a} = \frac{z^* - \frac{1}{a}}{\frac{a-b}{ab}} \Rightarrow z - a = -(z^*ab - b) \Rightarrow z = a + b - abz^* \qquad \square$$

Theorem 3.2: Let Z_1 and Z_2 be two points on the Argand plane represented by the complex numbers z_1 and z_2 respectively. Then if a point Z, representing the complex number z, divides the segment Z_1Z_2 in a ratio $\frac{Z_1Z}{ZZ_2} = \frac{k}{l}$ then z is given by

$$z = \frac{lz_1 + kz_2}{k+l} \tag{3.8}$$

Proof: If we let $z_1 = x_1 + iy_1$, $z_2 = x_2 + iy_2$ and $z = x + iy$ and substitute these into $\frac{z_1z}{zz_2} = \frac{k}{l}$ we get

$$x - x_1 = \frac{k}{l}(x_2 - x) \text{ AND } y - y_1 = \frac{k}{l}(y_2 - y)$$

and solving for x and y we get that

$$x = \frac{lx_1 + kx_2}{k+l} \quad y = \frac{ly_1 + ky_2}{k+l} \Rightarrow z = \frac{lz_1 + kz_2}{k+l} \qquad \square$$

Proposition 3.10: Given three points $A(a), B(b)$ and $C(c)$ representing the points of a triangle $\triangle ABC$, the point G with complex number

$$z_G = \frac{a+b+c}{3}$$

is the barycentre or centroid of the triangle.
Proof: The midpoint $M(m)$ of AB has $m = (a+b)/2$. As the barycentre of the triangle is at a ratio 2 to 1 from the $C(c)$ vertex, we must

have $\frac{CG}{GM} = \frac{2}{1}$ and

$$z_G = \frac{c+2m}{3} = \frac{a+b+c}{3}$$ □

3.8 Perpendicular Lines

If you want to prove that two complex numbers or vectors are perpendicular the following might become very handy!

Proposition 3.11: Two complex numbers z_1 and z_2 represented by their complex vectors are perpendicular if the complex number $z = \frac{z_1}{z_2}$ is purely imaginary or equivalently $\frac{z_1}{z_2} + \frac{z_1^*}{z_2^*} = 0$

Proof: If the two complex numbers are perpendicular then their in-between angle must be $\theta_1 - \theta_2 = \pm\pi/2$. Since the argument of $z = z_1/z_2$ is equal to $\arg(z) = \theta_1 - \theta_2 = \pm\pi/2$ the real part of $\Re(z) = 0$ and hence z is purely imaginary. □

Exercise 3.13: Prove that the diagonals of a rhombus intersect at right angles.

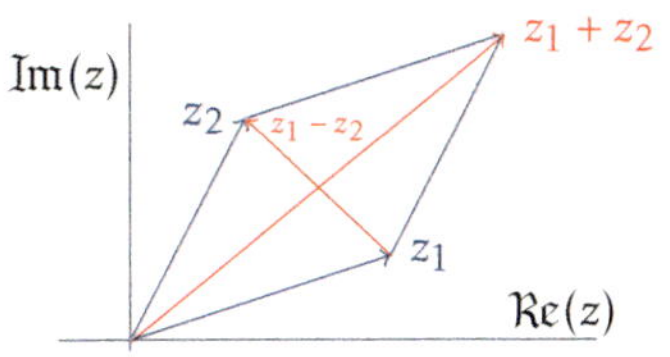

Figure 3.10: The diagonals of a rhombus intersect at right angles

Ans: Let z_1 and z_2 be the sides of the rhombus. See Figure (3.10). Then one diagonal is $z_1 - z_2$ and the other one is $z_1 + z_2$. According to our previous result the two vectors are perpendicular if the complex number $z = \frac{z_1 - z_2}{z_1 + z_2}$ is purely imaginary, or if $z + z^* = 0$. We thus have

$$z + z^* = \frac{z_1 - z_2}{z_1 + z_2} + \frac{z_1^* - z_2^*}{z_1^* + z_2^*} = \frac{2(|z_1|^2 - |z_2|^2)}{|z_1 + z_2|^2} = 0$$

And since it is a rhombus we have $|z_1| = |z_2|$ and thus z is purely imaginary and the diagonals intersect at right angles. □

Proposition 3.12: The orthocenter h (point where the three altitudes meet) of a triangle $\triangle ABC$ is given by $h = a + b + c$. See Figure (3.11)

Proof: We have that $AH \perp BC$, $BH \perp AC$ and $CH \perp AB$ and hence

$$\frac{h-a}{b-c} + \frac{h^*-a^*}{b^*-c^*} = 0, \quad \frac{h-b}{c-a} + \frac{h^*-b^*}{c^*-a^*} = 0, \quad \frac{h-c}{a-b} + \frac{h^*-c^*}{a^*-b^*} = 0 \quad (3.9)$$

Without loss of generality we can assume that centre of the circumscribed circle of the triangle is the origin of the Argand plane and that the radius of the circle is 1. We therefore have, $aa^* = bb^* = cc^* = 1$. Using these relations Eqs (3.9) become

$$ha - a^2 - h^*abc + cb = 0$$
$$hb - b^2 - h^*abc + ac = 0$$
$$hc - c^2 - h^*abc + ba = 0$$

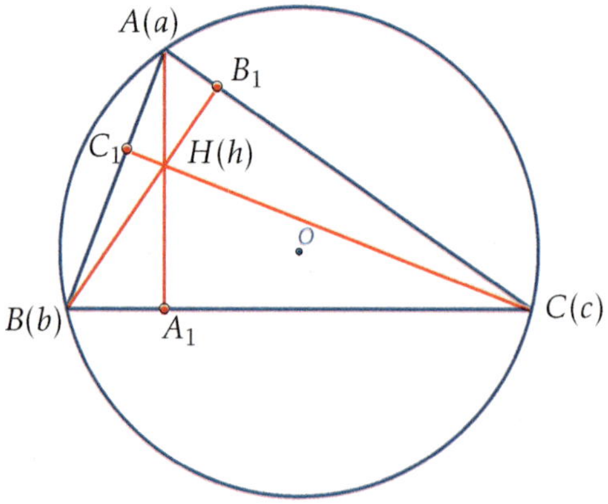

Figure 3.11: The orthocenter of a triangle is given by $h = a + b + c$.

Subtracting the second from the first we get $h(a-b)-(a^2-b^2)+c(b-a) = 0 \Rightarrow h = a + b + c$. We can now verify that the third equation is also satisfied. □

Exercise 3.14: Show that the centre $N(n)$ of the nine-point circle of a triangle $\triangle ABC$ is given by

$$n = \frac{a+b+c}{2}$$

and that its radius is half the radius of the circumscribed circle.

Proof: The nine point circle passes through the mid points of sides of the triangle. If $N(n)$ is the centre of the circle we must have $|n - \frac{a+b}{2}| = |n - \frac{b+c}{2}| = |n - \frac{c+a}{2}| = r$, where r is the radius of the nine-point circle. See Figure (3.12). Without loss of generality, we can assume that the centre of our Argand plane is the origin of the circumscribed circle and that its radius is one. We then have $|a| = |b| = |c| = 1$. Squaring and expanding

$$\begin{aligned}
\left|n - \frac{a+b}{2}\right|^2 &= \left|n - \frac{b+c}{2}\right|^2 \Rightarrow \\
n^*(b-c) + n(b^* - c^*) &= \frac{a(c^* - b^*) + a^*(c-b)}{2} \\
2n^*(c-b) + 2n\frac{b-c}{cb} &= a\frac{b-c}{cb} + \frac{c-b}{a} \\
2n^*abc - 2na &= cb - a^2
\end{aligned} \tag{3.10}$$

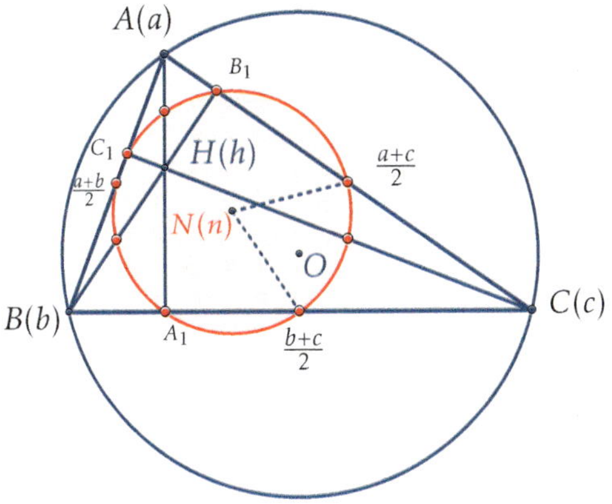

Figure 3.12: The nine-point circle passes through the mid-points of the sides, the feet of the altitudes and the mid points of the segments joining the vertices with the orthocenter.

Similarly, we get from the other two relations

$$2n^*abc - 2nb = ac - b^2 \tag{3.11}$$

$$2n^*abc - 2nc = ba - c^2 \tag{3.12}$$

Subtracting (3.11) from (3.10) we find $-2n(a-b) = -c(a-b) - (a^2 - b^2) \Rightarrow 2n = c + a + b$. Therefore $n = (a + b + c)/2$ and we can verify that the last equation (3.12) is also satisfied. The radius is then $|n - \frac{a+b}{2}| = |c|/2 = 1/2$. Hence, the radius of the nine-point circle is half the radius of the circumscribed circle. □

Exercise 3.15: Show that the Centroid K, the Orthocenter H, the centre of a the circumscribed circle O, and the centre of the Euler circle N, lie on the same line. This is the Euler line. See Figure (3.13).
Ans: If we choose the centre of the circumscribed circle as the centre of our Argand plane and the radius as unity we have that

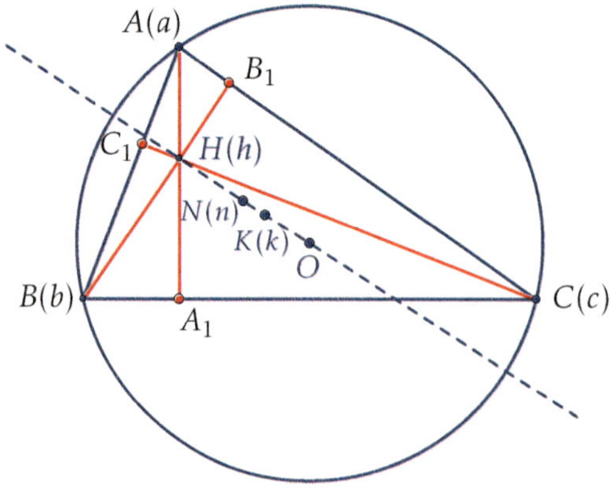

Figure 3.13: In a triangle $\triangle ABC$, the centroid K, the centre of the circumscribed circle O, the orthocenter H and the centre of the nine-point circle N are all collinear. This is the Euler line.

Forming the ratio

$$\frac{OK}{OH} = \frac{k}{h} = \frac{\frac{1}{3}(a+b+c)}{a+b+c} = \frac{1}{3}, \quad \text{Real number.}$$

And since the ratio is real, the points are collinear. Similarly, the centre of the nine point circle is at $n = (a+b+c)/2$ and $\frac{ON}{OH} = \frac{1}{2}$, which is real and therefore O, N, K and H are collinear. □

3.9 Concyclic Points

In many advanced questions you are given four points and you are asked to prove that they are concyclic (all lying on the same circle). The following proposition and its consequences make regular appearances in advanced exams. It concerns points on a circle.

Proposition 3.13: (Concyclic points) Four points P_1, P_2, P_3, P_4 representing the complex numbers z_1, z_2, z_3, z_4 respectively, see Figure (3.14) are concyclic (they fall on a circle) if the following condition holds

$$\arg\frac{z_1 - z_3}{z_2 - z_3} = \arg\frac{z_1 - z_4}{z_2 - z_4}$$

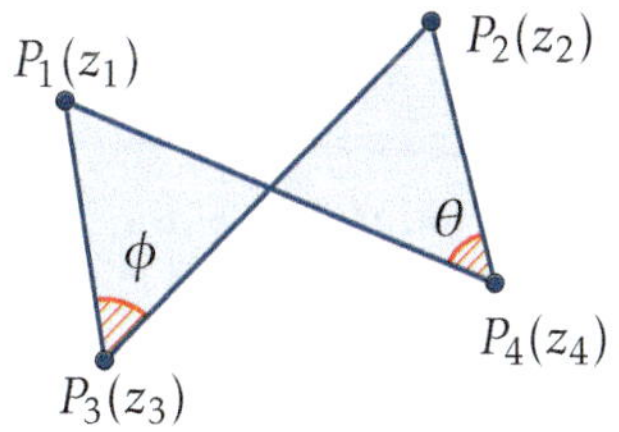

Figure 3.14: Four points are concyclic if the angle $\phi = \theta$. Namely they subtend the same arc.

Proof: The angle between $\overrightarrow{P_3P_2}$ and $\overrightarrow{P_3P_1}$ is ϕ and similarly the angle between $\overrightarrow{P_4P_1}$ and $\overrightarrow{P_4P_2}$ is θ. For the four points to by on a circle we must have that $\phi = \theta$. Since $\overrightarrow{P_3P_2}$ is represented by $z_2 - z_3$ and $\overrightarrow{P_3P_1}$ by $z_1 - z_3$ and similarly for $\overrightarrow{P_4P_1}$ and $\overrightarrow{P_4P_2}$ we must have

$$\arg\frac{z_1 - z_3}{z_2 - z_3} = \phi = \theta = \arg\frac{z_1 - z_4}{z_2 - z_4} \qquad \square$$

Thus, if you want to prove that four points are on the periphery of a circle, all you need to do is show that the angles of the two triangles with the same base are equal. There are other ways, all of them equivalent. For example, opposite angle of the quadrilateral must sum up to π, or the exterior angle is equal to the opposite interior angle of the quadrilateral.

Corollary 3.3: Four points P_1, P_2, P_3, P_4 representing the complex numbers z_1, z_2, z_3, z_4 respectively, see Figure (3.14) are concyclic if the following condition holds

$$\arg\frac{z_2 - z_1}{z_3 - z_1} + \arg\frac{z_3 - z_4}{z_2 - z_4} = \pi \Rightarrow \frac{(z_2 - z_1)(z_3 - z_4)}{(z_3 - z_1)(z_2 - z_4)} \text{ IS REAL}$$

DAD'S SOS NOTE: You do not need memorise the above conditions for concyclic points. All you need to remember is that if the angles subtending the same chord are equal then the points are concyclic, or that opposite angles in an inscribed quadrilateral sum up to π. The rest would follow. ♥

3.10 Similar and Equilateral Triangles

Before we examine the equilateral triangle, I should mention one more time that triangles have orientation. This comes from the symmetries of the Euclidean plane that leave a triangle invariant (another word for congruence or sameness). We can translate or rotate a triangle and we get back the same triangle with the same orientation. If on the other hand, we reflect a triangle we actually change its orientation even if none of the other properties of the triangle like the length of the sides or the value of the angles has changed.

DAD'S SOS NOTE: Triangles and other shapes have orientation. In a triangle $\triangle ABC$ if we swap any two the letters, say B and C, to form another triangle $\triangle ACB$, we would get back the same triangle but with opposite orientation. I usually write the triangle in the anti-clockwise direction. ♥

3.10.1 Similar Triangles and Reflected Triangles

Let me remind you of the conditions for two triangles to be similar. Two triangles are called similar if one of the following conditions hold true

(i) They have their corresponding angles equal

(ii) They have the ratios of the corresponding sides equal

(iii) They have one angle equal and the ratios of the two sides enclosing the angle are also equal.

These relations define similarity between two triangles. However, they say nothing about the possible orientation of the two triangles. Now that we deal with the complex plane and we know that angles and triangles have orientation we need to be slightly more careful.

Proposition 3.14: (Similar Triangles) Two triangles $\triangle Z_1 Z_2 Z_3$ and $\triangle W_1 W_2 W_3$ with the *same orientation* are similar if

$$\arg\left(\frac{z_3 - z_1}{z_2 - z_1}\right) = \arg\left(\frac{w_3 - w_1}{w_2 - w_1}\right) \quad \text{AND} \quad \left|\frac{z_3 - z_1}{z_2 - z_1}\right| = \left|\frac{w_3 - w_1}{w_2 - w_1}\right|$$

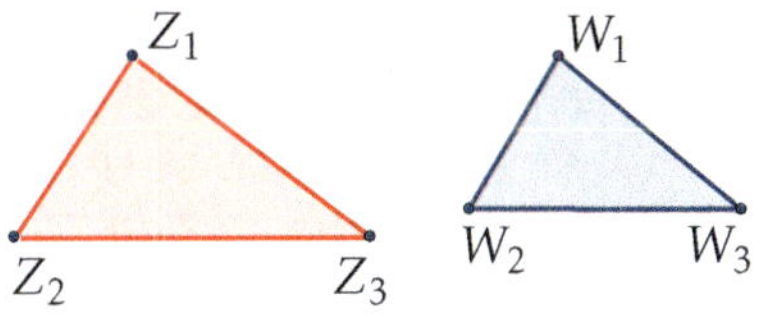

The first relation says that the angle between the complex numbers $z_3 - z_1$ and $z_2 - z_1$ is the same as then angle between $w_3 - w_1$ and $w_2 - w_1$ and the second relation says that the ratio of the lengths of their corresponding sides is also equal. Hence the two triangles are similar if

$$\frac{z_3 - z_1}{z_2 - z_1} = \frac{w_3 - w_1}{w_2 - w_1} \tag{3.13}$$

If two triangles are similar but *do not have the same orientation*, say $\triangle Z_1 Z_2 Z_3$ and $\triangle W_1 W_3 W_2$, then they are related by a *reflection*.

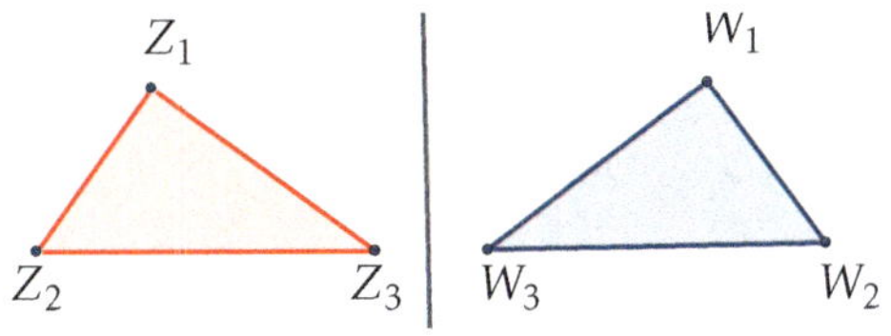

And as we have learnt, reflection in the complex plane is the complex conjugation operation. Hence the condition for two triangles to be similar if they have the opposite orientation is

$$\frac{z_3 - z_1}{z_2 - z_1} = \frac{w_3^* - w_1^*}{w_2^* - w_1^*} \tag{3.14}$$

Corollary 3.4: We can rewrite the equation of similarity (3.13) also with a determinant. Thus, two triangles with the same orientation are similar if

$$\begin{vmatrix} z_1 & w_1 & 1 \\ z_2 & w_2 & 1 \\ z_3 & w_3 & 1 \end{vmatrix} = 0 \tag{3.15}$$

If, on the other hand, the two triangles have opposite orientation then we can rewrite equation (3.14) as

$$\begin{vmatrix} z_1 & w_1^* & 1 \\ z_2 & w_2^* & 1 \\ z_3 & w_3^* & 1 \end{vmatrix} = 0 \tag{3.16}$$

Exercise 3.16: Consider a positive oriented triangle $\triangle ABC$. On the sides of the triangle we construct three positively oriented similar triangles $\triangle PAC$, $\triangle QBA$ and $\triangle RCB$. Prove that the centroid $G(g)$, of the triangle $\triangle ABC$, $g = (a+b+c)/3$ coincides with the centroid of $\triangle PQR$. See Figure (3.15).

Ans: Using Equation 3.13 for the similar triangles $\triangle PAC$, $\triangle QBA$ and $\triangle RCB$ we must have

$$\lambda = \frac{a-q}{b-q} = \frac{c-p}{a-p} = \frac{b-r}{c-r} \Rightarrow a-c = \lambda(b-q),\ c-p = \lambda(a-p),\ b-r = \lambda(c-r)$$

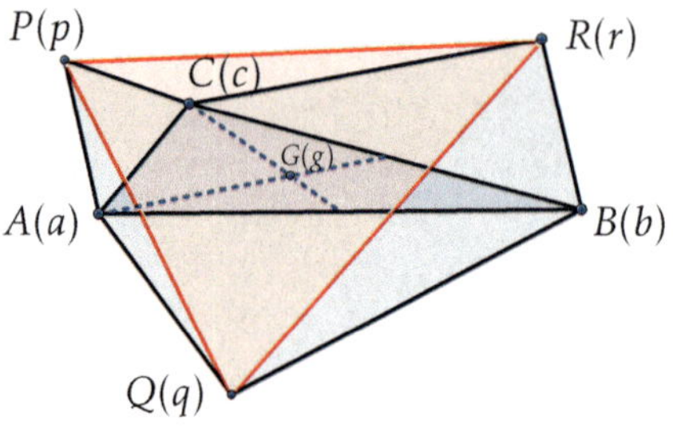

Figure 3.15

for some $\lambda \in \mathbb{C}$. Adding the last three equations together we find

$$a+b+c-(p+q+r) = \lambda(a+b+c) - \lambda(p+q+r) \Rightarrow a+b+c = p+q+r$$

Hence the centroid of $\triangle PQR$ is $(p+q+r)/3 = g$ which coincides with thepoint $G(g)$. The $\lambda = 1$ case corresponds to the degenerate case where the original triangle collapses to a point. □

3.10.2 Equilateral Triangles

The equilateral triangle has made many guest-star appearances in the exams in many different guises. Study it! It has many forms, and we have already encountered it in Exercise (2.9).

Proposition 3.15: Let z_1, z_2 and z_3 be three complex numbers corresponding to points Z_1, Z_2 and Z_3 in the Argand plane.

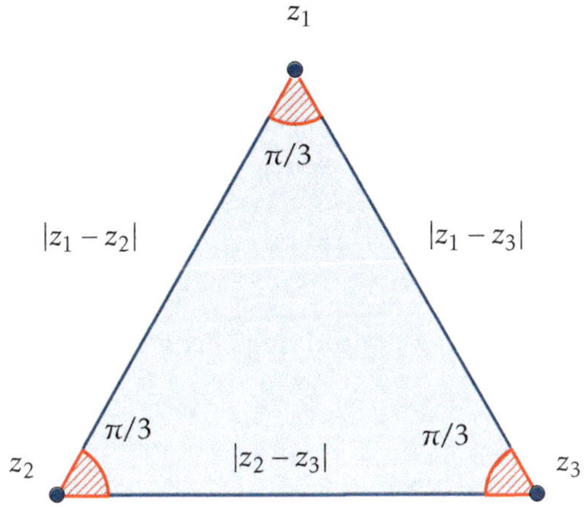

Figure 3.16

Then, any of the following relations is a necessary and sufficient condition for the three points to be the corners of an equilateral triangle (see Figure 3.16):

(i) $|z_1 - z_2| = |z_2 - z_3| = |z_3 - z_1| = k$

(ii) $\dfrac{1}{z_1 - z_2} + \dfrac{1}{z_2 - z_3} + \dfrac{1}{z_3 - z_1} = 0$

(iii) $z_1^2 + z_2^2 + z_3^2 = z_1z_2 + z_1z_3 + z_2z_3$

(iv) $\dfrac{z_3 - z_1}{z_2 - z_1} = \dfrac{z_1 - z_2}{z_3 - z_2}$,

(v) $\dfrac{1}{z - z_1} + \dfrac{1}{z - z_2} + \dfrac{1}{z - z_3} = 0$, where $z = (z_1 + z_2 + z_3)/3$

Proof: Part (i) is obvious since $|z_1 - z_2| = |z_2 - z_3| = |z_3 - z_1| = k$ are the lengths of the sides of the triangle. For part (ii) we use part (i).

$$(z_1 - z_2)(z_1^* - z_2^*) = k^2 \Rightarrow z_1^* - z_2^* = \frac{k^2}{z_1 - z_2}$$

and similarly for the other sides. Substituting into the equation we get

$$\frac{1}{z_1 - z_2} + \frac{1}{z_2 - z_3} + \frac{1}{z_3 - z_1} = \frac{1}{k^2}\left[(z_1^* - z_2^*) + (z_2^* - z_3^*) + (z_3^* - z_1^*)\right] = 0$$

and the last expression in the brackets is zero as all terms cancel out.

For (iii), all we need to do is use (ii) to get

$$\frac{(z_2 - z_3)(z_3 - z_1) + (z_1 - z_2)(z_3 - z_1) + (z_1 - z_2)(z_2 - z_3)}{(z_1 - z_2)(z_2 - z_3)(z_3 - z_1)} = 0$$

And the numerator after simplifying becomes

$$z_1^2 + z_2^2 + z_3^2 - z_1 z_2 - z_2 z_3 - z_3 z_1 = 0$$

Part (iii) and part (iv) can also be proved using the equations for similar triangles (3.13- 3.15). Since, the equilateral triangle $\Delta Z_1 Z_2 Z_3$ is similar to itself $\Delta Z_2 Z_3 Z_1$ with the same orientation (This is a beautiful argument, see [6], [1]) we must have

$$\frac{z_3 - z_1}{z_2 - z_1} = \frac{z_1 - z_2}{z_3 - z_2}$$

We have thus proved (iv) and by doing the algebra we also get (iii). I leave the last part (v) as an algebraic exercise. □

Exercise 3.17: Show that the three roots of $z^3 + 3kz^2 + 3lz + m = 0$ form an equilateral triangle if $k^2 = l$.

Ans: We would use the Vieta relations, see Equations (B.3-B.5) in the Appendix. If z_1, z_2, z_3 are the three roots then we must have $z_1 + z_2 + z_3 = -3k$ and $z_1 z_2 + z_2 z_3 + z_1 z_3 = 3l$. So, by squaring we get

$$(z_1 + z_2 + z_3)^2 = 9k^2 \Rightarrow (z_1^2 + z_2^2 + z_3^2) + 2(z_1 z_2 + z_2 z_3 + z_3 z_1) = 9k^2$$

$$3(z_1 z_2 + z_2 z_3 + z_3 z_1) = 9k^2 \Rightarrow 9l = 9k^2 \Rightarrow k^2 = l$$

□

Exercise 3.18: Show that the distinct complex numbers z, w and γ represent the vertices of an equilateral triangle (in clockwise or anti-clockwise order) if and only if

$$z^2 + w^2 + \gamma^2 - w\gamma - \gamma z - zw = 0.$$

Show that the roots of the equation

$$z^3 + az^2 + bz + c = 0 \qquad (*)$$

represent the vertices of an equilateral triangle if and only if $a^2 = 3b$.

Under the transformation $z = pw + q$, where p and q are given complex numbers with $p \neq 0$, the equation $(*)$ becomes

$$w^3 + Aw^2 + Bw + C = 0. \qquad (**)$$

Show that if the roots of equation $(*)$ represent the vertices of an equilateral triangle, then the roots of equation $(**)$ also represent the vertices of an equilateral triangle. **(STEP III 2006Q5)**

Ans: The first part was proved in Proposition (3.15). For example consider the similar triangles $\triangle zw\gamma$ and $\triangle w\gamma z$. For the second part, we need to use Vieta's relations for a cubic.

If we write the three roots as z_1, z_2, z_3 then their sum is $-a$, so $z_1 + z_2 + z_3 = -a$ and if we square this we get $z_1^2 + z_2^2 + z_2^2 + 2(z_1z_2 + z_2z_3 + z_1z_3) = a^2$. From the first part of the question we know that $z_1^2 + z_2^2 + z_2^2 = z_1z_2 + z_2z_3 + z_1z_3$. Hence $a^2 = 3(z_1z_2 + z_2z_3 + z_1z_3)$. But the sum-product of the roots using again Vieta's relations is equal to b. Hence $a^2 = 3b$.
Now for the last part. If we substitute $z = pw + q$ in the cubic and collect terms we get the following equation:

$$w^3 + \frac{1}{p}(3q + a)w^2 + \frac{1}{p^2}(3q^2 + 2qa + b)w + \frac{1}{p^3}(q^3 + q^2 + bq) = 0$$

In order for the solutions of these equation to also be the vertices of an equilateral triangle we must have

$$3\left[\frac{1}{p}(3q + a)\right]^2 = 3\frac{1}{p^2}(3q^2 + 2qa + b)$$
$$9q^2 + a^2 + 6qa = 9q^2 + 6qa + 3b \Rightarrow a^2 = 3b$$

And the last equation is true by the given assumption. □

3.11 Geometry on the Complex Plane

If you are a Euclidean geometry fanatic, like I am, then you will find that complex numbers provide an excellent tool for solving some problems that are very hard with the traditional methods. I will illustrate some of the techniques with few examples. A very important trick is to know how to "move" around the complex plane. If two points are the same distance from the origin then they are related by a rotation $\cos\theta + i\sin\theta = e^{i\theta}$ (We will learn the Euler's formula in Chapter 6) where θ is the angle. The particular case when $\theta = \pi/2$ is the rotation by i.

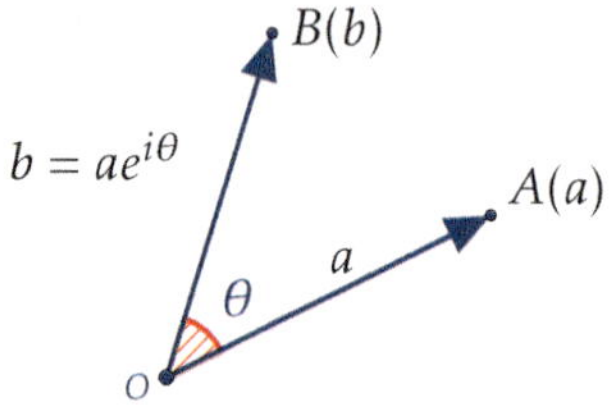

Figure 3.17: Points A and B have complex numbers a and b and are of the same distance from the origin O. Since their in-between angle is θ they are related by a rotation. The point B is the complex number $b = a(\cos\theta + i\sin\theta) = ae^{i\theta}$. In the special case that the angle was 90 degrees we would have $b = ia$.

Proposition 3.16: If we rotate anticlockwise, a point z around another point $A(\alpha)$ by an angle θ then then new point z' would be

$$z' = \alpha + (z - \alpha)e^{i\theta} \tag{3.17}$$

Proof: You can think of this as follows. Translate the axis to the point A. This means z is mapped to $z - a$. See Figure (3.18). Now rotate anticlockwise by θ and afterwards translate back by adding α. □

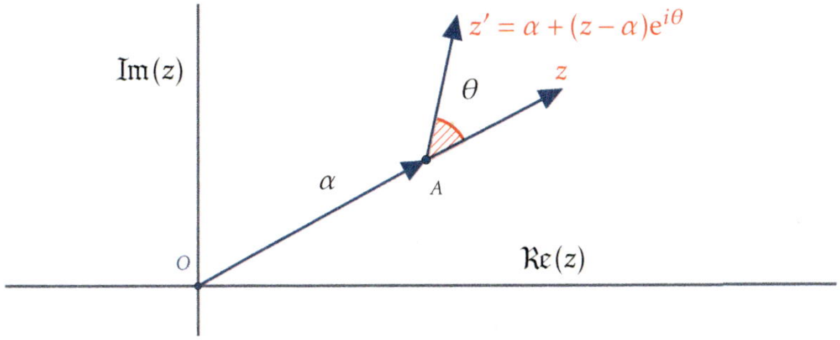

Figure 3.18

DAD'S SOS NOTE: In many geometry questions we would make use of this property to move around the diagram in the complex plane. The following example illustrates the technique. ♥

Exercise 3.19: Let A,B and C be the vertices of a positively oriented (meaning that going from $A \to B \to C$ we turn anti-clockwise) triangle $\triangle ABC$. On the sides, AB and AC we construct the squares $\square ADEB$ and $\square ACFG$ with sides the size of $|AB|$ and $|AC|$ respectively. If M is the midpoint of the side BC show that the line AM when extended is perpendicular to the line DG and furthermore that $|DG| = 2|AM|$.

Ans: This problem is typical of the problems that can be handled using complex plane tools. The first part is asking you to prove that two lines are perpendicular. From Proposition (3.11) we know that two line segments are perpendicular if we can prove that the ratio of their complex numbers is purely imaginary.

The next thing to do is to set up our complex plane and find the ratio. The question says nothing about the origin of our complex plane, so we are free to choose any point as our origin. The point A looks like a good choice since it lies in one of the lines that we want to prove perpendicular and also is in the second part of the question that asks us to prove that $|EG| = 2|AM|$. So, let the origin of our complex plane be the point A. We would also let the points B, C, D, E, F, G and M to represent the complex numbers b, c, d, e, f, g and m. See Figure (3.19).

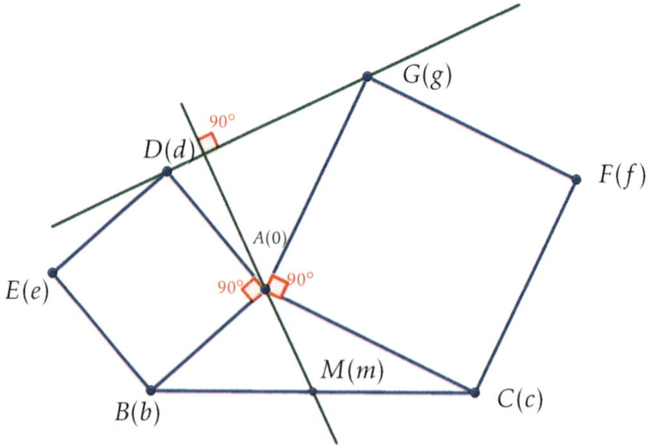

Figure 3.19: Point A is chosen as the origin of our complex plane and the various points are represented by complex numbers with lower case letters.

Next, the complex number representing DG is $g - d$ and the complex number representing AM is m, since A is the origin. Notice however, that the g is at a right angle with respect to c (anticlockwise) whilst d is at a right angle from b, but this time clockwise. We must therefore have that $g = ic$ and $d = -ib$. Furthermore, since m is the midpoint of b and c we must have that $m = (b + c)/2$. We now form the ratio AM/DG

$$\frac{AM}{DG} = \frac{m}{g-d} = \frac{b+c}{2(ic+ib)} = -\frac{i}{2}$$

Since the argument is purely imaginary the two lines are perpendicular. Moreover, if we take the modulus of the above relation we get $2|AM| = |DG|$. □

Dad's SOS Note: Study the above example. There are three elements that you need to know in order to tackle the majority of questions that might come up in an exam.

(i) Draw or rather sketch a diagram if you are not given one.

(ii) Question may ask you that two lines are perpendicular or that three points are collinear or four points are concyclic. You need to know the respective results. Usually, they form the first part of these questions.

(iii) If the origin of the complex plane is not given or suggested, try to make a judicious choice that would simplify your algebra. Usually, the best point is the one where most lines go through or is part of the answer.

(iv) VERY-VERY important. "Move" around the diagram using the right angles or any angles that the problem gives you. ♥

The next exercise uses the principles outlined in the previous sos note.

Exercise 3.20: Given a quadrilateral $ABCD$ we construct the squares on its four sides. Show that the lines joining the centres of the squares of opposite sides are perpendicular. See Figure (3.20)

Ans: This problem is similar to the previous one. All we need to do is choose point A as the origin of our complex plane. We also let all the points to be represented by complex numbers with lower case letters. Our next task is starting from point A to find the complex numbers representing the centre of the squares and then show that the ratio NP/MQ is imaginary. Lets start

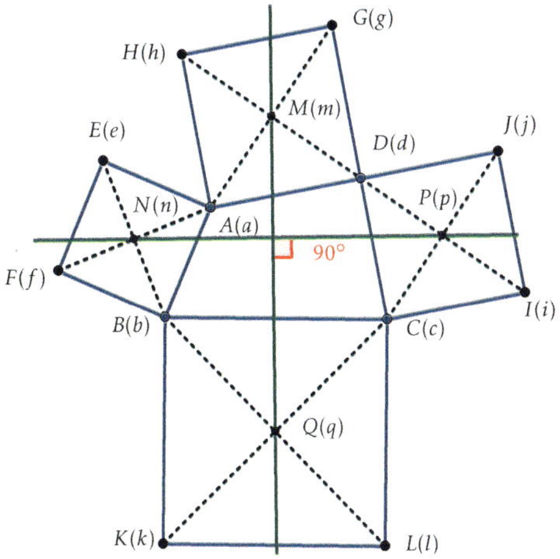

Figure 3.20: Diagram for Exercise (3.20)

- We get to the point M from A by going $d/2$ and then turning anticlockwise by 90 degrees and travel a $d/2$. So, point M is represented by $d/2 + id/2$
- We reach the point P if we go to d then add half $c - d$ to get to the midpoint of DC and then turn anticlockwise by 90 degrees and

travel a $(d-c)/2$. Hence, point P is represented by $d+(c-d)/2+i(c-d)/2$

- We get to the point Q by going to c and then travel half of $b-c$ and then turn anticlockwise by 90 degrees and travel a $(b-c)/2$. Hence, point Q is $c+(b-c)/2+i(b-c)/2$

- Finally, to reach the point N we just go half b and then turn clockwise by 90 degrees and travel a $b/2$ distance. Hence N is $b/2-ib/2$

Now that we have all the points we need to calculate NP and MQ

$$\begin{aligned} NP &= d+\frac{c-d}{2}+i\frac{c-d}{2}-\frac{b}{2}+i\frac{b}{2}=\frac{c+d-b}{2}+i\frac{b+c-d}{2} \\ MQ &= c+\frac{b-c}{2}+i\frac{b-c}{2}-\frac{d}{2}-i\frac{d}{2}=\frac{b+c-d}{2}+i\frac{b-c-d}{2} \end{aligned}$$

If we multiply MQ by i we see that it is equal to NP. Hence $\frac{NP}{MQ}=i$ and this shows that the two lines are perpendicular. Moreover, the two line segments are equal since $|NP|=|MQ|$. □

3.12 Geometrical Questions

Q 3.10 By considering $(5+i)^2$ show that

$$\arctan\frac{1}{5}=\frac{1}{2}\arctan\frac{5}{12}$$

Q 3.11 Show that the condition for the two lines $\epsilon_1: A_1 z+{A_1}^* z^*+B_1=0$ and $\epsilon_2: A_2 z+{A_2}^* z^*+B_2=0$ to be perpendicular is

$$\frac{{A_1}^*}{A_1}+\frac{{A_2}^*}{A_2}=0$$

Q 3.12 Using the fact that the area A of a triangle with three vertices $A(x_1,y_1)$, $B(x_2,y_2)$ and $C(x_3,y_3)$ is

$$A=\frac{1}{2}\begin{vmatrix} x_1 & y_1 & 1 \\ x_2 & y_2 & 1 \\ x_3 & y_3 & 1 \end{vmatrix}$$

Show that the equivalent expression in the complex plane is

$$A = \frac{i}{4}\begin{vmatrix} z_1 & z_1{}^* & 1 \\ z_2 & z_2{}^* & 1 \\ z_3 & z_3{}^* & 1 \end{vmatrix}$$

where $z_1 = x_1 + iy_1$, $z_2 = x_2 + iy_2$ and $z_3 = x_3 + iy_3$.

Q 3.13 Let AB be a chord on a unit circle. The points A and B have complex representations a and b. The tangents to the points A and B meet at a point $P(p)$. Show that $p = 2ab/(a+b)$.

Q 3.14 If $A(a)$ and $B(b)$ are the endpoints of a chord in a unit circle, show that the equation of the line through A and B is $z = a + b - abz^*$. Let $C(c)$ and $D(d)$ be the endpoints of another chord on the same circle. Show that the point of intersection $P(p)$ is given by

$$p = \frac{(c+d)ab - cd(a+b)}{ab - cd}$$

What does $ab = cd$ corresponds to?

Q 3.15 If $z_1^2 + z_2^2 = z_1 z_2$ then show that $|z_1| = |z_2|$ and that the points z_1, z_2 together with the origin form an equilateral triangle.

Q 3.16 The points A, B, C and D are the anticlockwise vertices of a quadrilateral. Show that if M, N, P and Q are the midpoints of AB, BC, CD and DA respectively then $MNPQ$ is a parallelogram. See below.

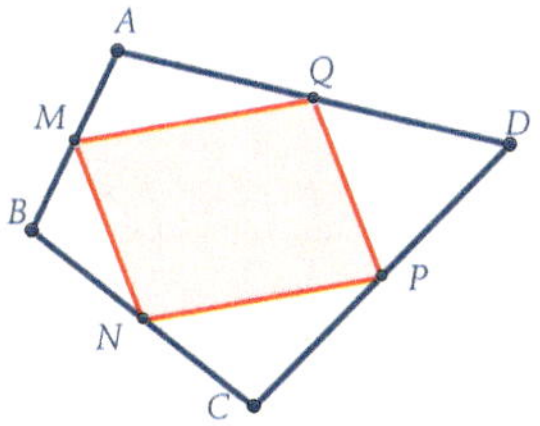

Q 3.17 On the sides AB and AC of a positively oriented triangle $\triangle ABC$ construct the squares $\square ADEB$ and $\square ACFG$ with sides AB and AC. If K and N are the centres of the squares as shown in diagram (3.17) and M is the midpoint of the AB side, show that KM is perpendicular to NM.

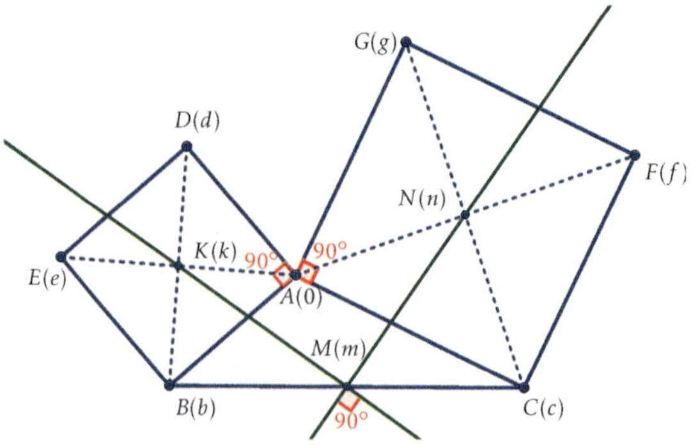

Figure 3.21: Diagram for question 3.17

Q 3.18 The points $A(a)$, $B(b)$ and $C(c)$ form a positively oriented triangle $\triangle ABC$. On the sides AB, BC and CA we construct similar and positively oriented triangles $\triangle AP_1B$, $\triangle BP_2C$ and $\triangle AP_3C$. The points $P_1(p_1)$ and $P_2(p_2)$ are outside the triangle $\triangle ABC$, whereas the point $P_3(p_3)$ is in the interior of the triangle $\triangle ABC$, see Figure (3.22).

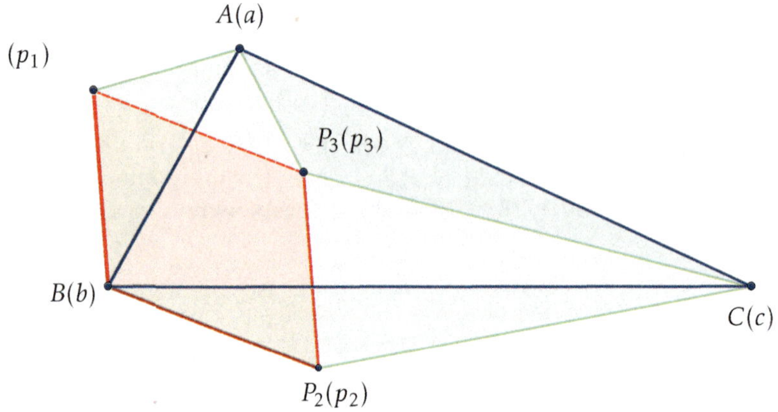

Figure 3.22: Diagram for Question (3.18).

Show that $P_1BP_2P_3$ is a parallelogram.

Q 3.19 The points Z_1, Z_2 and Z_3 are distinct and are represented by the complex numbers z_1,z_2 and z_3 respectively. Show that if $\dfrac{z_1 - z_2}{z_3 - z_2} = \dfrac{1}{2} + i\dfrac{\sqrt{3}}{3}$ then the points form an equilateral triangle.

Q 3.20 Show that the triangle with vertices $z_1 = 1, z_2 = 3+3i$ and $z_3 = 4+4i$ is similar to the triangle with vertices $w_1 = 1+i, w_2 = 7-3i, w_3 = 9-5i$.

Q 3.21 A quadrilateral drawn in the complex plane has vertices A, B, C and D, labelled anticlockwise. These vertices are represented, respectively, by the complex numbers a, b, c and d. Show that $ABCD$ is a parallelogram (defined as a quadrilateral in which opposite sides are parallel and equal in length) if and only if $a + c = b + d$. Show further that, in this case, $ABCD$ is a square if and only if i $(a - c) = b - d$. Let $PQRS$ be a quadrilateral in the complex plane, with vertices labelled anticlockwise, the internal angles of which are all less than 180. Squares with centres X, Y , Z and T are constructed externally to the quadrilateral on the sides PQ, QR, RS and SP, respectively.

(i) If P and Q are represented by the complex numbers p and q, respectively, show that X can be represented by

$$\frac{1}{2}(p(1+i)+q(1-i))$$

(ii) Show that $XYZT$ is a square if and only if $PQRS$ is a parallelogram.

(STEP III Jun2014)

Q 3.22 Let z_1, z_2 and z_3 be the vertices of an isosceles right-angled triangle with the right angle at z_2. Show that

$$z_1^2 + 2z_2^2 + z_3^2 = 2z_2(z_1 + z_3)$$

Q 3.23 In an Argand diagram, O is the origin and P is the point $2 + 0\mathrm{i}$. The points Q, R and S are such that the lengths OP, PQ, QR and RS are all equal, and the angles OPQ, PQR and QRS are all equal to $5\pi/6$, so that the points O, P, Q, R and S are five vertices of a regular 12-sided polygon lying in the upper half of the Argand diagram. Show that Q is the point $2 + \sqrt{3} + \mathrm{i}$ and find S.

The point C is the centre of the circle that passes through the points O, P and Q. Show that, if the polygon is rotated anticlockwise about O until C first lies on the real axis, the new position of S is

$$-\tfrac{1}{2}(3\sqrt{2}+\sqrt{6})(\sqrt{3}-\mathrm{i})\,.$$

(STEP II 2001Q7)

Q 3.24 Show that if z is a complex number, then the points $A(1)$, $B(-1)$, $C(z)$ and $D(1/z)$ are concyclic.

Q 3.25 The four points A, B, C, D in the Argand diagram (complex-plane) correspond to the complex numbers a, b, c, d respectively. The point P_1 is mapped to P_2 by rotating about A through $\pi/2$ radians. Then P_2 is mapped to P_3 by rotating about B through $\pi/2$ radians, P_3 is mapped to P_4 by rotating about C through $\pi/2$ radians and P_4 is mapped to P_5 by rotating about D through $\pi/2$ radians, each rotation being in the positive sense. If z_i is the complex number corresponding to P_i, find z_5 in terms of a, b, c, d and z_1.

Show that P_5 will coincide with P_1, irrespective of the choice of the latter if, and only if

$$a - c = \mathrm{i}(b - d)$$

and interpret this condition geometrically.

The points A, B and C are now chosen to be distinct points on the unit circle and the angle of rotation is changed to θ, where $\theta \neq 0$, on each occasion. Find the necessary and sufficient condition on θ and the points A, B and C for P_4 always to coincide with P_1. **(STEP III 1994)**

Q 3.26 By considering the product $(k + l + i)(k^2 + kl + 1 + il)$ show that

$$\arctan\left(\frac{1}{k+l}\right) + \arctan\left(\frac{l}{k^2 + kl + 1}\right) = \arctan\left(\frac{1}{k}\right)$$

Hence show that $\arctan \frac{1}{5} + \arctan \frac{2}{3} = \frac{\pi}{4}$.

4. Locus on the Complex Plane

Let no one ignorant of Mathematics enter here.
Ἀγεωμέτρητος μηδεὶς εἰσίτω

Plato

Finding the locus of points on the complex plane is no harder than in the real plane. In this chapter we would describe some basic loci that come up in the exams frequently. If z is an arbitrary point on the complex plane then any constraint or restriction on z would produce a curve on the complex plane. We will do a few examples to see how it works.

4.1 Locus is a Circle

Exercise 4.1: Find the locus of points for which $|z| = 4$.

Ans: Intuitively speaking the equation $|z| = 4$ says that all the points z have distance from the origin equal to 4. This clearly describes a circle with radius 4 on the complex plane. If you want to convince yourself of this just substitute $z = x + iy$. We then have $|x + iy| = 4 \Rightarrow \sqrt{x^2 + y^2} = 4 \Rightarrow x^2 + y^2 = 4^2$. The last equation is the equation of a circle with origin the point $(0, 0)$ and radius 4. □

If instead of $|z| = 4$ we had $|z - 2| = 4$ (say) then the equation would describe a circle with radius 4 but with center the point $(2, 0)$. In general, an equation of the type $|z - z_1| = c$, where $z_1 = a + bi$ a complex number would describe a circle with center (a, b) and radius c

We thus have:

Theorem 4.1: The equation $|z - z_1| = c$, with $z_1 = a + bi$ and $a, b, c \in \mathbb{R}$ describes a circle with radius c and centre the point z_1 on the complex plane.
Proof: If we let $z = x + iy$ we get $|(x - a) + i(y - b)| = c$ and the modulus of this complex number is $(x - a)^2 + (y - b)^2 = c^2$. This however, is the equation of a circle with radius c and centre the point (a, b). □

4.2 Locus is a Perpendicular Bisector

Exercise 4.2: Find the locus of points for which $|z - 2| = |z + 4|$.

Ans: We can substitute for $z = x + iy$ and then solve to find the equation in terms of x, y. However, it is easier to think geometrically. The equation $|z-2| = |z+4|$ says that the point z on the complex plane is equidistant from the point 2 and the point -4.

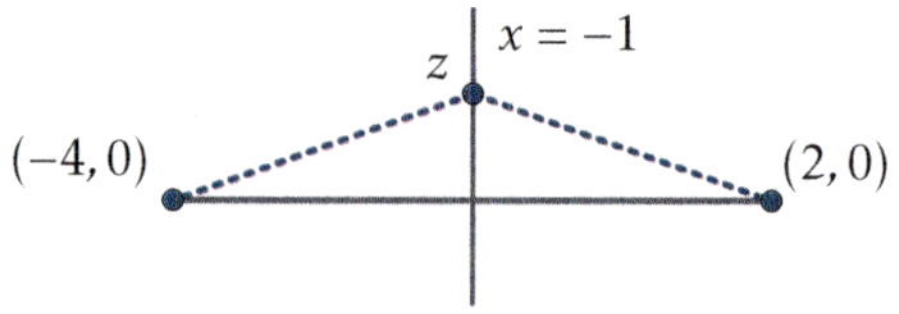

Figure 4.1: The locus of points that are equidistant from two points are the points on the perpendicular bisector of the segment joining these points

So it must be on the perpendicular bisector of the line joining the two points, see figure (4.1). Namely it must be a distance of $(2-(-4))/2 = 3$ from either side,and so $2-3 = -1 = -4+3$. This is the line $x = -1$. It must therefore lie on the perpendicular bisector of the line segment from -3 to 2.
Algebraically, we get $|x-2+iy| = |x+4+iy|$ which implies $(x-2)^2 + y^2 = (x+4)^2 + y^2 \Rightarrow -4x+4 = 8x+16 \Rightarrow -12 = 12x$. Hence the equation of the line is $x = -1$ as expected. □

> **Theorem 4.2:** The locus of points with equation $|z-z_1| = |z-z_2|$ is the perpendicular bisector to the line segment joining the points z_1 and z_2.

4.3 Locus is a Ray Line

In case you do not remember the terminology, a "ray line" is a line emanating from a given point. In other words, it is half a line. See the diagram below.

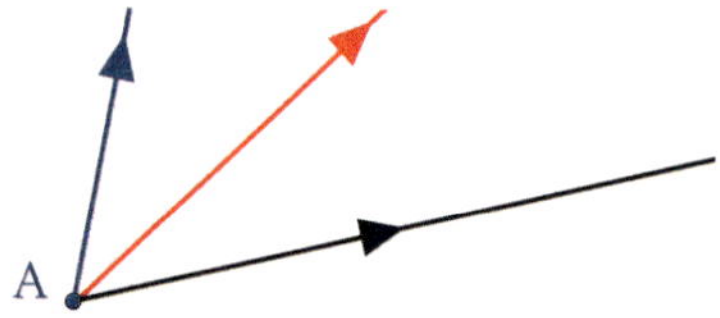

Exercise 4.3: Find the locus of the points z for which $\arg(z) = \pi/6$.

Ans: Since the argument is constant and equal to $\pi/6$ the locus of the points would be the straight line that makes $\pi/6$ with the x-axis. However, and this point is very important, it is NOT the whole line, but only the points that are on the positive y-axis. This is because the points below have principal argument $-5\pi/6$ and not $\pi/6$. □

Exercise 4.4: Find the locus of points z for which $\arg(z-2) = \pi/3$.

Ans: Doing a quick sketch always helps. In Figure (4.2) the point B is represented by the complex number z and $\overrightarrow{AB}$ is the $z-2$ complex number. The argument of this vector is the positive angle $\pi/3$. Hence the locus of points is the ray starting from point A in the upper half of the plane. Note that, if the point z was on the ray in the lower half of the plane then the angle would have been $-2\pi/3$ and not $\pi/3$. This is because, the vector $\overrightarrow{AB}$ is now pointing in the other directions and hence its principal argument is $-2\pi/3$. See Figure (4.3)

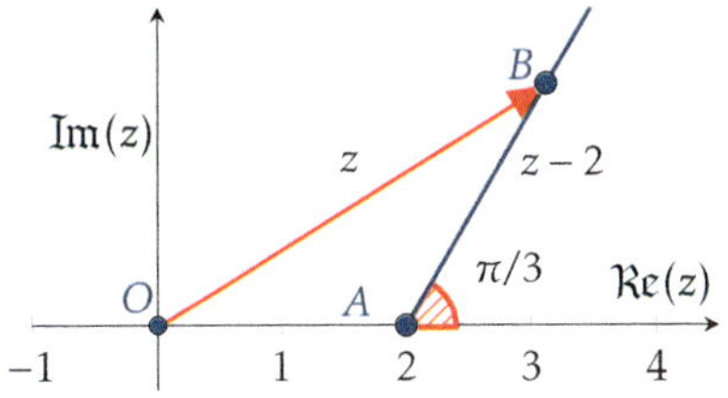

Figure 4.2: The locus of points z satisfying $\arg(z-2) = \pi/3$

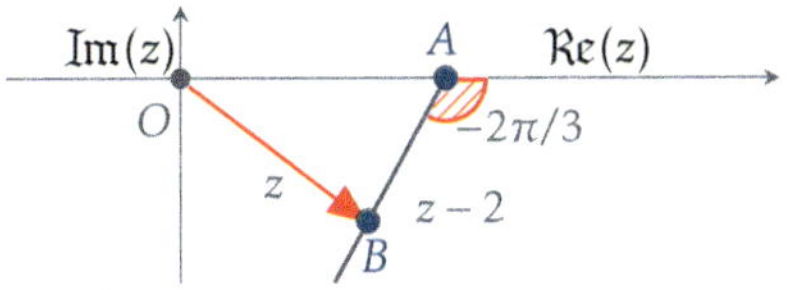

Figure 4.3: The locus of points z satisfying $\arg(z-2) = -2\pi/3$ is the ray in the lower half of the plane.

□

Exercise 4.5: Show on an Argand diagram the locus of points for which

$$\pi/2 < \arg(z-2)^2 < \pi$$

Ans: You should remember that $\arg(z-2)^2 = 2\arg(z-2)$. Once you do this the rest is easy since $\pi/2 < 2\arg(z-2) < \pi$ and this implies $\pi/4 <$

$\arg(z-2) < \pi/2$. Hence the region of points is the interior of the two ray lines starting from $z = 2$ and having angles $\pi/2$ and $\pi/4$.

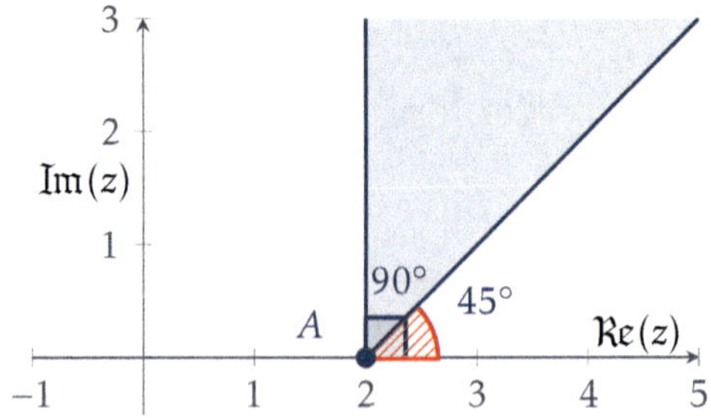

Theorem 4.3: If $A(a)$ is a point on the complex plane represented by the complex number a, then the locus of the points $P(z)$ with equation $\arg(z-a) = \theta$, where θ is a constant angle, are the points lying on a straight line going through the point $A(a)$, making an angle angle θ with the x-axis. Note, that this will be a ray-line rather than a whole line at an angle θ with the x-axis.

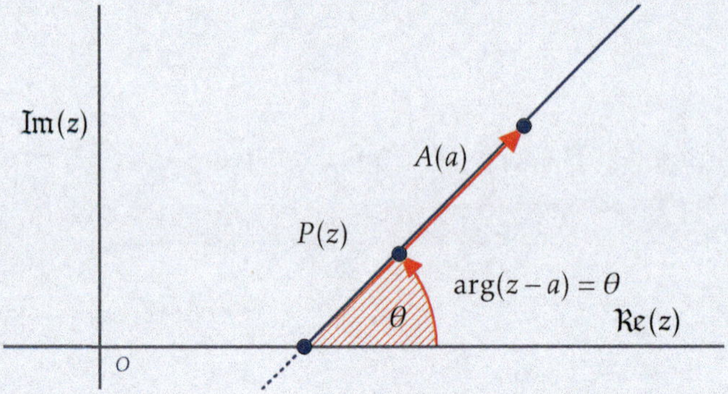

Figure 4.4: The locus of points that have Principal argument θ with the vector PA is the solid line. Points on the dotted line have Principal argument $-\pi + \theta$ and thus are not part of the locus.

Proof: If we let $x = x + iy$ and $a = a_1 + ia_2$ then

$$\arg(z-a) = \theta \Rightarrow \arctan\frac{y-a_2}{x-a_1} = \theta$$

and therefore $y - a_2 = \tan\theta(x - a_1)$ which is the equation of a line through a at an angle θ. □

4.4 Locus is an Arc of a Circle

Exercise 4.6: Find the locus of points z for which

$$\arg\left(\frac{z}{z+5}\right) = \frac{\pi}{2}$$

Ans: If we substitute $z = x + iy$ and do the algebra, we find that

$$\arg\left(\frac{x^2+5x+y^2}{(x+5)^2+y^2} + i\frac{5y}{(x+5)^2+y^2}\right) = \frac{\pi}{2}$$

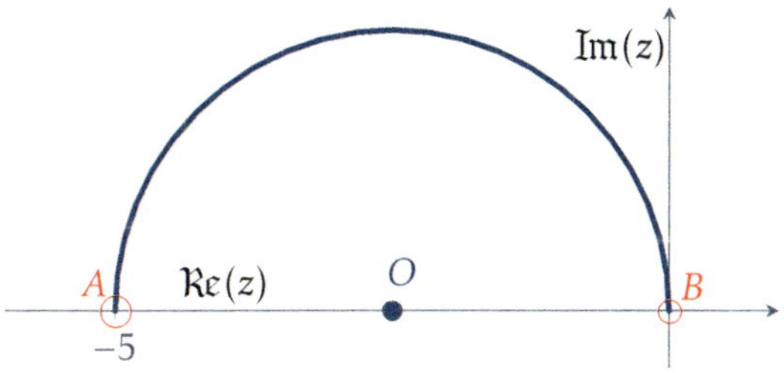

Figure 4.5: The locus of points for which $\arg\left(\frac{z}{z+5}\right) = \frac{\pi}{2}$

But the tangent of $\pi/2$ is ∞. Hence we must have $x^2 + 5x + y^2 = 0 = (x+5/2)^2 + y^2 - 25/4$ which is a circle with centre $(-5/2, 0)$ and radius $r = 5/2$. On the other hand $y > 0$, since if it is zero the argument is $0/0$ and thus undefined. Similarly, if $y < 0$ then argument would have been $-\pi/2$. So, the locus of points is the half-circle on the positive y axis. See Figure (4.5). □

The following theorem formalises this result.

Theorem 4.4: If z_1, z_2 are the complex numbers of the points A and B respectively, then the locus of points represented by the complex number z, that satisfy $\arg\left(\frac{z-z_2}{z-z_1}\right) = \phi$, with $-\pi \leq \phi \leq \pi$, is the circular arc which subtends the line segment AB at an angle ϕ. see Figure (4.6)

Proof: We know that the angle between two vectors $z - z_1$ and $z - z_2$ is given by $\arg\left(\frac{z-z_2}{z-z_1}\right)$ (see Proposition (3.7)) and since it is a constant real number between $-\pi \leq \phi \leq \pi$ the point z must move on the circular arc that subtends the AB. □

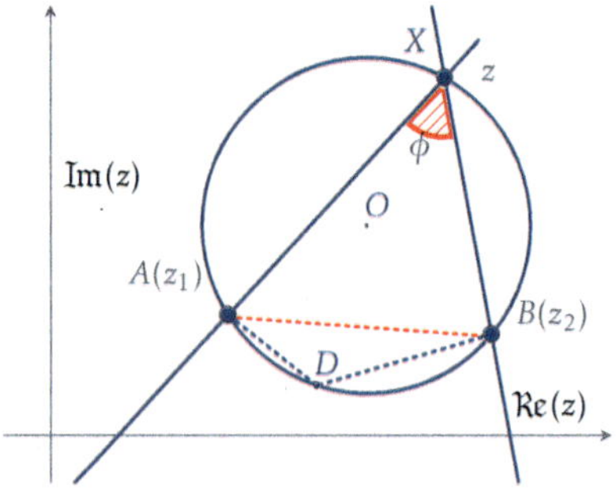

Figure 4.6: The locus of points that have $\arg\left(\frac{z-z_2}{z-z_1}\right) = \phi$, is the circular arc that subtends the line segment AB at an angle ϕ.

We can thus revisit Exercise (4.6). Using the above theorem with $\phi = \pi/2$ and $z_1 = 0, z_2 = 5$ the locus must be a semicircle with diameter the points -5 and 0. The centre of the circle is at -5/2 and the radius 5/2.

Exercise 4.7: The for points P_1, P_2, P_3 and P_4 are represented by the complex numbers z_1, z_2, z_3 and z_4. Show that the points are concyclic if the cross ratio

$$\text{Cross ratio} = \frac{(z_1 - z_2)(z_3 - z_4)}{(z_4 - z_1)(z_2 - z_3)}$$

is real.

Ans: Let P_1, P_2, P_3, P_4 be the points on the circle representing the complex numbers z_1, z_2, z_3 and z_4 respectively, see figure (4.7).

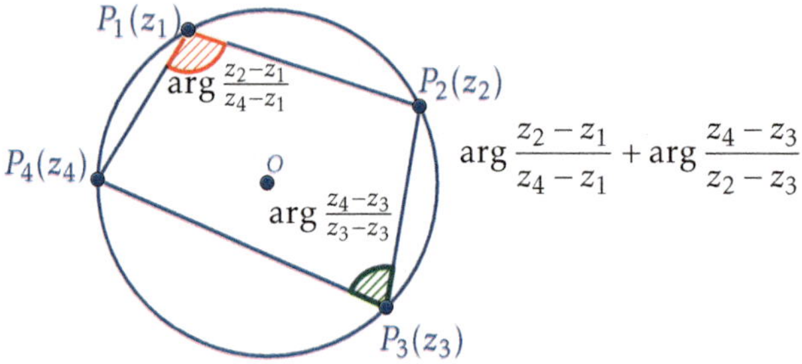

Figure 4.7: As the points are concyclic the sum of the opposite angles of the quadrilateral must by π.

Since the points are on a circle then the $\arg \frac{z_2 - z_1}{z_4 - z_1}$ is the angle $\angle Z_4 Z_1 Z_2$

and the arg $\frac{z_4 - z_3}{z_2 - z_3}$ is the angle $\angle Z_2Z_3Z_4$. As the sum must be π we have

$$\begin{aligned} \arg\frac{z_2 - z_1}{z_4 - z_1} + \arg\frac{z_4 - z_3}{z_2 - z_3} &= \pi \\ \arg\left(\frac{z_2 - z_1}{z_4 - z_1}\frac{z_4 - z_3}{z_2 - z_3}\right) &= \pi \\ \arg\left(\frac{(z_1 - z_2)(z_3 - z_4)}{(z_4 - z_1)(z_2 - z_3)}\right) &= \pi \end{aligned}$$

Since the argument of w is π, the imaginary part of this complex number is zero and hence w is real. This essentially is another proof of the concyclic points Proposition (3.13) we did earlier. □

4.5 Other Loci. Apollonian Circle. Ellipse

The circle of Apollonius[1] is the locus of points P that have the property $|AP| = \kappa|BP|$, with A and B two fixed points and κ is a number different from 1 (if it is equal to 1 the circle collapses to the perpendicular bisector of the segment AB). Another way to view this, is that the ratio of distances from two points is fixed. The following example illustrates the Apollonian circle.

Exercise 4.8: Find the locus of points for which $|z-1| = 3|z-2|$.

Ans: Substituting for $z = x + iy$ we get

$$\begin{aligned} (x-1)^2 + y^2 &= 9\left[(x-2)^2 + y^2\right] \\ x^2 - 2x + 1 + y^2 &= 9\left[x^2 - 4x + 4 + y^2\right] \\ 0 &= 8x^2 + 8y^2 - 34x + 35 \\ \left(x - \frac{34}{16}\right)^2 + y^2 &= \left(\frac{3}{8}\right)^2 \end{aligned}$$

Clearly, this is a circle. It is the locus of points that move with a constant ratio from two points and that is exactly the definition of the Apollonian circle! □

[1]Apollonius of Perga, 262BC-190BC, was a Greek mathematician known as "The Great Geometer". His works had a very great influence on the development of mathematics and his famous book Conics introduced the terms parabola, ellipse and hyperbola.

The ellipse is the locus of points P that have the sum of the distances between two points constant. The following example illustrates the locus.

Exercise 4.9: Find the locus of points for which $|z-1|+|z+1|=9$.

Ans: If you remember the definition of an ellipse you can easily identify this as an ellipse with focal points the $x=1$ and $x=-1$ and eccentricity $e=2/9$. If you want to get the equation of the ellipse the algebraic way, you are in for some messy algebra. You would finally get that the equation is

$$\frac{x^2}{\frac{81}{4}-1}+\frac{y^2}{\frac{81}{4}}=1$$

The geometric way is not only fast but also the smart way to do it. □

Theorem 4.5: The locus of points z with $|z-c|+|z+c|=2a$, with $c,a\in\mathbb{R}$ and $a>c$, is an ellipse with foci on $(c,0)$ and $(-c,0)$.

Proof: Substituting $z=x+iy$ we get

$$\begin{aligned}
\sqrt{(x+c)^2+y^2}+\sqrt{(x-c)^2+y^2} &= 2a \\
\left(\sqrt{(x+c)^2+y^2}\right)^2 &= \left(2a-\sqrt{(x-c)^2+y^2)}\right)^2 \\
a^2-xc &= a\sqrt{(x-c)^2+y^2} \\
\text{SQUARING AGAIN } a^2(a^2-c^2) &= x^2(a^2-c^2)+a^2y^2 \\
\frac{x^2}{a^2}+\frac{y^2}{a^2-c^2} &= 1
\end{aligned}$$

And this is an ellipse with eccentricity $e=c/a$ and foci at $(c,0)$ and $(-c,0)$. □

Exercise 4.10: Show that if $|z|=l$, where $l>1$ then the locus of the complex number $w=z+1/z$ is an ellipse.

Ans: We need to find the locus of points of w. If we substitute $z=x+iy$ into w we get

$$w=x+iy+\frac{1}{x+iy}=x+iy+\frac{x-iy}{x^2+y^2}=x+\frac{x}{x^2+y^2}+i\left(y-\frac{y}{x^2+y^2}\right)$$

But we know that $|z| = \sqrt{x^2 + y^2} = l$ and if we substitute back into w we get

$$w = x + \frac{x}{l^2} + i\left(y - \frac{y}{l^2}\right)$$

We are almost there. In order to find the equation that w describes, let $w = X + iY$ we then have $X = x + \dfrac{x}{l^2}$ and $Y = y - \dfrac{y}{l^2}$. If we solve these for x and y we get

$$x = \frac{l^2 X}{l^2 + 1}, \quad y = \frac{l^2 Y}{l^2 - 1}$$

Using the fact the $|z|^2 = x^2 + y^2 = l^2$ we finally get

$$\left(\frac{l^2}{l^2+1}\right)^2 X^2 + \left(\frac{l^2}{l^2-1}\right)^2 Y^2 = l^2 \Rightarrow \frac{X^2}{\left(l + \frac{1}{l}\right)^2} + \frac{Y^2}{\left(l - \frac{1}{l}\right)^2} = 1$$

And this is the equation of an ellipse. □

Theorem 4.6: The locus of points z with $|z-c|-|z+c| = 2a$, with $c, a \in \mathbb{R}$ and $c > a$, is an hyperbola with foci on $(c, 0)$ and $(-c, 0)$.
Proof: Substituting $z = x + iy$ we get

$$\begin{aligned}
\sqrt{(x-c)^2 + y^2} &= 2a + \sqrt{(x+c)^2 + y^2} \Rightarrow \\
(x-c)^2 + y^2 &= 4a^2 + (x+c)^2 + y^2 + 4a\sqrt{(x+c)^2 + y^2} \Rightarrow \\
-(a^2 + xc) &= \sqrt{(x+c)^2 + y^2} \Rightarrow \\
x^2(a^2 - c^2) + y^2 a^2 &= a^2(a^2 - c^2)
\end{aligned}$$

Dividing by $(a^2 - c^2)a^2$ we get

$$\frac{x^2}{a^2} - \frac{y^2}{c^2 - a^2} = 1, \quad c > a$$

And this is the standard equation of a hyperbola with foci on $(-c, 0)$ and $(c, 0)$. □

4.6 Questions on Loci

Q 4.1 Show that the equation of the circle with center z_0 and radius R can also be written as

$$|z|^2 - 2\Re(z^* z_0) + |z_0|^2 = R^2$$

Q 4.2 Find the locus of z if $zz^* + i(z - z^*) = 1$.

Q 4.3 Show that the hyperbola $x^2 - y^2 = 1$ can be written as $z^2 + (z^*)^2 = 2$

Q 4.4 Sketch, on a single Argand diagram, the loci given by $|z - \sqrt{3} - i| = 2$ and $\arg z = \pi/6$. [6] **(OCR FP1 Jan2012)**

Q 4.5 The loci C_1 and C_2 are given by $|z - 2i| = 2$ and $|z + 1| = |z + i|$ respectively.

(i) Sketch, on a single Argand diagram, the loci C_1 and C_2. [5]

(ii) Hence write down the complex numbers represented by the points of intersection of C_1 and C_2. [2]

(OCR FP1 Jun2005)

Q 4.6 In an Argand diagram the loci C_1 and C_2 are given by

$$|z| = 2, \text{ and } \arg(z) = \frac{\pi}{3}$$

respectively.

(i) Sketch, on a single Argand diagram, the loci C_1 and C_2. [5]

(ii) Hence find, in the form $x + iy$, the complex number representing the point of intersection of C_1 and C_2. [2]

(OCR FP1 Jun2006)

Q 4.7 The point z moves on a circle with radius R and centre a, where $a \in \mathbb{C}$. If we let $w = \frac{1}{z}$ show that the locus of points of w is a line if $|a| = R$ and a circle otherwise.

Q 4.8 Sketch the locus defined by $|z| = 3$. If $a = 5 + i$ and $|z| = 3$ find the greatest and least values of $|z + a|$. **(C) part**

Q 4.9 Given that $\arg(z_1 - z_2) - \arg(z_1 + z_2) = \pi/2$, prove that $|z_1| = |z_2|$. **(JMB part)**

Q 4.10 (i)Sketch the locus of the point z that satisfies $|z-1| = 3|z+i|$ and express the equation of the locus in Cartesian form. (ii) Find the points on the locus which satisfy the equation $|z| = |z - 1 + i|$. **(UL)**

Q 4.11 (i) Sketch, on an Argand diagram, the locus given by $|z-1+i| = \sqrt{2}$. [3]

(ii) Shade on your diagram the region given by $1 \le |z-1+i| \le \sqrt{2}$. [3]

(OCR FP1 Jan2007)

Q 4.12 The loci C_1 and C_2 are given by $|z-3| = 3$ and $\arg(z-1) = \pi/4$ respectively.

(i) Sketch, on a single Argand diagram, the loci C_1 and C_2. [6]

(ii) Indicate, by shading, the region of the Argand diagram for which $|z-3| \le 3$ and $0 \le \arg(z-1) \le \pi/4$. [2]

(OCR FP1 Jun2007)

Q 4.13 Show that if $\lambda zz^* + Az^* + A^*z + \mu = 0$ with $\lambda, \mu \in \mathbb{R}$ and $A \in \mathbb{C}$ then

(i) If $\lambda \neq 0$ and $|A|^2 > \lambda\mu$ then z describes a circle.

(ii) If $\lambda = 0$ and $A \neq 0$, then z describes as straight line.

Q 4.14 The loci C_1 and C_2 are given by $|z| = |z-4i|$ and $\arg z = \pi/6$ respectively.

(i) Sketch, on a single Argand diagram, the loci C_1 and C_2. [5]

(ii) Hence find, in the form $x + iy$, the complex number represented by the point of intersection of C_1 and C_2. [3]

(OCR FP1 Jan2008)

Q 4.15 The complex number $3 + 4i$ is denoted by a.

(i) Find $|a|$ and $\arg a$. [2]

(ii) Sketch on a single Argand diagram the loci given by

(a) $|z-a| = |a|$ [2]

(b) $\arg(z-3) = \arg a$. [3]

(OCR FP1 Jun2008)

Q 4.16 If $\dfrac{z-i}{z+1}$ is purely imaginary, show that the z lies on a circle with center $(1/2, -1/2)$ and radius $1/\sqrt{2}$

Q 4.17 (i) Use an algebraic method to find the square roots of the complex number $2 + i\sqrt{5}$. Give your answers in the form $x + iy$, where x and y are exact real numbers. [6]

(ii) Hence find, in the form $x+iy$ where x and y are exact real numbers, the roots of the equation $z^4 - 4z^2 + 9 = 0$. [4]

(iii) Show, on an Argand diagram, the roots of the equation in part (ii). [1]

(iv) Given that a is the root of the equation in part (ii) such that $0 < \arg a < \pi/2$, sketch on the same Argand diagram the locus given by $|z-a| = |z|$. [3]

(OCR FP1 Jan2009)

Q 4.18 (i) Sketch on a single Argand diagram the loci given by
(a) $|z| = |z-8|$, [2]
(b) $\arg(z+2i) = \pi/4$. [3]

(ii) Indicate by shading the region of the Argand diagram for which

$$|z| \leq |z-8| \text{ AND } 0 \leq \arg(z+2i) \leq \pi/4 \quad [3]$$

(OCR FP1 Jan2011)

Q 4.19 The complex number $1 + i\sqrt{3}$ is denoted by a.

(i) Find $|a|$ and $\arg a$. [2]

(ii) Sketch on a single Argand diagram the loci given by $|z-a| = |a|$ and $\arg(z-a) = \pi/2$. [6]

(OCR FP1 Jun2011)

Q 4.20 The loci C_1 and C_2 are given by $|z-3-4i| = 4$ and $|z| = |z-8i|$ respectively.

(i) Sketch, on a single Argand diagram, the loci C_1 and C_2. [6]

(ii) Hence find the complex numbers represented by the points of intersection of C_1 and C_2. [2]

(iii) Indicate, by shading, the region of the Argand diagram for which

$$|z-3-4i| \leq 4 \text{ AND } |z| \geq |z-8i| \quad [2]$$

(OCR FP1 Jun2012)

Q 4.21 (i) Sketch on a single Argand diagram the loci given by
(a) $z = 2$, [2]
(b) $\arg(z-3-i) = \pi$. [3]

(ii) Indicate, by shading, the region of the Argand diagram for which

$$|z| \leq 2 \text{ and } 0 < \arg(z - 3 - i) \leq \pi \qquad [2]$$

(OCR FP1 Jan2013)

Q 4.22 The loci C_1 and C_2 are given by $\arg(z - 2 - 2i) = \pi/4$ and $|z| = |z - 10|$ respectively.

(i) Sketch on a single Argand diagram the loci C_1 and C_2. [4]

(ii) Indicate, by shading, the region of the Argand diagram for which

$$0 \leq \arg(z - 2 - 2i) \leq \pi/4 \text{ and } |z| \geq |z - 10| \qquad [3]$$

(OCR FP1 Jun2014)

Q 4.23 The loci C_1 and C_2 are given by $|z + 2| = 2$ and $\arg(z + 2) = \dfrac{5\pi}{6}$ respectively.

(i) Sketch, on a single Argand diagram, the loci C_1 and C_2. [4]

(ii) Find the complex number represented by the intersection of C_1 and C_2. [2]

(iii) Indicate, by shading, the region of the Argand diagram for which

$$|z + 2| \leq 2 \text{ and } \frac{5\pi}{6} \leq \arg(z + 2) \leq \pi \qquad [2]$$

(OCR FP1 Jun2015)

Q 4.24 In an Argand diagram the points A and B represent the complex numbers 5+4i and 1+2i respectively.

(i) Given that A and B are the ends of a diameter of a circle C, find the equation of C in complex number form. [4]
The perpendicular bisector of AB is denoted by l.

(ii) Sketch C and l on a single Argand diagram. [2]

(iii) Find the complex numbers represented by the points of intersection of C and l. [3]

(OCR FP1 Jun2016)

Q 4.25

(i) Show on an Argand diagram the locus of z when

   (a) $|z-1-i|=2$,

   (b) $\Re(z)=1$ and $-\pi/3 \le \arg(z) \le \pi/4$.
   In each case find the greatest value of $|z|$

(ii) The co-ordinates of the point P in one Argand diagram are (x,y) and are expressed in the complex form $z=x+iy$. If the co-ordinates of a point Q in a second Argand diagram are (u,v) express the co-ordinates of Q in complex form w.
If $z=w^2$, find x and y in terms of u and v and show that, if P lies on the circle $x^2+y^2=16$, then Q lies on the circle $u^2+v^2=4$.

(AEB 132/2 Jun1973)

Q 4.26

(a) If $z=x+iy$, $x \neq 0$ and $y \neq 0$, show that $\dfrac{z}{1+z^2}$ is real provided z is a point on the circle $x^2+y^2=1$.
Show that $\dfrac{z}{1+z^2}$ can never be entirely imaginary.

(b) The complex numbers z_1, z_2 and z_3 are represented on an Argand diagram by the points A, B and C respectively. The complex numbers t_1, t_2 and t_3 are represented on an Argand diageam by K, L and M respectively. Show that triangle ABC is similar to triangle KLM provided

$$\frac{z_2-z_1}{z_3-z_1}=\frac{t_2-t_1}{t_3-t_1}$$

(AEB 632/2 Nov1976)

Q 4.27 The roots of the equation $(z-4)^3=8$ are z_1, z_2 and z_3. Find the roots and represent them by the points P_1, P_2, P_3 on an Argand diagram. State the values of $|z_1|$, $|z_2|$ and $|z_3|$.
A complex number z is such that $|z|=k|z-4|$. Obtain the Cartesian equation of the locus of z when

(i) $k=1$

(ii) $k=3$.

In each case sketch the locus.
For each of the points P_1, P_2 and P_3 find the value of k for which the point lies on the locus given by $|z|=k|z-4|$. **(AEB 632/2 Jun1980)**

Q 4.28 The complex numbers z_1, z_2, z_3 are represented on an Argand diagram by the points A, B, C and

$$z_1 = 4i,\ z_2 = 2\sqrt{3} - 2i,\ z_3 = -2\sqrt{3} - 2i$$

(i) Show that the triangle ABC is equilateral

(ii) Show that z_1^2 and $z_2 z_3$ are represented by the same point in the Argand diagram.

(iii) Find the equation of the circle OBC, where O is the origin, in the $|z - a| = b$ form and also in the $f(x, y) = 0$ form.

(iv) Describe the locus of the point P, given that P represents the complex number z in the Argand diagram and

$$\arg\left(\frac{z - z_1}{z - z_2}\right) = \frac{\pi}{2}$$

(AEB 632/2 Jun1981)

Q 4.29 If $z = x + iy$, interpret on an Argand diagram the locus of z given that $\arg\left(\frac{z-2}{z+2}\right) = \frac{\pi}{3}$. **(AEB 132/2 Nov1970p)**

Q 4.30 (i) Show that if $(z-2)(z^* - 2) + |z-2| - 2 = 0$ then the locus of points if z is a circle C with centre $(0, 2)$ and radius 1.

(ii) Show further for any complex number on C we have $|z| \leq 3$.

(iii) If a, b and c are complex numbers that lie on the circle C and w is a complex number satisfying

$$w^3 + aw^2 + bw + c = 0$$

show that $|w| < 4$.

Q 4.31 Let a be a positive real number ($a > 0, a \in \mathbb{R}$). The complex numbers w, z, w_1 are such $w = z - zi$ and $w_1 = \frac{1}{a} + ai$. Show that if $w = w_1{}^*$ then the complex number z moves into a hyperbola.

Q 4.32 If P represents the complex number z on an Argand diagram, find the Cartesian equation of the locus of P

(i) when $\frac{|z+i|}{|z+1|} = 3$,

(ii) when $\frac{z+i}{z+1}$ is real.

(AEB 632/2 Jun1976p)

5. De Moivre's Theorem

> The shortest path between two truths in the real domain passes through the complex domain.
>
> Jacques Hadamard

5.1 De Moivre's Theorem

The following theorem by De Moivre[1] is one of the most useful and striking theorems on complex numbers.

Theorem 5.1: (De Moivre) For any complex number $z = r(\cos\theta + i\sin\theta)$, with $n \in \mathbb{N}$, the following relation holds

$$z^n = [r(\cos\theta + i\sin\theta)]^n = r^n(\cos n\theta + i\sin n\theta) \tag{5.1}$$

Proof: We would formally prove this using induction and a bit of trigonometry. First, we note that the relation is true for $n = 1$ by definition. Namely, $n = 1 \Rightarrow z = r(\cos\theta + i\sin\theta)$. Next, we assume that the relation is true for $n = k$, so $z^k = r^k(\cos k\theta + i\sin k\theta)$. We would prove that it is also true for $n = k+1$. We thus have

$$\begin{aligned}
z^{k+1} &= r^k \ (\cos k\theta + i\sin k\theta) \times r(\cos\theta + i\sin\theta) \\
&= r^{k+1}(\cos k\theta + i\sin k\theta) \times (\cos\theta + i\sin\theta) \\
&= r^{k+1}\left[\cos k\theta\cos\theta - \sin k\theta\sin\theta + i(\sin k\theta\cos\theta + \cos k\theta\sin\theta)\right] \\
&= r^{k+1}\left[\cos(k\theta + \theta) + i\sin(k\theta + \theta)\right] \\
&= r^{k+1}\left[\cos(k+1)\theta + i\sin(k+1)\theta\right]
\end{aligned}$$

Hence, the relation is true for all $n \in \mathbb{N}$. We can similarly prove that (5.1) is true for negative integers and hence for all integers (for all $n \in \mathbb{Z}$) and we can further prove that it also holds true for rational numbers (this has been in the past an exam question). However, for irrational numbers it is not always the case. □

Exercise 5.1: Show that $(\cos 3\theta + i\sin 3\theta)(\cos 3\theta - i\sin 3\theta) = 1$.

[1] Abraham De Moivre 1667-1754, was a French-born mathematician who pioneered the development of analytic geometry and the theory of probability.

Ans: Using De Moivre's theorem we have that $(\cos 3\theta + i\sin 3\theta) = (\cos\theta + i\sin\theta)^3$ and $\cos 3\theta - i\sin 3\theta = \cos(-3\theta) + i\sin(-3\theta)) = (\cos\theta + i\sin\theta)^{-3}$. Combining the two we get the desired result. □

Exercise 5.2: Show that

$$\frac{\cos\theta - i\sin\theta}{\cos 5\theta - i\sin 5\theta} = \cos 4\theta + i\sin 4\theta$$

Ans: Using De Moivre's theorem the numerator becomes $\cos\theta - i\sin\theta = (\cos\theta + i\sin\theta)^{-1}$. The denominator becomes $\cos 5\theta - i\sin 5\theta = (\cos\theta + i\sin\theta)^{-5}$. Combining

$$\frac{\cos\theta - i\sin\theta}{\cos 5\theta - i\sin 5\theta} = \frac{(\cos\theta + i\sin\theta)^{-1}}{(\cos\theta + i\sin\theta)^{-5}} = (\cos\theta + i\sin\theta)^4 = \cos 4\theta + i\sin 4\theta$$

□

Another question that comes up often, is to ask you to compute some ridiculous high power polynomial or complex number. In most cases, De Moivre comes to the rescue.

Exercise 5.3: Show that $(\sqrt{3} + i)^{150} = -2^{150}$.

Ans: Clearly we cannot expand to the 150th power, so we must use De Moivre's theorem. But before we do this we need to write the complex number in its trigonometric form. So let $z = \sqrt{3} + i$. We have $|z| = \sqrt{(\sqrt{3})^2 + 1^2} = 2$. We can now write $z = 2\left(\frac{\sqrt{3}}{2} + i\frac{1}{2}\right)$. The sine is 1/2 at $\pi/6$ or 30 degrees and so

$$\begin{aligned} z &= 2\left(\frac{\sqrt{3}}{2} + i\frac{1}{2}\right) = 2\left(\cos\frac{\pi}{6} + i\sin\frac{\pi}{6}\right) \Rightarrow \\ z^{150} &= 2^{150}\left(\cos\frac{\pi}{6} + i\sin\frac{\pi}{6}\right)^{150} = 2^{150}\left(\cos\frac{150\pi}{6} + i\sin\frac{150\pi}{6}\right) \\ &= 2^{150}(\cos 25\pi + i\sin 25\pi) = 2^{150}(-1+0) = -2^{150} \end{aligned}$$

□

The following expression is encountered many times in questions that involve summation of geometric series. It is a good idea to master it.

Exercise 5.4: Show that if $z = (1 + \cos\theta + i\sin\theta)$ then

$$z^n = 2^n \cos^n\frac{\theta}{2}\left(\cos\frac{n\theta}{2} + i\sin\frac{n\theta}{2}\right)$$

Ans: In order to use De Moivre's theorem (5.1) we need somehow to get rid of the 1 inside the bracket. The way to do this is by using the double-angle trigonometric identities. We can simplify the expression using $\cos\theta = 2\cos^2\theta/2 - 1$ and $\sin\theta = 2\sin\theta/2\cos\theta/2$

$$
\begin{aligned}
z = (1+\cos\theta + i\sin\theta)^n &= \left(1 - 1 + 2\cos^2\frac{\theta}{2} + 2i\sin\frac{\theta}{2}\cos\frac{\theta}{2}\right)^n \\
&= 2^n\cos^n\frac{\theta}{2}\left(\cos\frac{\theta}{2} + i\sin\frac{\theta}{2}\right)^n \\
\text{De Moivre} \quad &= 2^n\cos^n\frac{\theta}{2}\left(\cos\frac{n\theta}{2} + i\sin\frac{n\theta}{2}\right) \qquad \square
\end{aligned}
$$

Exercise 5.5: Find the value of (i) $(-1)^{3/4}$ and (ii) $(1+i)^{1/2}$.
Ans: In order to compute these, we need to first convert the complex number into their polar form and then apply De Moivre's theorem.

$$
(-1)^{3/4} = (\cos(-\pi) + i\sin(-\pi))^{3/4} = \cos\left(-\frac{3\pi}{4}\right) + i\sin\left(-\frac{3\pi}{4}\right) = -\frac{1}{2} - i\frac{\sqrt{3}}{2}
$$

and

$$
\begin{aligned}
(1+i)^{1/2} = 2^{1/4}\left(\frac{1}{\sqrt{2}} + i\frac{1}{\sqrt{2}}\right)^{1/2} &= 2^{1/4}\left(\cos\frac{\pi}{4} + i\sin\frac{\pi}{4}\right)^{1/2} \\
&= 2^{1/4}\left(\cos\frac{\pi}{8} + i\sin\frac{\pi}{8}\right) \qquad \square
\end{aligned}
$$

Exercise 5.6: Show that, for $n \in \mathbb{Z}$ the following relation is true

$$
(\sin\theta + i\cos\theta)^n = \cos n\left(\frac{\pi}{2} - \theta\right) + i\sin n\left(\frac{\pi}{2} - \theta\right)
$$

Ans: Notice that, the left hand side is not exactly what we expect from De Moivre's theorem. The sine and cosine are reversed. So, in order to use the theorem we need to get it into the usual form. We can use the complementary angles, so that $\cos\theta = \sin(\pi/2 - \theta)$ and $\sin\theta = \cos(\pi/2-\theta)$

$$
\begin{aligned}
(\sin\theta + i\cos\theta)^n &= \left[\cos\left(\frac{\pi}{2} - \theta\right) + i\sin\left(\frac{\pi}{2} - \theta\right)\right]^n \\
&= \cos n\left(\frac{\pi}{2} - \theta\right) + i\sin n\left(\frac{\pi}{2} - \theta\right) \qquad \square
\end{aligned}
$$

De Moivre's theorem connects complex numbers with trigonometry and also with the binomial theorem. A very important result that is used very often is the following,

Proposition 5.1: If $z = \cos\theta + i\sin\theta$, use De Moivre theorem to show that

$$z + \frac{1}{z} = 2\cos\theta \quad \text{AND} \quad z - \frac{1}{z} = 2i\sin\theta \tag{5.2}$$

$$z^n + \frac{1}{z^n} = 2\cos n\theta \quad \text{AND} \quad z^n - \frac{1}{z^n} = 2i\sin n\theta \tag{5.3}$$

Proof: Since $z = \cos\theta + i\sin\theta$, we also have that $z^{-1} = (\cos\theta + i\sin\theta)^{-1} = \cos(-\theta) + i\sin(-\theta) = \cos\theta - i\sin\theta$, as the cosine is an even function and the sine an odd function. If we add them we get

$$z + \frac{1}{z} = \cos\theta + i\sin\theta + \cos\theta - i\sin\theta = 2\cos\theta$$

Similarly, $z^n = \cos n\theta + i\sin n\theta$ and $z^{-n} = \cos n\theta - i\sin n\theta$ and when we add them we get

$$z^n + \frac{1}{z^n} = \cos n\theta + i\sin\, n\theta + \cos n\theta - i\sin n\theta = 2\cos n\theta$$

and similarly for $z^n - 1/z^n$. □

DAD'S SOS NOTE: This way of writing $\cos\theta$ and $\sin\theta$ in terms of complex numbers is more than useful. It is a MUST KNOW! ♥

A straightforward application of these results is used in the following examples.

Exercise 5.7: If $|z| = 1$ and $z + 1/z = \sqrt{2}$ show that, $z^4 + z^{-4} = -2$.
Ans: If we let $z = \cos\theta + i\sin\theta$ and using (5.2) we get $2\cos\theta = \sqrt{2}$. Hence, $\theta = \pi/4$. Now using equation (5.3) we get $z^4 + z^{-4} = 2\cos 4\theta = 2\cos\pi = -2$. □

The following example is slightly trickier but uses the same principles.
Exercise 5.8: Find the all the solutions to the equation

$$\cos\theta + \cos 2\theta - \cos 3\theta = 1$$

where $0 \le \theta \le \pi$.
Ans: By inspection one can verify that $\theta = 0$ or π satisfy the above equation. But are these the full set of solutions? We are going to re-write the

equation using $2\cos\theta = z + 1/z$ where $z = \cos\theta + i\sin\theta$. We then have

$$\cos\theta = \frac{1}{2}\left(z+\frac{1}{z}\right),\quad \cos 2\theta = \frac{1}{2}\left(z^2+\frac{1}{z^2}\right),\quad \cos 3\theta = \frac{1}{2}\left(z^3+\frac{1}{z^3}\right)$$

Substituting these we get

$$\begin{aligned}\left(z+\frac{1}{z}\right)+\frac{1}{2}\left(z^2+\frac{1}{z^2}\right)-\frac{1}{2}\left(z^3+\frac{1}{z^3}\right) &= 1\\ -z^6+z^5+z^4+z^2+z-1 &= 2z^3\end{aligned}$$

The last equation looks a bit daunting and we need to solve this if we are to find the roots. The only option is to factorise the expression. We know from inspection that $z = 1, -1$ are roots so we can use this fact to factorise the expression. But perhaps the fastest route is to attempt to factorize it.

$$\begin{aligned}-z^6+z^5+z^4+z^2+z-1-2z^3 &= 0\\ -z^6-z^3+z^5+z^2+z^4+z-1-z^3 &= 0\\ -z^3(z^3+1)+z^2(z^3+1)+z(z^3+1)-(1+z^3) &= 0\\ (z^3+1)(-z^3+z^2+z-1) &= 0\\ (z^3+1)\left[z(1-z^2)-(1-z^2)\right] &= 0\\ (z^3+1)(1-z^2)(z-1) &= 0\\ (z^3+1)(1+z)(1-z)^2 &= 0\end{aligned}$$

We thus recover the solutions $z = \pm 1$ as expected. The values of θ are zero and π (the question restricts θ, otherwise we would have multiples of 2π added). The extra solution is $z^3 = -1$ and this gives $\theta = \pi/3$, since θ is restricted to $0 \le \theta \le \pi$.
Another way, not using complex numbers is to use the formula for the difference of cosines $\cos A - \cos B = -2\cos(A+B)/2\cos(A-B)/2$ and after some algebra you will end up with the same answer. □

5.2 Trigonometric Applications of De Moivre

By far the most interesting applications are in proving trigonometric identities. By a clever application of De Moivre's theorem we can get many results very efficiently. The following are the most typical trigonometric applications that make exam appearances. Needless to say that they are a MUST KNOW.

5.2.1 Express $\cos n\theta$, $\sin n\theta$ in term of powers of $\cos\theta$ or $\sin\theta$

One of the most frequently asked questions is to express $\cos n\theta$ in term of powers of $\cos\theta$ (similarly for $\sin n\theta$, $\tan n\theta$ and $\cot n\theta$). In this case, we use both De Moivre's theorem and the binomial expansion. If we write

$$(\cos\theta + i\sin\theta)^n = \cos n\theta + \sin n\theta$$

and then expand the binomial n^{th}-power we get the required identity by equating real and imaginary parts.

The following example is a typical question asked time and time again in high school exams (like the A-level).

Exercise 5.9: Using De Moivre's theorem (5.1) find $\cos 3\theta$ in terms of powers of $\cos\theta$.

Ans: Start with

$$\begin{aligned}
\cos 3\theta + i\sin 3\theta &= (\cos\theta + i\sin\theta)^3 = \\
&= \cos^3\theta + 3i\cos^2\theta\sin\theta + 3\cos\theta(i\sin\theta)^2 + (i\sin\theta)^3 \\
&= \cos^3\theta - 3\cos\theta\sin^2\theta + i(3\cos^2\theta\sin\theta - \sin^3\theta)
\end{aligned}$$

In the last step, if we equate the real and imaginary parts we get:

$$\begin{aligned}
\cos 3\theta &= \cos^3\theta - 3\cos\theta(1-\cos^2\theta) = 4\cos^3\theta - 3\cos\theta \\
\sin 3\theta &= 3(1-\sin^2\theta)\sin\theta - \sin^3\theta = 3\sin\theta - 4\sin^3\theta
\end{aligned}$$

By application of De Moivre not only we found $\cos 3\theta$ but we also got $\sin 3\theta$ as a bonus! Fast and neat. □

DAD'S SOS NOTE: In the high school exams they may ask for either the sin or the cos or even tan and cot. Usually they go up to the fifth power or even the seventh, so you will need to do the binomial expansion. Do Pascal's triangle (see p. 188) to get the coefficients. ♥

We could also write the general formula for $\cos n\theta$, $\sin n\theta$ and $\tan n\theta$ using the binomial theorem.

Exercise 5.10: Obtain the general formula for $\cos n\theta$ and $\sin n\theta$ and hence find the $\tan n\theta$.

Ans: You just need to write the binomial expansion formula using equation

$$(\cos\theta + i\sin\theta)^n = {}^nC_0\cos^n\theta + {}^nC_1\cos^{n-1}\theta(i\sin\theta) + ...{}^nC_n(i\sin\theta)^n$$
$$= \left[{}^nC_0\cos^n\theta - {}^nC_2\cos^{n-2}\sin^2\theta + {}^nC_4\cos^{n-4}\theta\sin^4\theta + ...\right]$$
$$+i\left[{}^nC_1\cos^{n-1}\theta\sin\theta - {}^nC_3\cos^{n-3}\theta\sin^3\theta + {}^nC_5\cos^{n-5}\theta\sin^5\theta + ...\right]$$

Comparing real and imaginary parts we get

$$\cos n\theta = {}^nC_0\cos^n\theta - {}^nC_2\cos^{n-2}\theta\sin^2\theta + {}^nC_4\cos^{n-4}\theta\sin^4\theta + ...$$
$$\sin n\theta = {}^nC_1\cos^{n-1}\theta\sin\theta - {}^nC_3\cos^{n-3}\theta\sin^3\theta + {}^nC_5\cos^{n-5}\theta\sin^5\theta + ...$$

Notice that, all the even powers give the cosine and all the odd powers the sine with the plus and minus sign alternating. This is a manifestation of the even and odd nature of the cosine and the sine function. We can now get the $\tan n\theta$ by dividing the two.

$$\tan n\theta = \frac{{}^nC_1\cos^{n-1}\theta\sin\theta - {}^nC_3\cos^{n-3}\theta\sin^3\theta + {}^nC_5\cos^{n-5}\theta\sin^5\theta + ...}{{}^nC_0\cos^n\theta - {}^nC_2\cos^{n-2}\theta\sin^2\theta + {}^nC_4\cos^{n-4}\theta\sin^4\theta + ...}$$

Divide by $\cos^n\theta$ to get

$$\tan n\theta = \frac{{}^nC_1\tan\theta - {}^nC_3\tan^3\theta + {}^nC_5\tan^5\theta + ...}{{}^nC_0 - {}^nC_2\tan^2\theta + {}^nC_4\tan^4\theta + ...}$$ □

Another type of question, is to use De Moivre's theorem to find the roots of equations and then using the Vieta relations to obtain trigonometric sums.

Exercise 5.11: (i) Use De Moivre's theorem to find an expression for $\tan 4\theta$ in terms of $\tan\theta$. [4]

(ii) Deduce that

$$\cot 4\theta = \frac{\cot^4\theta - 6\cot^2\theta + 1}{4\cot^3\theta - 4\cot\theta}$$ [1]

(iii) Hence show that one of the roots of the equation $x^2 - 6x + 1 = 0$ is $\cot^2 \pi/8$. [3]

(iv) Hence find the value of $\operatorname{cosec}^2\frac{\pi}{8} + \operatorname{cosec}^2\frac{3\pi}{8}$, justifying your answer. [5]**(OCR FP3 Jan2007)**

Ans: For part (i) see Exercise (5.10). For $n = 4$ we get

$$\tan 4\theta = \frac{{}^nC_1 \tan\theta - {}^4C_3 \tan^3\theta}{{}^4C_0 - {}^4C_2 \tan^2\theta + {}^4C_4 \tan^4\theta} = \frac{4\tan\theta - 4\tan^3\theta}{1 - 6\tan^2\theta + \tan^4\theta}$$

By using $\tan\theta\cot\theta = 1$ and after some simplifications we get

$$\cot 4\theta = \frac{\cot^4\theta - 6\cot^2\theta + 1}{4\cot^3\theta - 4\cot\theta} \tag{5.4}$$

Part (iii) is the interesting one. If you substitute $\theta = \pi/8$ in the above equation you will get zero since $\cot 4\pi/8 = \cot\pi/2 = 0$. This means that the numerator must be zero and so you get that one of the solutions to the quartic $t^4 - 6t^2 + 1 = 0$ is $\cot\frac{\pi}{8}$.

$$\cot^4\frac{\pi}{8} - 6\cot^2\frac{\pi}{8} + 1 = 0$$

If you now let $x = \cot^2\frac{\pi}{8}$ you get $x^2 - 6x + 1 = 0$.
The last part asks us to find the value of $\operatorname{cosec}^2\frac{\pi}{8} + \operatorname{cosec}^2\frac{3\pi}{8}$. From the previous part you have $\cot^2\frac{\pi}{8}$ but not anything with $\frac{3\pi}{8}$. But notice that if you let $\theta = \frac{3\pi}{8}$ into Eq (5.4), you also get zero. In other words both $\cot^2\frac{\pi}{8}$ and $\cot^2\frac{3\pi}{8}$ are roots of the equation $x^2 - 6x + 1 = 0$. And the sum of the roots must be equal to minus the coefficient of x from the Vieta relations. Hence, $\cot^2\frac{\pi}{8} + \cot^2\frac{3\pi}{8} = 6$. Re-writing cot in terms of cosec (use $1 + \cot^2\theta = \operatorname{cosec}^2\theta$) we find that

$$\operatorname{cosec}^2\frac{\pi}{8} + \operatorname{cosec}^2\frac{3\pi}{8} = 2 + \cot^2\frac{\pi}{8} + \cot^2\frac{3\pi}{8} = 8$$ □

DAD'S SOS NOTE: These type of mixed questions using Vieta relations are very appealing since they examine many different parts of the curriculum. Work through them. ♥

5.2.2 Express $\cos^n\theta$ or $\sin^n\theta$ in terms of $\cos k\theta$ and $\sin k\theta$

In order to express $\cos^n\theta$ in terms of multiples of θ we would again use Eq. (5.2) and the binomial theorem. If we are asked to express $\cos^n\theta$ then we can use the $z + z^{-1} = 2\cos\theta$ and raise it to the nth power. Lets see how with an example.

Exercise 5.12: Show that $\cos^3\theta = \frac{1}{4}(\cos 3\theta + 3\cos\theta)$.

Ans: Using (5.2) and raising it to the power of 3 we get the $\cos^3\theta$ that we want. So,

$$\left(z+\frac{1}{z}\right)^3 = \left(z^3+3z+3\frac{1}{z}+\frac{1}{z^3}\right) = 2^3\cos^3\theta$$

$$\left(z^3+\frac{1}{z^3}\right)+3\left(z+\frac{1}{z}\right) = 8\cos^3\theta$$

$$\text{Using Eq. (5.3)}\quad \cos 3\theta + 3\cos\theta = 4\cos^3\theta$$

□

> Dad's SOS Note: Exactly the same procedure is done in the case of $\sin^n\theta$. We just use the $z - z^{-1}$ instead of the $z + z^{-1}$. In the exam it is not uncommon to ask you to evaluate powers up to 7. So be prepared to do the binomial expansion fast and without errors. Remember that the *coefficients in the binomial expansion are symmetric* which is why we can use equations (5.3). ♥

Questions that ask you to find $\cos^n\theta$ or $\sin^n\theta$ in terms of cosines or sines of multiples of theta give rise to many more interesting applications which is why they are actually asked in the exam. For example, they may ask you to evaluate the integral of some power of $\cos\theta$ or $\sin\theta$.

Exercise 5.13: Show that

$$\sin^4\theta \equiv \frac{1}{8}(\cos 4\theta - 4\cos 2\theta + 3)$$

and hence evaluate

$$\int_0^{\pi/3} \sin^4\theta \, d\theta$$

Ans: The first part should be done in 3 minutes:

$$(2i)^4\sin^4\theta = \left(z-\frac{1}{z}\right)^4 = \left(z^4+\frac{1}{z^4}\right)-4\left(z^2+\frac{1}{z^2}\right)+6 \Rightarrow$$

$$16\sin^4\theta = 2\cos 4\theta - 8\cos 2\theta + 6 \Rightarrow$$

$$\sin^4\theta = \frac{1}{8}(\cos 4\theta - 4\cos 2\theta + 3)$$

The integral is now easy to evaluate

$$\int_0^{\pi/3} \sin^4\theta \; d\theta = \frac{1}{8}\int_0^{\pi/3} (\cos 4\theta - 4\cos 2\theta + 3) \; d\theta$$
$$= \frac{1}{8}\,\frac{\sin 4\theta}{4} - 2\sin 2\theta + 3\theta\Big|_0^{\pi/3} = \frac{1}{8}\left(\frac{1}{4}\sin\frac{4\pi}{3} - 2\sin\frac{2\pi}{3} + \pi\right)$$
$$= \frac{1}{8}\left(-\frac{\sqrt{3}}{8} - \sqrt{3} + \pi\right) = \frac{1}{8}\left(\pi - \frac{9\sqrt{3}}{8}\right) \qquad \square$$

Exercise 5.14: Express $\sin^6\theta\cos^2\theta$ in terms of multiple angles and show that

$$\int_0^{\pi/2} \sin^6\theta\cos^2\theta \, d\theta = \frac{5}{256}\pi$$

Ans: Using the relations for the sine and cosine we can write

$$(2i\sin\theta)^6(2\cos\theta)^2 = (z - 1/z)^6(z + 1/z)^2$$
$$= (z^8 + 1/z^8) - 4(z^6 + 1/z^6) + 4(z^4 + 1/z^4)$$
$$+ 4(z^2 + 1/z^2) - 10$$
$$= 2\cos 8\theta - 8\cos 6\theta + 8\cos 4\theta + 8\cos 2\theta - 10 \Rightarrow$$
$$\sin^6\theta\cos^2\theta = \frac{-1}{256}(2\cos 8\theta - 8\cos 6\theta + 8\cos 4\theta + 8\cos 2\theta - 10)$$

The second part of doing the integral now becomes elementary.... □

5.2.3 Obtain trigonometric series expansions

If the question asks you to prove some mean-looking trigonometric series with multiple angles, chances are that you need to use De Moivre's theorem. Usually, you assume that $z = \cos\theta + i\sin\theta$ and you sum the series using the known formulae of arithmetic or geometric series. Do not be intimidated by the looks. Usually, ugly looking questions are the easiest to do. The following example is typical.

Exercise 5.15: (i) Prove that

$$S_n = 1 + z^2 + z^3 + \ldots + z^n = \frac{1 - z^{n+1}}{1 - z}$$

(ii) Using the previous result show Lagrange's[2] trigonometric identity:

$$1 + \cos\theta + \cos 2\theta + ... + \cos n\theta = \frac{1}{2} + \frac{\sin(2n+1)\theta/2}{2\sin\theta/2}$$

Ans: (i) The RHS is the sum of a geometric progression with common ratio z. Hence the result follows immediately. If you wish you can prove this result with the usual method of considering $zS_n - S_n$
(ii) If we use $z = \cos\theta + i\sin\theta$ and apply De Moivre's theorem we get

$$1+(\cos\theta+i\sin\theta)+...+(\cos n\theta+i\sin n\theta) = \frac{1-(\cos(n+1)\theta+i\sin(n+1)\theta)}{1-(\cos\theta+i\sin\theta)}$$

$$1+\cos\theta+...+\cos n\theta+i(\sin\theta+...+\sin n\theta) = \frac{1-\cos(n+1)\theta-i\sin(n+1)\theta}{2\sin\theta/2(\sin\theta/2-i\cos\theta/2)}$$

We can now compare the real and imaginary parts on both sides to get

$$1 + \cos\theta + ... + \cos n\theta = \frac{\sin\frac{\theta}{2} + \left[-\cos(n+1)\theta\sin\frac{\theta}{2} + \sin(n+1)\theta\cos\frac{\theta}{2}\right]}{2\sin\frac{\theta}{2}}$$

Finally,

$$1 + \cos\theta + ... + \cos n\theta = \frac{1}{2} + \frac{\sin\frac{(2n+1)\theta}{2}}{2\sin\frac{\theta}{2}}$$

And you can also get the similar relation for the sine, by comparing the imaginary parts

$$\sin\theta + \sin 2\theta + ... + \sin n\theta = \frac{1}{2}\cot\frac{\theta}{2} - \frac{\cos\frac{(2n+1)\theta}{2}}{2\sin\frac{\theta}{2}} \qquad \square$$

Exercise 5.16: Show that

$$\cos\alpha + \binom{n}{1}\cos(\alpha+\beta) + \binom{n}{2}\cos(\alpha+2\beta) + ... + \cos(\alpha+n\beta) =$$

$$= \left(2\cos\frac{\beta}{2}\right)^n \cos\left(\alpha + \frac{n\beta}{2}\right)$$

[2]Joseph-Louis Lagrange 1736-1813, was an Italian-born French mathematician who excelled in all fields of analysis and number theory and analytical and celestial mechanics.

Ans: Again, you will need to get this into complex form. If you let $z = \cos\alpha + i\sin\alpha$ and $x = \cos\beta + i\sin\beta$ then you can write the given equation as

$$z + \binom{n}{1}zx + \binom{n}{2}zx^2 + \ldots + \binom{n}{n}zx^n = z\left[1 + \binom{n}{1}x + \binom{n}{2}x^2 + \ldots + \binom{n}{n}x^n\right] = z(1+x)^n$$

Where, I have used $(\cos\alpha + i\sin\alpha)(\cos n\beta + i\sin n\beta) = \cos(a + n\beta)$ and the binomial expansion of $(1+x)^n$. You need now to compare the real and imaginary parts. Using the double angle identities (see Exercise (5.4)) you can write the RHS as

$$\begin{aligned}
z(1+x)^n &= (\cos\alpha + i\sin\alpha)(1 + \cos\beta + i\sin\beta)^n \\
&= (\cos\alpha + i\sin\alpha)\left(2\cos^2\frac{\beta}{2} + 2i\cos\frac{\beta}{2}\sin\frac{\beta}{2}\right)^n \\
&= 2^n\cos^n\frac{\beta}{2}(\cos\alpha + i\sin\alpha)\left[\cos\frac{\beta}{2} + i\sin\frac{\beta}{2}\right]^n \\
&= 2^n\cos^n\frac{\beta}{2}(\cos\alpha + i\sin\alpha)\left[\cos\frac{n\beta}{2} + i\sin\frac{n\beta}{2}\right] \\
&= 2^n\cos^n\frac{\beta}{2}\left[\cos\left(\alpha + \frac{n\beta}{2}\right) + i\sin\left(\alpha + \frac{n\beta}{2}\right)\right]
\end{aligned}$$

Comparing now the real and imaginary parts, you obtain the result and you also have the similar expression for the sine. □

Exercise 5.17: Show that

$$\cos\frac{\pi}{9} + \cos\frac{3\pi}{9} + \cos\frac{5\pi}{9} + \cos\frac{7\pi}{9} = \frac{1}{2}$$

Ans: As it looks, it is a hard question. You could apply the sum of cosines formula and get the answer after some very tedious algebra. The complex way is however very elegant. Let $z = \cos\frac{\pi}{9} + i\sin\frac{\pi}{9}$, namely $z^9 = -1$. You can then write the LHS of the equation as $A = z + z^3 + z^5 + z^7$ and after computing this you can take the real part. Lets see how it works. The A expression is a geometric series with z^2 as its step. For some unknown psychological reason I never remember the formula and I always re-derive it. So, $Az^2 = z^3 + z^5 + z^7 + z^9$, and subtracting this from A you get

$$A - Az^2 = z - z^9 \Rightarrow A = \frac{z - z^9}{1 - z^2} = \frac{z+1}{(1-z)(1+z)} = \frac{1}{1-z}$$

So now you need to take the real part of A.

$$\begin{aligned}\Re(A) &= \Re\frac{1}{1-z} = \Re\left[\frac{1}{1-\cos\frac{\pi}{9} - i\sin\frac{\pi}{9}}\right] \\ &= \Re\left[\frac{1-\cos\frac{\pi}{9} + i\sin\frac{\pi}{9}}{1+\cos^2\frac{\pi}{9}+\sin^2\frac{\pi}{9} - 2\cos\frac{\pi}{9}}\right] = \Re\left[\frac{1}{2} + i\frac{\sin\frac{\pi}{9}}{2(1-\cos\frac{\pi}{9})}\right]\end{aligned}$$

And the result follows as the real part is $1/2$ and this is precisely

$$\cos\frac{\pi}{9} + \cos\frac{3\pi}{9} + \cos\frac{5\pi}{9} + \cos\frac{7\pi}{9} = \frac{1}{2} \qquad \square$$

DAD'S SOS NOTE: Questions involving De Moivre's theorem involve trigonometry and binomial expansions. In order to tackle these type of questions you should be very familiar with the following:

(I) Know the binomial expansion $(a+b)^n$ using Pascal's triangle, see p. 188.

(II) Remember that the expansion $(z+1/z)^n$ is symmetric and group terms like $(z^n \pm 1/z^{n-1})$ to make $\cos n\theta$ and $\sin n\theta$

(III) Remember how to add geometric progression terms like $S_n = 1 + x + x^2 + \ldots + x^{n-1} = \dfrac{1-x^n}{1-x}$. If you cannot remember the formula, derive it by forming $S_n - xS_n$. This is the fastest and error-free way.

(IV) Know the double angle identities $2\cos^2\theta - 1 = \cos 2\theta$ and $2\sin\theta\cos\theta = \sin 2\theta$ and use them to simplify expressions like $(1+\cos\theta + i\sin\theta)$, see Exercise (5.4).

(V) Know the Vieta relations for the quadratic and the cubic (B.3-B.5) by heart (p. 187). ♥

5.3 Question on De Moivre

Q 5.1 If $z = \cos\theta + i\sin\theta$ show that $z + \frac{1}{z} = 2\cos\theta$ and $z - \frac{1}{z} = 2i\sin\theta$. Show also that

$$z^n + \frac{1}{z^n} = 2\cos n\theta$$
$$z^n - \frac{1}{z^n} = 2i\sin n\theta$$

Q 5.2 If $z = 1 - (\cos\theta + i\sin\theta)$ show that

$$z^{-1} = \frac{1}{2} + \frac{i}{2}\cot\frac{\theta}{2}$$

and that

$$z^n = 2^n(-i)^n \sin^n\frac{\theta}{2}\left(\cos\frac{n\theta}{2} + i\sin\frac{n\theta}{2}\right)$$

Q 5.3 Show using De Moivre's theorem that

$$\left(\frac{1 + i\tan\theta}{1 - i\tan\theta}\right)^n = \frac{1 + \tan n\theta}{1 - i\tan n\theta}$$

Q 5.4 If $|z| = 1$ and $\left(z - z^{-1}\right)^2 = -3$ find the values of $z^3 + z^{-3}$.

Q 5.5 (i) Solve the equation $z^2 - 6z + 36 = 0$, and give your answers in the form $r(\cos\theta \pm i\sin\theta)$, where $r > 0$ and $0 \le \theta \le \pi$. [4]

(ii) Given that z is either of the roots found in part (i), deduce the exact value of z^{-3}. [3]

(OCR FP3 Jan2007)

Q 5.6 Show that

$$1 + x\cos\theta + x^2\cos 2\theta + \ldots + x^{n-1}\cos(n-1)\theta = \\ = \frac{1 - x\cos\theta - x^n\cos n\theta + x^{n+1}\cos(n-1)\theta}{1 - 2x\cos\theta + x^2}$$

and

$$x\sin\theta + x^2\sin 2\theta + \ldots + x^{n-1}\sin(n-1)\theta = \\ = \frac{x\sin\theta - x^n\sin n\theta + x^{n+1}\sin(n-1)\theta}{1 - 2x\cos\theta + x^2}$$

Deduce further that when $|x| < 1$ the summation to infinity is

$$\sum_{r=1}^{\infty} x^{r-1}\cos(r-1)\theta = \frac{1 - x\cos\theta}{1 - 2x\cos\theta + x^2}$$

and

$$\sum_{r=1}^{\infty} x^{r-1}\sin(r-1)\theta = \frac{x\sin\theta}{1 - 2x\cos\theta + x^2}$$

Q 5.7 Using De Moivre's theorem show that

$$\frac{\sin 5\theta}{\sin\theta} = 16\cos^4\theta - 12\cos^2\theta + 1$$

By using a suitable angle show that $\cos^2 \pi/5 = \frac{6+\sqrt{20}}{16}$.

Q 5.8 Prove that

$$(\cos\theta + \mathrm{i}\sin\theta)(\cos\phi + \mathrm{i}\sin\phi) = \cos(\theta+\phi) + \mathrm{i}\sin(\theta+\phi)$$

and that, for every positive integer n,

$$(\cos\theta + \mathrm{i}\sin\theta)^n = \cos n\theta + \mathrm{i}\sin n\theta.$$

By considering $(5-\mathrm{i})^2(1+\mathrm{i})$, or otherwise, prove that

$$\arctan\left(\frac{7}{17}\right) + 2\arctan\left(\frac{1}{5}\right) = \frac{\pi}{4}.$$

Prove also that

$$3\arctan\left(\frac{1}{4}\right) + \arctan\left(\frac{1}{20}\right) + \arctan\left(\frac{1}{1985}\right) = \frac{\pi}{4}.$$

[Note that $\arctan\theta$ is another notation for $\tan^{-1}\theta$.] **(STEP II 2000Q4)**

Q 5.9 (i) (a) Verify, without using a calculator, that $\theta = \pi/8$ is a solution of the equation $\sin 6\theta = \sin 2\theta$. [1]

(b) By sketching the graphs of $y = \sin 6\theta$ and $y = \sin 2\theta$ for $0 \le \theta \le \pi/2$, or otherwise, find the other solution of the equation $\sin 6\theta = \sin 2\theta$ in the interval $0 < \theta < \pi/2$. [2]

(ii) Use De Moivre's theorem to prove that

$$\sin 6\theta \equiv \sin 2\theta(16\cos^4\theta - 16\cos^2\theta + 3) \qquad [5]$$

(iii) Hence show that one of the solutions obtained in part (i) satisfies $\cos^2\theta = \frac{1}{4}(2-\sqrt{2})$, and justify which solution it is. [3]

(OCR FP3 Jan2008)

Q 5.10 Show that

$$\frac{1+\sin\theta+i\cos\theta}{1+\sin\theta-i\cos\theta} = \sin\theta + i\cos\theta$$

Use this result to show that

$$\left(1+\sin\frac{\pi}{5}+i\cos\frac{\pi}{5}\right)^5 + i\left(1+\sin\frac{\pi}{5}-i\cos\frac{\pi}{5}\right)^5 = 0$$

Q 5.11 (i) Use De Moivre's theorem to show that

$$\sin 6\theta \equiv \cos\theta(6\sin\theta - 32\sin^3\theta + 32\sin^5\theta) \qquad [5]$$

(ii) Hence show that, for $\sin 2\theta \neq 0$, [7]

$$-1 \leq \frac{\sin 6\theta}{\sin 2\theta} < 3$$

(OCR FP3 Jun2016)

Q 5.12 (i) Use De Moivre's theorem to prove that $\cos 6\theta = 32\cos^6\theta - 48\cos^4\theta + 18\cos^2\theta - 1$. [4]

(ii) Hence find the largest positive root of the equation

$$64x^6 - 96x^4 + 6x^2 - 3 = 0,$$

giving your answer in trigonometrical form. [4]

(OCR FP3 Jun2007)

Q 5.13 Show that

$$\cos\frac{\pi}{11} + \cos\frac{3\pi}{11} + \cos\frac{5\pi}{11} + \cos\frac{7\pi}{11} + \cos\frac{9\pi}{11} = \frac{1}{2}$$

Hint: Look at example (5.17).

Q 5.14 (i) Use De Moivre's theorem to express $\cos 4\theta$ as a polynomial in $\cos\theta$. [4]

(ii) Hence prove that $\cos 4\theta\cos 2\theta \equiv 16\cos^6\theta - 24\cos^4\theta + 10\cos^2\theta - 1$. [1]

(iii) Use part (ii) to show that the only roots of the equation $\cos 4\theta \cos 2\theta = 1$ are $\theta = n\pi$, where n is an integer. [3]

(iv) Show that $\cos 4\theta \cos 2\theta = -1$ only when $\cos\theta = 0$. [3]

(OCR FP3 Jun2011)

Q 5.15 (i) Use De Moivre's theorem to prove that

$$\tan 5\theta \equiv \frac{5\tan\theta - 10\tan^3\theta + \tan^5\theta}{1 - 10\tan^2\theta + 5\tan^4\theta} \qquad [4]$$

(ii) Solve the equation $\tan 5\theta = 1$, for $0 \le \theta < \pi$. [3]

(iii) Show that the roots of the equation $t^4 - 4t^3 - 14t^2 - 4t + 1 = 0$ may be expressed in the form $\tan\alpha$, stating the exact values of α, where $0 \le \alpha < \pi$. [5]

(OCR FP3 Jan2012)

Q 5.16 Show the identity $(x^3 + y^3 + z^3) - 3xyz = (x + y + z)(x^2 + y^2 + z^2 - xy - xz - yz)$.
If $\cos a + \cos b + \cos c = 0 = \sin a + \sin b + \sin c$ show that

$$\cos 3a + \cos 3b + \cos 3c = 3\cos(a + b + c)$$
$$\sin 3a + \sin 3b + \sin 3c = 3\sin(a + b + c)$$

Q 5.17 Prove that for all $n \in \mathbb{N}$

(i) $(1 + i)^n + (1 - i)^n = 2^{\frac{n+2}{2}} \cos\dfrac{n\pi}{4}$

(ii) $(1 + i)^n - (1 - i)^n = i2^{\frac{n+2}{2}} \sin\dfrac{n\pi}{4}$

Q 5.18 (i) Use De Moivre's theorem to show that $\cos 5\theta \equiv 16\cos^5\theta - 20\cos^3\theta + 5\cos\theta$. [5]

(ii) Hence find the roots of $16x^4 - 20x^2 + 5 = 0$ in the form $\cos\alpha$ where $0 \le \alpha \le \pi$. [4]

(iii) Hence find the exact value of $\cos \pi/10$. [3]

(OCR FP3 Jun2013)

Q 5.19 (i) Solve the equation $\cos 6\theta = 0$, for $0 < \theta < \pi$. [3]

(ii) By using de Moivre's theorem, show that

$$\cos 6\theta \equiv (2\cos^2\theta - 1)(16\cos^4\theta - 16\cos^2\theta + 1) \qquad [5]$$

(iii) Hence find the exact value of

$$\cos\left(\frac{\pi}{12}\right)\cos\left(\frac{5\pi}{12}\right)\cos\left(\frac{7\pi}{12}\right)\cos\left(\frac{11\pi}{12}\right)$$

justifying your answer. [5]

(OCR FP3 Jun2010)

Q 5.20 Express in the form $a + ib$ the expression A

$$A = \left[1 + i\tan\frac{4k+1}{4n}\pi\right]^n$$

where $n, m \in \mathbb{Z}$

Q 5.21 Show that the polynomial $x^n \sin\theta - x\sin n\theta + \sin(n-1)\theta$, where $\theta \in \mathbb{R}$, $n \in \mathbb{N}$ and $n \geq 2$ has a factor $x^2 - 2x\cos\theta + 1$.
Hint: Show that the roots of the quadratic are $\cos\theta \pm i\sin\theta$ and show that they are also roots of the polynomial.

Q 5.22 Show that

$$\cos\theta + \frac{1}{2}\cos 2\theta + \frac{1}{4}\cos 3\theta + \frac{1}{8}\cos 4\theta + \ldots =$$
$$= \frac{4\cos\theta - 2 + 2^{1-n}\cos n\theta - 2^{2-n}\cos(n+1)\theta}{5 - 4\cos\theta}$$

Q 5.23 Prove that

$$\frac{\sin 7\theta}{\sin\theta} = x^3 + x^2 - 2x - 1$$

where $x = 2\cos 2\theta$.

6. Euler's Identity $e^{i\theta} = \cos\theta + i\sin\theta$

> Like a Shakespearean sonnet that captures the very essence of love, or a painting that brings out the beauty of the human form that is far more than just skin deep, Euler's equation reaches down into the very depths of existence.
>
> Keith Devlin

6.1 An Intriguing Identity

One of the most famous identities in mathematics was derived by Euler. It seems however, that the identity bearing his name was also known, in a slightly different form to Roger Cotes[1].

Theorem 6.1: The following relation holds

$$e^{i\theta} = \cos\theta + i\sin\theta \tag{6.1}$$

Stare at this mathematical formula for few minutes. It is amazingly simple and beautiful. It combines complex numbers, trigonometry and the transcendental number $e = 2.718281828459045....$

Proof: In order to demonstrate this relation we would rely on the series expansion of e^x given by equation

$$e^x = 1 + x + \frac{x^2}{2!} + \frac{x^3}{3!} + ... + \frac{x^n}{n!}$$

and on the expansions of sin and cos given by

$$\begin{aligned} \sin x &= x - \frac{x^3}{3!} + \frac{x^5}{5!} + ... + \frac{(-1)^n x^{2n+1}}{(2n+1)!}, \quad n = 0, 1, 2... \\ \cos x &= 1 - \frac{x^2}{2!} + \frac{x^4}{4!} + ... + \frac{(-1)^n x^{2n}}{(2n)!}, \quad n = 0, 1, 2... \end{aligned}$$

[1] Roger Cotes 1682-1716, was an English mathematician who edited the second edition of Newton's Principia. He made advances in the theory of logarithms, the integral calculus and in numerical methods, particularly interpolation. Newton who was not known for complimenting others said on hearing of Cotes death, "If he had lived we might have known something".

If you replace x with $x = i\theta$ in the power series of e^x you will get

$$\begin{aligned}
\mathrm{e}^{i\theta} &= 1 + i\theta + \frac{(i\theta)^2}{2!} + \frac{(i\theta)^3}{3!} + \ldots + \frac{(i\theta)^n}{n!} \\
&= 1 + i\theta - \frac{\theta^2}{2!} - i\frac{\theta^3}{3!} + \ldots \\
&= \underbrace{\left(1 - \frac{\theta^2}{2} + \frac{\theta^4}{4!} + \ldots\right)}_{\cos\theta} + i\underbrace{\left(\theta - \frac{\theta^3}{3!} + \frac{\theta^5}{5!} + \ldots\right)}_{\sin\theta} \\
&= \cos\theta + i\sin\theta
\end{aligned}$$

One can see this result most beautifully, with a simple geometric diagram (see Needham [9]). The terms of the expansion of $\mathrm{e}^{i\theta}$ are:

$$\mathrm{e}^{i\theta} = 1 + i\theta - \frac{\theta^2}{2!} - i\frac{\theta^3}{3!} + \frac{\theta^4}{4!}$$

If you draw this sum on the complex plane, see Figure (6.1), by moving one term at a time, you can see how it converges to the point on the unit circle at an angle θ. The first term which is 1, moves from point A to point B. The next term is $i\theta$, so you will need to move anticlockwise by $\pi/2$ and at a distance θ. Continuing this way you converge to the point on the circle.

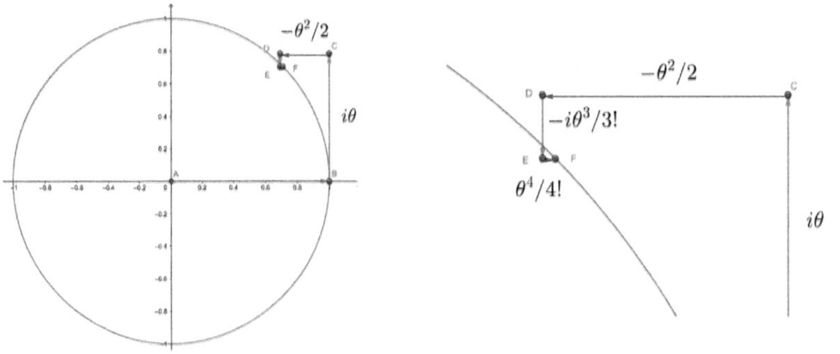

Figure 6.1: Every real term in the expansion moves the point parallel to the real axis (left or right) and every i-term moves it along the imaginary axis (up or down) homing in on the point on the circle.

DAD'S SOS NOTE: Euler's identity is perhaps the second most famous equation after $E = mc^2$. The main reason is the fact that if you plug $\theta = \pi$ you get

$$e^{i\pi} = -1$$

This is a remarkable identity since it involves two transcendental irrational numbers e, π the square root of -1, i, giving the simple answer of minus unity. Many have tried to give this identity some inner hidden mystical meaning. Although very beautiful and neat one needs to distance themselves from such "higher" meanings. It is just another formula that shows the deep interrelations of different mathematical concepts. Geometrically, if we multiply any number by $e^{i\pi}$ it just rotates everything by π or maps it to the symmetrical point about the origin. In our case, $e^{i\pi}\,1$ sends the 1 into -1. Nothing mystical about that. ♥

In fact the $e^{i\pi} + 1 = 0$ is not the only surprising result. Try to calculate $1^{\sqrt{-1}} = 1^i$. You would think that 1 raised to any power is 1. Wrong! Try $1^i = (e^{2ik\pi})^i = e^{-2k\pi}$. The solution $k = 0$ gives us 1, but this is not the only one! There are plenty more. In fact, an infinite number of solutions for $k \in \mathbb{Z}$.

6.2 "Complexification" Trick

When doing calculus questions that involve trigonometric functions a very cool trick is to express the sine or cosine as a complex number. This is sometimes called the "Complexification" trick and it can be very useful as it speeds up calculations.

We can also take derivatives or integrate functions that contain i in the usual way.

Proposition 6.1: The derivative of e^{ikx}, where x is real and k is a constant is just

$$\frac{d}{dx}e^{ikx} = ike^{ix} \tag{6.2}$$

And the integral of e^{ikx} is

$$\int e^{ikx}\,dx = \frac{1}{ik}e^{ikx} + c = -\frac{i}{k}e^{ikx} + c \tag{6.3}$$

Exercise 6.1: Show that $\dfrac{\mathrm{d}}{\mathrm{d}x}\mathrm{e}^x\cos x = \sqrt{2}\mathrm{e}^x\cos\left(x+\dfrac{\pi}{4}\right)$.
We would prove in two ways. One by applying the standard rules of differentiation and second by using the "Complexification" trick.
Using the standard differentiation we get

$$(\mathrm{e}^x\cos x)' = \mathrm{e}^x\cos x - \mathrm{e}^x\sin x = \mathrm{e}^x(\cos x - \sin x)$$

In order to get this into the form required you can either expand the RHS of the answer and show that it is equal to the derivative since $\cos(x+\pi/4) = \cos x\cos\pi/4 - \sin x\sin\pi/4 = \frac{\sqrt{2}}{2}(\cos x - \sin x)$ or work backwards and write

$$\mathrm{e}^x(\cos x - \sin x) = \sqrt{2}\mathrm{e}^x\left(\frac{1}{\sqrt{2}}\cos x - \frac{1}{\sqrt{2}}\sin x\right) = \sqrt{2}\mathrm{e}^x\cos(x+45)$$

Ans: Now for the magic. Instead of $\cos x$ write e^{ix}. In the end, we will take the real part of e^{ix} which of course is $\cos x$. So lets see how we can differentiate this

$$\begin{aligned}
\frac{\mathrm{d}}{\mathrm{d}x}(\mathrm{e}^x\mathrm{e}^{ix}) &= \frac{\mathrm{d}}{\mathrm{d}x}\mathrm{e}^{(1+i)x} = (1+i)\mathrm{e}^{(1+i)x}\\
\text{WRITE IN POLAR FORM} &= \sqrt{2}\left(\frac{1}{\sqrt{2}} + i\frac{1}{\sqrt{2}}\right)\mathrm{e}^{(1+i)x}\\
&= \sqrt{2}\mathrm{e}^{i\pi/4}\mathrm{e}^{(1+i)x} = \sqrt{2}\mathrm{e}^x\mathrm{e}^{i(x+\pi/4)}
\end{aligned}$$

Now, if we take the real part of the above we get

$$\frac{\mathrm{d}}{\mathrm{d}x}\mathrm{e}^x\cos x = \sqrt{2}\mathrm{e}^x\cos\left(x+\frac{\pi}{4}\right)$$

And if you compare the imaginary part we also get a similar expression for the derivative of $e^x\sin x$ as a bonus. □

Exercise 6.2: Show that, for any integer m,

$$\int_0^{2\pi}\mathrm{e}^x\cos mx\,\mathrm{d}x = \frac{1}{m^2+1}\left(\mathrm{e}^{2\pi}-1\right).$$

Ans: You can do the integral By-Parts and this is what is expected from you. But if you are a badass you can use the "complexification" trick to get the real part of $\int_0^{2\pi} e^{x+imx}\,dx$

$$
\begin{aligned}
\int_0^{2\pi} e^x \cos mx\,dx &= \Re\left(\int_0^{2\pi} e^{x+imx}\,dx\right) \\
&= \Re\left(\frac{1}{1+im} e^{x+imx}\Big|_0^{2\pi}\right) \\
&= \Re\frac{1-im}{1+m^2}(e^{2\pi}-1) = \frac{1}{1+m^2}(e^{2\pi}-1) \qquad \square
\end{aligned}
$$

One can use the Euler representation to compute strange looking expressions like i^i. Although, as the following example shows, one must be very careful....

Exercise 6.3: Show that $i^i = e^{-\pi/2}$. Explain why your answer is not unique.

Ans: Write $i = e^{i\pi/2}$ and on taking the exponent

$$
i^i = (e^{i\pi/2})^i = e^{ii\pi/2} = e^{-\pi/2}
$$

This is an interesting example because the answer is not unique. You could have chosen as your $i = e^{5\pi/2}$ and the result would be different. Still a real number, but different. One has to be very careful with taking exponents with complex numbers. The answer $i^i = e^{-\pi/2}$ is only valid for the principal argument of i.

The next exercise is absolutely amazing, see Nahin [8].

Exercise 6.4: By writing $2\cos\theta e^{i\theta} = 1 + e^{2i\theta}$, show that

$$
\int_0^{\pi} \cos^n\theta \cos n\theta\,d\theta = \frac{\pi}{2^n}
$$

Ans: From $2\cos\theta = e^{i\theta} + e^{-i\theta}$ you get $2\cos\theta e^{i\theta} = 1 + e^{2i\theta}$. The integral has $\cos^n\theta$. So, you can raise the relation to get $2^n\cos^n\theta e^{in\theta} = (1+e^{2i\theta})^n$. You still need to get the term $\cos n\theta$, that is in the integral. Notice however, that if you let $\theta \to -\theta$, you also get $2^n\cos^n\theta e^{-in\theta} = (1+e^{-2i\theta})^n$. If you add these two together you will get

$$
\begin{aligned}
2^n\cos^n\theta e^{in\theta} &= (1+e^{2i\theta})^n \\
2^n\cos^n\theta e^{-in\theta} &= (1+e^{-2i\theta})^n \Rightarrow \\
2^n\cos^n\theta\left(e^{in\theta}+e^{-in\theta}\right) &= (1+e^{2i\theta})^n + (1+e^{-2i\theta})^n \\
2^{n+1}\cos^n\theta\cos n\theta &= (1+e^{2i\theta})^n + (1+e^{-2i\theta})^n
\end{aligned}
$$

Now the integral becomes

$$2^{n+1}\int_0^{\pi}\cos^n\theta\cos n\theta\,\mathrm{d}\theta=\int_0^{\pi}\left[(1+\mathrm{e}^{2i\theta})^n+(1+\mathrm{e}^{-2i\theta})^n\right]\mathrm{d}\theta$$

Even though it looks formidable it is not. When you do the binomial expansion you will pick terms

$$\int_0^{\pi}\mathrm{e}^{2in\theta}\,\mathrm{d}\theta=\frac{1}{2ni}\mathrm{e}^{2ni\theta}\Big|_0^{\pi}=0$$

So all the terms apart from the 1 drop to zero. And the RHS evaluates to $\int_0^{\pi}2\,\mathrm{d}\theta=2\pi$. So finally,

$$2^{n+1}\int_0^{\pi}\cos^n\theta\cos n\theta\,\mathrm{d}\theta=2\pi\Rightarrow\int_0^{\pi}\cos^n\theta\cos n\theta\,\mathrm{d}\theta=\frac{\pi}{2^n}\qquad\square$$

6.3 Applications to Trigonometry

Using Euler's formula we can now do a much faster proof of the trigonometric identities of $\cos(A+B)$ and $\sin(A+B)$. But before we do this we would express the sine and cosine using complex numbers and Euler's formula.

Proposition 6.2: If $z=\cos\theta+i\sin\theta=\mathrm{e}^{i\theta}$ then

$$\begin{aligned}z+\frac{1}{z}&=2\cos\theta=\mathrm{e}^{i\theta}+\mathrm{e}^{-i\theta}\Rightarrow\cos\theta=\frac{\mathrm{e}^{i\theta}+\mathrm{e}^{-i\theta}}{2}\\z-\frac{1}{z}&=2i\sin\theta=\mathrm{e}^{i\theta}-\mathrm{e}^{-i\theta}\Rightarrow\sin\theta=\frac{\mathrm{e}^{i\theta}-\mathrm{e}^{-i\theta}}{2i}\end{aligned}$$

Proof: Summing $\mathrm{e}^{i\theta}+\mathrm{e}^{-i\theta}=2\cos\theta$ and similarly for $\mathrm{e}^{i\theta}-\mathrm{e}^{-i\theta}=2\sin\theta$. □

These relations have a very nice geometrical analogue, see figure (6.2)

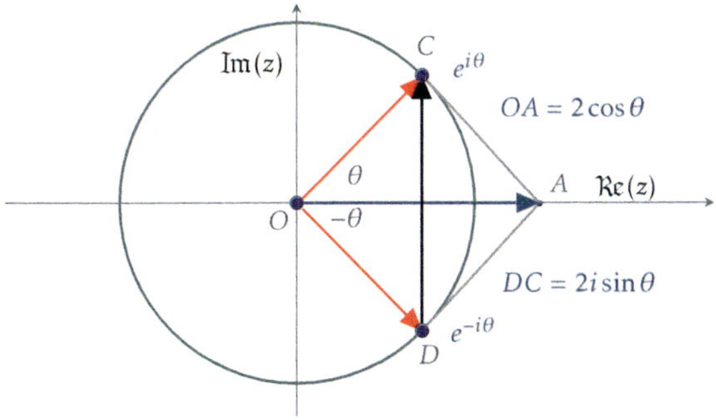

Figure 6.2: The resultant of the two vectors is the length OA which is equal to $2\cos\theta$, whereas the difference is the vertical vector $DC = 2i\sin\theta$

The following is a variation of De Moivre's method we did in the previous Chapter 5.

Exercise 6.5: Express $\cos n\theta$ and $\sin n\theta$ in terms of $e^{\pm in\theta}$ using Euler's formula (6.1). Hence, show that $\cos^3\theta = \frac{1}{4}(\cos 3\theta + 3\cos\theta)$.

Ans: If you raise (6.1) to the nth power and use De Moivre's theorem (5.1) you will get

$$e^{in\theta} = (\cos\theta + i\sin\theta)^n = \cos n\theta + i\sin n\theta$$

Similarly, if you raise it to $-n^{\text{th}}$ you will get $e^{-in\theta} = \cos n\theta - i\sin n\theta$. Adding these two together

$$e^{in\theta} + e^{-in\theta} = 2\cos n\theta$$

and subtracting

$$e^{in\theta} - e^{-in\theta} = 2i\sin n\theta$$

For the second part, you have that $\cos\theta = \frac{1}{2}(e^{i\theta} + e^{-i\theta})$. Raising to the third power

$$\begin{aligned}\cos^3\theta &= \frac{1}{2^3}(e^{i\theta} + e^{-i\theta})^3 = \frac{1}{2^3}(e^{3i\theta} + 3e^{2i\theta}e^{-i\theta} + 3e^{i\theta}e^{-2i\theta} + e^{-3i\theta})\\ &= \frac{1}{2^3}\underbrace{(e^{3i\theta} + e^{-3i\theta})}_{2\cos 3\theta} + 3\underbrace{(e^{i\theta} + e^{-i\theta})}_{2\cos\theta} = \frac{1}{4}(\cos 3\theta + 3\cos\theta)\end{aligned}$$

□

Exercise 6.6: Using Euler's formula you can easily obtain the $\sin(\theta + \phi)$ and $\cos(\theta + \phi)$. You know that $e^{i\theta}e^{i\phi} = e^{i(\theta+\phi)}$ and hence

$$(\cos\theta + i\sin\theta)(\cos\phi + i\sin\phi) = \cos(\theta+\phi) + i\sin(\theta+\phi)$$

Expanding

$$\cos\theta\cos\phi - \sin\theta\sin\phi + i(\sin\theta\cos\phi + \cos\theta\sin\phi) = \cos(\theta+\phi) + i\sin(\theta+\phi)$$

If you now compare real and imaginary parts, you will obtain the well known trigonometric identities for the sum of two angles

$$\cos(\theta+\phi) = \cos\theta\cos\phi - \sin\theta\sin\phi$$
$$\sin(\theta+\phi) = \sin\theta\cos\phi + \cos\theta\sin\phi$$

□

Exercise 6.7: Prove that

$$S = n\sin\theta + \frac{n(n-1)}{2!}\sin 2\theta + \frac{n(n-1)(n-2)}{3!}\sin 3\theta + ... + \sin n\theta = 2^n \cos\frac{\theta}{2}\sin\frac{n\theta}{2}$$

Ans: It is clear that you will need to apply De Moivre's theorem. But you are only given the sines. You could, however, write the full complex number and then take only the imaginary part. You may also notice that the formula looks very much like the binomial expansion and that gives you a big hint. If you expand $(1 + e^{i\theta})^n$ and take the imaginary part you actually get the S expression.

$$(1 + e^{i\theta})^n = 1 + ne^{i\theta} + \frac{n(n-1)}{2!}e^{2i\theta} + \frac{n(n-1)(n-2)}{3!}e^{3i\theta} + ... + e^{ni\theta}$$

But

$$\left[e^{i\theta/2}(e^{i\theta/2} + e^{-i\theta/2})\right]^n = e^{in\theta/2}\left(2\cos\frac{\theta}{2}\right)^n = 2^n\cos^n\frac{\theta}{2}\left(\cos\frac{n\theta}{2} + i\sin\frac{n\theta}{2}\right)$$

Now, if you take the imaginary part of this equation

$$S = 2^n\cos^n\frac{\theta}{2}\sin\frac{n\theta}{2}$$

□

Another nice example is the so-called Poisson Kernel.

Exercise 6.8: Prove that for $0 \le r < 1$ the following holds

$$1 + 2\sum_{n=1}^{\infty} r^n \cos n\theta = 1 + 2(r\cos\theta + r^2\cos 2\theta + ... + r^n\cos n\theta + ...) =$$

$$= \frac{1-r^2}{1-2r\cos\theta + r^2}$$

Complexifying, we get that $\sum_{n=1}^{\infty} r^n \cos n\theta = \mathfrak{Re}(\sum_{n=1}^{\infty} r^n e^{in\theta})$. So we have

$$1 + 2\sum_{n=1}^{\infty} r^n \cos n\theta = 1 + 2\mathfrak{Re}\sum_{n=1}^{\infty}(r^n e^{in\theta}) = 1 + 2\mathfrak{Re}\sum_{n=1}^{\infty}(re^{i\theta})^n$$

In order to compute the infinite sum notice that this is a geometric series. If we let $S_n = re^{i\theta} + ... + r^n e^{in\theta}$ then forming $S_n - re^{i\theta}S_n = re^{i\theta} - r^{n+1}e^{i(n+1)\theta}$ we get that

$$S_n = \frac{re^{i\theta} - r^{n+1}e^{(n+1)i\theta}}{1 - re^{i\theta}}$$

Taking the limit as $n \to \infty$, the term $r^{n+1}e^{(n+1)i\theta} \to 0$ because $0 \le r < 1$ and therefore

$$S_\infty = \frac{re^{i\theta}}{1 - re^{i\theta}}$$

Taking the real part of this we have

$$\mathfrak{Re}\frac{re^{i\theta}}{1 - re^{i\theta}} = \frac{r\cos\theta - r^2}{1 - 2r\cos\theta + r^2}$$

So finally,

$$1 + 2\sum_{n=1}^{\infty} r^n \cos n\theta = 1 + 2\frac{r\cos\theta - r^2}{1 - 2r\cos\theta + r^2} = \frac{1-r^2}{1 - 2r\cos\theta + r^2} \qquad \square$$

6.4 Questions on Euler's Identity

Q 6.1 Show that $|1 - e^{i\theta}|^2 = 4\sin^2\theta/2$.

Q 6.2 (i) By expressing $\cos\theta$ in terms of $e^{i\theta}$ and $e^{-i\theta}$, show that

$$\cos^5\theta \equiv= \frac{1}{16}(\cos 5\theta + 5\cos 3\theta + 10\cos\theta) \qquad [5]$$

(ii) Hence solve the equation $\cos 5\theta + 5\cos 3\theta + 9\cos\theta = 0$ for $0 \le \theta \le \pi$. [4]

(OCR FP3 Jun2008)

Q 6.3 (i) Show that $(z^n - e^{i\theta})(z^n - e^{-i\theta}) \equiv z^{2n} - (2\cos\theta)z^n + 1$. [1]

(ii) Express $z^4 - z^2 + 1$ as the product of four factors of the form $z - e^{i\alpha}$, where $0 \le \alpha < 2\pi$. [6]

(OCR FP3 Jan2012)

Q 6.4 (i) By expressing $\sin\theta$ in terms of $e^{i\theta}$ and $e^{-i\theta}$, show that

$$\sin^6\theta \equiv -\frac{1}{32}(\cos 6\theta - 6\cos 4\theta + 15\cos 2\theta - 10) \qquad [5]$$

(ii) Replace θ by $\pi/2 - \theta$ in the identity in part (i) to obtain a similar identity for $\cos 6\theta$. [3]

(iii) Hence find the exact value of

$$\int_0^{\pi/4} (\sin^6\theta - \cos^6\theta)\,d\theta \qquad [4]$$

(OCR FP3 Jan2009)

Q 6.5 Show that

$$\cos(a+\theta) + \cos(a+2\theta) + \ldots + \cos(a+n\theta) = \cos\left(a + \frac{n+1}{2}\theta\right)\frac{\sin\frac{n\theta}{2}}{\sin\frac{\theta}{2}}$$

Derive a similar expression for the sine series.

Q 6.6 (i) Express $\frac{\sqrt{3}+i}{\sqrt{3}-i}$ in the form $re^{i\theta}$, where $r > 0$ and $0 \le \theta < 2\pi$. [3]

(ii) Hence find the smallest positive value of n for which $\left(\frac{\sqrt{3}+i}{\sqrt{3}-i}\right)^n$ is real and positive. [2]

(OCR FP3 Jan2009)

Q 6.7 In an Argand diagram, the complex numbers 0, z and $ze^{i\pi/6}$ are represented by the points O, A and B respectively.

(i) Sketch a possible Argand diagram showing the triangle OAB. Show that the triangle is isosceles and state the size of angle AOB. [4]
The complex numbers $1+i$ and $5+2i$ are represented by the points C and D respectively. The complex number w is represented by the point E, such that $CD = CE$ and angle $DCE = \pi/6$.

(ii) Calculate the possible values of w, giving your answers exactly in the form $a + bi$. [5]

(OCR FP3 Jun2015)

Q 6.8 Prove that

$$\cos\theta + \cos\left(\theta + \frac{2\pi}{3}\right)e^{\frac{2\pi}{3}i} + \cos\left(\theta - \frac{2\pi}{3}\right)e^{-\frac{2\pi}{3}i} = \frac{3}{2}e^{-i\theta}$$

(AEB 632/2 Jun1975p)

Q 6.9 (i) By expressing $\sin\theta$ in terms of $e^{i\theta}$ and $e^{-i\theta}$, show that

$$\sin^5\theta \equiv \frac{1}{16}(\sin 5\theta - 5\sin 3\theta + 10\sin\theta)$$ [4]

(ii) Hence solve the equation

$$\sin 5\theta + 4\sin\theta = 5\sin 3\theta$$

for $-\pi/2 \le \theta \le \pi/2$. [4]

(OCR FP3 Jun2014)

Q 6.10 Show that

$$e^x\cos x = \frac{e^{x(1+i)} + e^{x(1-i)}}{2}$$

Use this expression to show that the nth term in the expansion of $e^x\cos x$ is

$$\frac{x^n(\sqrt{2})^n}{n!}\cos\frac{n\pi}{4}$$

.

Q 6.11 Convergent infinite series C and S are defined by

$$C = 1 + \frac{1}{2}\cos\theta + \frac{1}{4}\cos 2\theta + \frac{1}{8}\cos 3\theta + \ldots$$

$$S = \frac{1}{2}\sin\theta + \frac{1}{4}\sin 2\theta + \frac{1}{8}\sin 3\theta + \ldots$$

(i) Show that $C + iS = \dfrac{2}{2 - e^{i\theta}}$. [4]

(ii) Hence show that $C = \dfrac{4 - 2\cos\theta}{5 - 4\cos\theta}$, and find a similar expression for S. [4]

(OCR FP3 Jun2010)

Q 6.12 (i) Express $\sin\theta$ in terms of $e^{i\theta}$ and $e^{-i\theta}$ and show that

$$\sin^4\theta \equiv \frac{1}{8}(\cos 4\theta - 4\cos 2\theta + 3) \qquad [4]$$

(ii) Hence find the exact value of $\int_0^{\pi/6} \sin^4\theta d\theta$. [4]

(OCR FP3 Jan2011)

Q 6.13 It is given that $z = e^{i\theta}$, where $0 < \theta < 2\pi$, and $w = \dfrac{1+z}{1-z}$

(i) Prove that $w = i\cot\theta/2$. [3]

(ii) Sketch separate Argand diagrams to show the locus of z and the locus of w. You should show the direction in which each locus is described when θ increases in the interval $0 < \theta < 2\pi$. [3]

(OCR FP3 Jun2011)

Q 6.14 (i) By expressing $\sin\theta$ and $\cos\theta$ in terms of $e^{i\theta}$ and $e^{-i\theta}$, prove that

$$\sin^3\theta\cos^2\theta \equiv -\frac{1}{16}(\sin 5\theta - \sin 3\theta - 2\sin\theta) \qquad [6]$$

(ii) Hence show that all the roots of the equation $\sin 5\theta = \sin 3\theta + 2\sin\theta$ are of the form $\theta = \dfrac{n\pi}{k}$, where n is any integer and k is to be determined. [3]

(OCR FP3 Jun2012)

Q 6.15 Using the "Complexification" technique as in example (6.1) show that

$$\frac{d^n}{dx^n}e^x\cos x = 2^{n/2}e^x\cos\left(x + \frac{n\pi}{4}\right)$$

and obtain a similar expression for the nth derivative of $e^x\sin x$.

Q 6.16 (a) Show that when $z = e^{i\theta}$ then $z^n + z^{-n} = 2\cos n\theta$. State a similar result for $z^n - z^{-n}$. Given that $\sin^3\theta\cos 3\theta = P\sin 2\theta + Q\sin 4\theta + R\sin 6\theta$, find the numerical values of P, Q and R.

(b) Find the moduli and the arguments of $\dfrac{1+i}{1-i}$ and $\dfrac{\sqrt{2}}{1-i}$. Represent these numbers on an Argand diagram and hence show that

$$\arg\left(\frac{1+\sqrt{2}+i}{1-i}\right) = \frac{3\pi}{8}$$

(AEB 632/2 Nov1978)

Q 6.17 (i) Prove that if $z = e^{i\theta}$, then $z^n + \dfrac{1}{z^n} = 2\cos n\theta$. [2]

(ii) Express $\cos^6\theta$ in terms of cosines of multiples of θ , and hence find the exact value of

$$\int_0^{\pi/3} \cos^6\theta \, d\theta$$ [8]

(OCR FP3 Specimen)

Q 6.18 The complex numbers 0, 3 and $3e^{i\pi/3}$ are represented in an Argand diagram by the points O, A and B respectively.

(i) Sketch the triangle OAB and show that it is equilateral. [3]

(ii) Hence express $3 - 3e^{i\pi/3}$ in polar form. [2]

(iii) Hence find $(3 - 3e^{i\pi/3})^5$, giving your answer in the form $a + b\sqrt{3}i$ where a and b are rational numbers. [3]

(OCR FP3 Jun2013)

7. The Nth root of a number

Irrationality is the Square Root of All Evil

Douglas Hofstadter

7.1 Taking Roots of Numbers

A very common application of the De Moivre's theorem is in finding the nth root of a number, real or complex. Let us start with an example.

Exercise 7.1: Find the three roots of the equation $z^3 = -1 + i\sqrt{3}$.
Ans: We first need to bring the complex number into its trigonometric form in order to apply De Moivre's theorem. So $|-1 + i\sqrt{3}| = 2$. The argument is $\arg(-1 + i\sqrt{3}) = \arctan(-\sqrt{3}) = 2\pi/3$ or 120 degrees. Hence, we can rewrite the equation as

$$z^3 = -1 + i\sqrt{3} = 2\left(\cos\frac{2\pi}{3} + i\sin\frac{2\pi}{3}\right)$$

If we now take the cube root of this we would find only one root, the

$$z_0 = 2^{1/3}\left(\cos\frac{2\pi}{3} + i\sin\frac{2\pi}{3}\right)^{1/3} = 2^{1/3}\left(\cos\frac{2\pi}{9} + i\sin\frac{2\pi}{9}\right)$$

In order to find all three roots we need to go back a step and realise that the expression does not change if we add $2k\pi$ inside the trig functions.

$$2\left[\cos\frac{2\pi}{3} + i\sin\frac{2\pi}{3}\right] = 2\left[\cos\left(\frac{2\pi}{3} + 2k\pi\right) + i\sin\left(\frac{2\pi}{3} + 2k\pi\right)\right]$$

We can now get all three roots if we let $k = 0, 1, 2$.

$$z_k = 2^{1/3}\left[\cos\left(\frac{2\pi}{9} + \frac{2k\pi}{3}\right) + i\sin\left(\frac{2\pi}{9} + \frac{2k\pi}{3}\right)\right], \quad k = 0, 1, 2$$

For any other values of k we just repeat the same roots.
If we place these roots on an Argand diagram we immediately see that they form an equilateral triangle. This is because every root differs by 120 degrees from the next one and they all have the same modulus. The first root is at 40 degrees ($k = 0$, $2\pi/9$) the next one at 160 degrees and the last one at 280 degrees ($k = 2$). The roots are on a circle with center the origin of the Argand diagram and radius $\sqrt[3]{2}$. □

The general solution to the n-th root of any number is given by:

Theorem 7.1: If $a = r(\cos\theta + i\sin\theta)$ with $r = |a|$, is a complex number then, the general solution to $z^n = a$ is

$$z_n = \sqrt[n]{r}\left[\cos\left(\frac{\theta + 2k\pi}{n}\right) + i\sin\left(\frac{\theta + 2k\pi}{n}\right)\right], \quad k = 0, 1, 2, ..., n-1 \quad (7.1)$$

All the roots fall on a circle with radius $\sqrt[n]{r}$. You can verify, that there are no more roots if $k = n, n+1, ...$ For example, if we let $k = n$, we get for the argument $\frac{\theta+2n\pi}{n} = \frac{\theta}{n} + 2\pi$ and this is the argument of the first root for $k = 0$ as the 2π does not matter. Hence, there are only k distinct roots.

Dad's SOS Note: All the roots of the equation $z^n = a$, where a is a complex number would lie on a circle with radius $\sqrt[n]{|a|}$ and the shape is a regular n–gon. Every root differs from the next one by the same amount, namely $\frac{2\pi}{n}$. The figure below shows the roots of a $z^9 = 1$. ♥

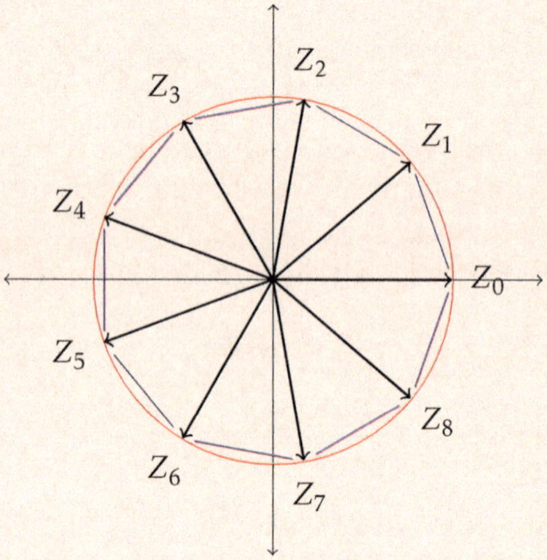

Figure 7.1: The roots of $z^9 = 1$ form a regular heptagon.

Exercise 7.2: Find the four roots of $z^4 + 81 = 0$

Ans: Rearranging, we get $z^4 = -81$, so now we need to write -81 in complex polar form. We know that $\cos\pi = -1$, $\sin\pi = 0$. So we can write,

$-81 = 81(\cos\pi + i\sin\pi)$ and by adding an integral multiple of 2π we get

$$z^4 = 81\left[\cos(2k+1)\pi + i\sin(2k+1)\pi\right]$$

Applying De Moivre's theorem we get the four roots for $k = 0, 1, 2, 3$

$$z_k = 3\left[\cos\frac{(2k+1)\pi}{4} + i\sin\frac{(2k+1)\pi}{4}\right]$$

The solutions are, $z_0 = \frac{3\sqrt{2}}{2}(1+i)$, $z_1 = \frac{3\sqrt{2}}{2}(-1+i)$, $z_2 = z_1^*$, $z_3 = z_0^*$. □

7.2 The Nth Roots of Unity

A very important case is the nth root of 1, $z^n = 1$. All roots are on the circumference of a unit circle and form a regular n-gon. Factorising

$$z^n = 1 \Rightarrow (z^n - 1) = 0 \Rightarrow (z-1)(z^{n-1} + z^{n-2} + ... + z + 1) = 0 \tag{7.2}$$

Clearly, one root is $z = 1$. The other roots satisfy the equation

$$z^{n-1} + z^{n-2} + ... + z + 1 = 0$$

If we use the polar form of 1, namely $1 = e^{2k\pi}$ with integer $k \in \mathbb{Z}$, we can re-write the solutions as

$$z^n = e^{2k\pi} \Rightarrow z = e^{2k\pi/n} = \cos\frac{2k\pi}{n} + i\sin\frac{2k\pi}{n} \tag{7.3}$$

And the n solutions are obtained if we let $k = 0, 1, 2, ..., n-1$.

Exercise 7.3: Find the solutions to $z^5 = 1$.
Ans: You could use the method suggested by Eq. (7.2) and try to solve the quartic but it is rather tedious and long. The fast way to do it is through Eq. (7.3). We thus have

$$z^5 = e^{2k\pi} \Rightarrow z = e^{2k\pi/5} = \cos\frac{2k\pi}{5} + i\sin\frac{2k\pi}{5}$$

The five solutions z_k are then given if we substitute $k = 0, 1, 2, 3, 4$. The $k = 0$ is the $z_0 = 1$ standard real solution. All the other ones are, however, complex. If you place $k = 5$ you fall back on the $z = 1$ solution. Hence, there are no more solution if we place higher values of k. □

DAD'S SOS NOTE: If we write

$$\epsilon = e^{\frac{2\pi}{n}} = \cos\frac{2\pi}{n} + i\sin\frac{2\pi}{n}$$

Then the set of solutions of $z^n = 1$ is

$$\{1, \epsilon, \epsilon^2, \ldots \epsilon^{n-1}\}$$

and we say that ϵ generates the full set of solutions (by taking powers of it). ♥

Definition 7.1: If $\{1, \epsilon, \epsilon^2, \ldots \epsilon^{n-1}\}$ are the n roots of unity, then a particular root of unity is called *Primitive* if when raised to a power $m < n$ it does not equal 1.
Alternatively, a root is called a *Primitive* root of unity if the smallest power k of the root that gives 1 is equal to n.

For example, in the case of $z^6 = 1$ the roots are $\{1, \epsilon, \epsilon^2, \ldots, \epsilon^5\}$, with $\epsilon = e^{i\pi/6}$. Then ϵ^5 is Primitive since $(\epsilon^5)^2 = \epsilon^4$, $(\epsilon^5)^3 = \epsilon^3$, $(\epsilon^5)^4 = \epsilon^2$ and $(\epsilon^5)^5 = \epsilon$ and none of these is 1. The lowest number that we can raise ϵ^5 to get 1 is 6.
On the other hand, the root ϵ^2 is not Primitive since $(\epsilon^2)^3 = \epsilon^6 = 1$ and 3 is less than 6.

Exercise 7.4: The five roots of unity $z^5 = 1$ are $\{1, \epsilon, \epsilon^2, \epsilon^3, \epsilon^4\}$, with $\epsilon = e^{2i\pi/5}$. Show that, ϵ^2 is a Primitive root.
Ans: Taking powers of ϵ^2, you have $(\epsilon^2)^2 = \epsilon^4$, $(\epsilon^2)^3 = \epsilon^6 = \epsilon$, $(\epsilon^2)^4 = \epsilon^8 = \epsilon^3$. Since none of these gives 1, and therefore ϵ^2 is a Primitive root. □

DAD'S SOS NOTE: Not all roots $\{1, \epsilon, \epsilon^2, \ldots, \epsilon^{n-1}\}$ are Primitive. For a root ϵ^m to be Primitive we must have that the Greatest Common Divisor of m and n must be 1, namely $\gcd(m, n) = 1$.
A *Primitive* root of unity also generates the full solution space (all solutions). ♥

Proposition 7.1: Show that if $z^n = 1$ and $z^m = 1$ are two different roots of unity, then they will have a common root $z^d = 1$ with d given by $d = \gcd(m,n)$.
Proof: The roots are $\epsilon = e^{2k\pi/n}$ and $\alpha = e^{2l\pi/m}$, for $k,l \in \mathbb{Z}$. In order to have a common root the arguments must be equal. Hence

$$\frac{2k\pi}{n} = \frac{2l\pi}{m} + 2t\pi$$

for some integer t. If d is the greatest common divisor of m and n, we have $n = pd$ and $m = p'd$ for some integers p and p' with $\gcd(p,p') = 1$. Substituting these we get

$$kp' - pl = pp'td$$

which means that p divides kp'. Since p and p' are coprime, this implies that p divides k and hence $k = gp$ for some integer g.
We now see that the common root would have argument

$$\frac{2k}{n}\pi = \frac{2gp}{pd}\pi = \frac{2g}{d}\pi$$

And this is the dth root, with $d = \gcd(m,n)$. □

Exercise 7.5: Two regular polygons inscribed on a circle have have 2006 and 2023 sides respectively. How many, common vertices do they have, if they at have at least 1?
Ans: The vertices of the two polygons are the roots of $z^{2006} - 1 = 0$ and $z^{2023} - 1 = 0$, respectively. Using the previous proposition the number of common roots is the greatest common divisor $n = \gcd(2006, 2023)$. And using a calculator we obtain $d = 17$. □

Exercise 7.6: If ρ_1, ρ_2, ρ_3 and ρ_4 are the roots of $z^4 + z^3 + z^2 + z + 1 = 0$, show that the expression $\rho_1^n + \rho_2^n + \rho_3^n + \rho_4^n$ with $n \in \mathbb{N}$ is either equal to 4 if $5|n$, or -1 otherwise.
Ans: It is clear that all the ρ are roots of $\rho^5 = 1$. Hence if 5 divides n you can set $n = 5m$ and the expression becomes

$$(\rho_1)^{5m} + (\rho_2)^{5m} + (\rho_3)^{5m} + (\rho_4)^{5m} = (\rho_1^5)^m + (\rho_2^5)^m + (\rho_3^5)^m + (\rho_4^5)^m = 4$$

For the next part, you can write the roots as $\rho_1 = \epsilon$, $\rho_2 = \epsilon^2$, $\rho_3 = \epsilon^3$, $\rho_4 = \epsilon^4$ where $\epsilon = e^{2\pi/5}$. Using these for $n = 5m + 1$ you will have

$$\epsilon^{5m+1} + \epsilon^{2(5m+1)} + \epsilon^{3(5m+1)} + \epsilon^{4(5m+1)} = \epsilon + \epsilon^2 + \epsilon^3 + \epsilon^4 = -1$$

and similarly for $n = 5m+2, 5m+3, 5m+4$. □

DAD'S SOS NOTE: The last exercise is a particular case of a well known result. Namely, for $n, m \in \mathbb{Z}$, if $z^n = 1$ then

$$1 + z^m + z^{2m} + \ldots + z^{(n-1)m} = \sum_{r=0}^{n-1} z^{rm} = \begin{cases} n; \text{ IF } n \text{ DIVIDES } m \\ 0; \text{ OTHERWISE} \end{cases} \quad (7.4)$$

Proof: If n divides m then $m = pn$ for some integer p. But then the terms z^{rm} in the sum become 1, since $z^{rm} = z^{rpn} = z^{rn/p} = (z^n)^{r/p} = 1$, thus making the sum equal to n. On the other hand, if n does not divide m we can write the sum as a geometric progression, $\frac{1-(z^m)^n}{1-z^m} = \frac{1-1}{1-z^m} = 0$. ♥

Exercise 7.7: Show that if $z^6 = 1$ and $z^{12} = 1$ then any root of $z^6 = 1$ is also a root of $z^{12} = 1$.
Ans: You can rewrite $z^{12} - 1 = 0 = (z^6 - 1)(z^6 + 1) = 0$. This shows that $z^6 = 1$ is also a root of $z^{12} = 1$. □

Proposition 7.2: The previous exercise can be generalised as follows. If $z^n = 1$ and $z^p = 1$ and n divides p then the roots of $z^n = 1$ are also roots of $z^p = 1$.
Proof: Since n divides p we must have $p = mn$ for some integer m. We then have

$$z^p - 1 = 0 = z^{mn} - 1 = (z^n)^m - 1 \Rightarrow (z^n - 1)(z^{(m-1)n} + z^{(m-2)n} + \ldots + 1) = 0$$

And the last equation shows that $z^n - 1$ is also a root of $z^p - 1 = 0$. □

Exercise 7.8: Show that the polynomial $P(z) = z^{20n+4} + z^{15n+3} + z^{10n+2} + z^{5n+1} + 1$ has as a factor the polynomial $Q(z) = z^4 + z^3 + z^2 + z + 1$.
Ans: This is another fun question. You can of course try to perform the division, but it will get messy. The trick is to realise that the roots of the polynomial $Q(z)$ are basically the 5th roots of unity apart from 1. Namely $z^5 - 1 = (z-1)(z^4 + z^3 + z^2 + z + 1)$. Similarly the roots of $P(z)$ are the roots

of

$$z^{25n+5}-1=\left[(z^{5n+1})^5-1\right]=$$
$$=(z^{5n+1}-1)\left[(z^{5n+1})^4+(z^{5n+1})^3+(z^{5n+1})^2+(z^{5n+1})^1+1\right]$$

And the expression in the square bracket is $P(z)=z^{20n+4}+z^{15n+3}+z^{10n+2}+z^{5n+1}+1$ and it has the roots of z^{25n+5}. According to Proposition (7.2) $z^5-1=0$ has common roots (namely, is a factor) with $z^{25n+5}-1=0$, if 5 divides $25n+5$ which is true. □

A second way is:

Ans: So the roots of Q, obey $r^5=1 \Rightarrow r^4+r^3+r^2+r+1=0$. We then only need to check if the roots of Q are also the roots of P.

$$\begin{aligned} P &= r^{20n+4}+r^{15n+3}+r^{10n+2}+r^{5n+1}+1 \\ &= (r^5)^{4n}r^4+(r^5)^{3n}r^3+(r^5)^{2n}r^2+(r^5)^{n}r+1 \\ \text{Since } r^5=1 \quad &= r^4+r^3+r^2+r+1=0 \end{aligned}$$

Hence every root of Q is also a root of P and so Q is a factor of P. □

Theorem 7.2: The polynomial z^n-1 can be factorised as

$$z^n-1=(z-1)(z-\epsilon)(z-\epsilon^2)...(z-\epsilon^{n-1})$$

Proof: : We saw earlier that the roots of the polynomial equation $z^n=1$ are in the set $\{1,\epsilon,\epsilon^2,...\epsilon^{n-1}\}$. We also know that any polynomial can be factorised in terms of its roots. Hence $z^n-1=\lambda(z-1)(z-\epsilon)...(z-\epsilon^{n-1})$ and by comparing coefficients we get that $\lambda=1$. □

Exercise 7.9: If ϵ is the nth-root of unity then

$$(1-\epsilon)(1-\epsilon^2)...(1-\epsilon^{n-1})=n$$

Ans: Factorizing $z^n-1=(z-1)(z^{n-1}+z^{n-2}+...+1)$ and using the previous result we get

$$(z-1)(z^{n-1}+z^{n-2}+...+1)=(z-1)(z-\epsilon)(z-\epsilon^2)...(z-\epsilon^{n-1})$$

After cancelling the $(z-1)$ factor we get

$$z^{n-1}+z^{n-2}+...+z+1=(z-\epsilon)(z-\epsilon^2)...(z-\epsilon^{n-1})$$

Letting $z = 1$ in the last equation we get the desired result. You may object to the fact that I cancelled out the $z-1$ and then set $z = 1$ back to get the result. But, what I did really, was to take the limit

$$\lim_{z\to 1}\frac{z^n-1}{z-1} = n = \lim_{z\to 1}\frac{(z-1)(z-\epsilon)(z-\epsilon^2)...(z-\epsilon^{n-1})}{z-1}$$

in order to get the result. Although we have not defined what we mean by $\lim_{z\to 1}$, for polynomial functions in complex numbers there are no convergence issues. □

Exercise 7.10: Find the roots of the equation

$$x^{2n} - 2x^n \cos n\alpha + 1 = 0$$

Hence, show that

$$x^{2n} - 2x^n \cos n\alpha + 1 = \prod_{k=0}^{k=n-1}\left[x^2 - 2x\cos\left(\alpha + \frac{2k\pi}{n}\right) + 1\right] \tag{7.5}$$

Ans: The given equation is a quadratic in x^n. Solving it, we get $x^n = \cos n\alpha \pm i \sin n\alpha$ and therefore the nth root is

$$x = \cos\left(\alpha + \frac{2k\pi}{n}\right) \pm i\sin\left(\alpha + \frac{2k\pi}{n}\right) = \mathrm{e}^{\pm i(\alpha+2k\pi/n)}$$

for $k = 0, 1, ..., n-1$. Now if we multiply the two complex conjugate roots we get

$$\left(x - \mathrm{e}^{\alpha+2k\pi/n}\right)\left(x - \mathrm{e}^{-(\alpha+2k\pi/n)}\right) = x^2 - 2x\cos\left(\alpha + \frac{2k\pi}{n}\right) + 1$$

Now, there would be n such pairs of factors and therefore the equation would be written as the product of these n pairs, for $k = 0, ..., n-1$

$$x^{2n} - 2x^n \cos n\alpha + 1 = \prod_{k=0}^{k=n-1}\left[x^2 - 2x\cos\left(\alpha + \frac{2k\pi}{n}\right) + 1\right]$$ □

Exercise 7.11: A regular n-gon $X_0X_1X_2..X_{n-1}$ is inscribed on a circle of unit radius. Show that

(i) $|X_0X_1| \times |X_0X_2| \times ... \times |X_0X_{n-1}| = n$

(ii) Show that $|1-\epsilon^k| = 2\sin\frac{k\pi}{n}, \quad k \in \mathbb{Z}$

(iii) Deduce that $\sin\frac{\pi}{n}\sin\frac{2\pi}{n}...\sin\frac{(n-1)\pi}{n} = \frac{n}{2^{n-1}}$

Ans: The first part was done in Exercise (7.9). Since we have a regular polygon of n sides, each point is the root of $z^n = 1$. Hence the points $X_0, X_1, ..., X_{n-1}$ are $\{1, \epsilon, \epsilon^2, ..., \epsilon^{n-1}\}$ with $\epsilon = e^{\frac{2\pi}{n}}$. The relation then becomes

$$|X_0X_1| \times |X_0X_2| \times ... \times |X_0X_{n-1}| = |(1-\epsilon)(1-\epsilon^2)...(1-\epsilon^{n-1})| = n$$

Now for the second part we need to calculate $|1-\epsilon^k|$. So

$$|1-\epsilon^k| = \left|1-\cos\frac{2k\pi}{n} - i\sin\frac{2k\pi}{n}\right| = \left|2\sin^2\frac{k\pi}{n} - 2\sin\frac{k\pi}{n}\cos\frac{k\pi}{n}\right|$$
$$= 2\sin\frac{k\pi}{n}\left|\sin\frac{k\pi}{n} - i\cos\frac{k\pi}{n}\right| = 2\sin\frac{k\pi}{n}$$

Now part (iii) becomes trivial since using part (i) we have

$$|(1-\epsilon)(1-\epsilon^2)...(1-\epsilon^{n-1})| = n$$
$$2\sin\frac{\pi}{n}2\sin\frac{2\pi}{n}...2\sin\frac{(n-1)\pi}{n} = n \Rightarrow$$
$$\sin\frac{\pi}{n}\sin\frac{2\pi}{n}...\sin\frac{(n-1)\pi}{n} = \frac{n}{2^{n-1}}$$ □

The roots of unity and their complex conjugates are related. For example, for the cube roots of unity $1, \omega, \omega^2$ we have that $\omega^* = \omega^2$ and $(\omega^2)^* = \omega$. This result generalises to the nth-root and it is a very useful fact to remember.

Proposition 7.3: If $\epsilon = e^{2\pi/n}$, namely $\epsilon^n = 1$ with $n \in \mathbb{N}$, then $\epsilon^* = \epsilon^{n-1}$ and in general if $\epsilon^k = e^{2ik\pi/n}$ then $(\epsilon^k)^* = \epsilon^{n-k}$ for $k = 1, 2, ..., n-1$.
Proof: The roots of $z^n = 1$ are $\{1, \epsilon, \epsilon^2, ..., \epsilon^{n-1}\}$ with $\epsilon = e^{2i\pi/n}$. Then $(\epsilon^k)^* = e^{-2ik\pi/n} = e^{2i\pi-2ik\pi/n} = e^{(n-k)2i\pi/n} = (\epsilon)^{n-k}$. □

Exercise 7.12: Let $z = e^{2i\pi/7}$. Show that $(z^*)^4 = z^3$.
Ans: Obviously $z^7 = 1$. Since $z = e^{2\pi/7}$, then

$$(z^*)^4 = e^{-8i\pi/7} = e^{14i\pi/7-8i\pi/7} = e^{6i\pi/7} = \left(e^{2i\pi/7}\right)^3 = z^3$$ □

7.3 Cube Roots of Unity

The cube roots of unity make frequent appearances in exam questions in several forms. Geometrically, they form an equilateral triangle. See Figure (7.2).

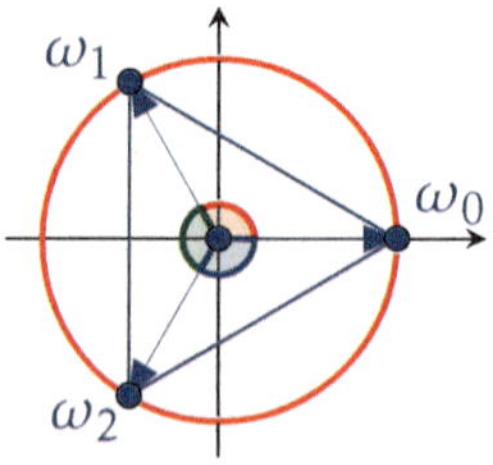

Figure 7.2: The roots of $z^3 - 1 = 0$ are 1, $\omega_1 = e^{2i\pi/3}$ and $\omega_2 = e^{4i\pi/3}$ form an equilateral triangle. $\omega_1^2 = \omega_2$ and $\omega_2^2 = \omega_1$

The equation $z^3 - 1 = 0$ has one obvious real root $z = 1$. The other two roots are the solutions to $z^2 + z + 1 = 0$ and they are

$$\omega_1 = \frac{-1}{2} + i\frac{\sqrt{3}}{2}, \quad \omega_2 = \frac{-1}{2} - i\frac{\sqrt{3}}{2}$$

We can also write them in polar form as $\omega_1 = e^{2i\pi/3} = \cos\frac{2\pi}{3} + i\sin\frac{2\pi}{3}$ and $\omega_2 = e^{4\pi/3} = \cos\frac{4\pi}{3} + i\sin\frac{4\pi}{3}$.
As expected, they form the vertices of an equilateral triangle with the origin at its barycentre (centroid). The roots $\omega_{1,2}$ also obey the following relations.

$$\omega_1^3 = \omega_2^3 = 1, \quad \omega_1^2 = \omega_2, \quad \omega_2^2 = \omega_1$$

Dad's SOS Note: If you remember the definition of Primitive roots you will recognise that since 3 is a prime number, both ω_1 and ω_2 are Primitive roots and hence they must generate the full spectrum of solutions. Hence, $\omega_1^2 = \omega_2$ and $\omega_2^2 = \omega_1$. ♥

Exercise 7.13: If $\omega \neq 1$ is a solution to $z^3 = 1$, namely a solution to $\omega^2 + \omega + 1 = 0$, show that the only possible values of the expression $A = \omega^{2n} + \omega^n$ are -1 and 2 for $n = 0, 1, 2...$

Ans: Since you are given that ω is the cube root of unity, it would be a good idea to try and form ω^3 as this would simplify to 1. The way to do it is by writing the natural number n as $n = 3k + p$ where $p = 0, 1, 2$. Doing this you will get

$$A = \omega^{6k+2p} + \omega^{3k+p} = (\omega^3)^{2k}\omega^{2p} + (\omega^3)^k\omega^p = \omega^{2p} + \omega^p$$

The last expression can now be evaluated for $p = 0,1,2$. Therefore, for $p = 0 \Rightarrow A = 2$, for $p = 1 \Rightarrow A = \omega^2 + \omega = -1$. Finally, for $p = 2 \Rightarrow A = \omega^4 + \omega^2 = \omega^3\omega + \omega^2 = \omega + \omega^2 = -1$. Hence the only possible values are indeed 2 and -1.
This question is just an application of Eq. (7.4). □

Proposition 7.4: In an equilateral triangle $\triangle ABC$ (written anticlockwise) with vertices represented by the complex numbers a, b and c the following relations are true

$$a = b + (c-b)e^{i\pi/3}, \quad b = c + (a-c)e^{i\pi/3}, \quad c = b + (a-b)e^{-i\pi/3}$$

Furthermore if $\omega = e^{2\pi/3}$, the triangle $\triangle ABC$ is equilateral if any of the following conditions hold

$$a + b\omega + c\omega^2 = 0, \quad b + c\omega + a\omega^2 = 0, \quad c + a\omega + b\omega^2 = 0$$

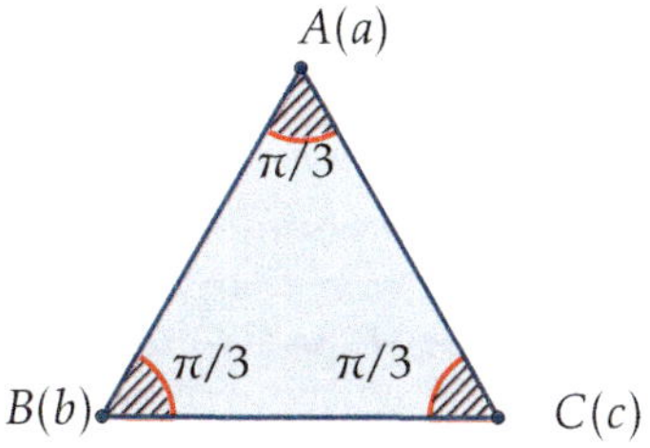

Proof: To reach the point $A(a)$ we can go to b and then add $(c-b)$ rotated anticlockwise by $\pi/3$. Hence $a = (c-b)e^{i\pi/3}$. Similarly, for the other two relations.
For the next part, starting from

$$\begin{aligned} a + b\omega + c\omega^2 &= a + bw + (b + (a-b)e^{-i\pi/3})\omega^2 \\ &= a + b\omega + b\omega^2 + (a-b)e^{4\pi/2 - i\pi/3} \\ &= a + b\omega + b\omega^2 + b - a = b(1 + \omega + \omega^2) = 0 \end{aligned}$$

Similarly for the other two relations. □

DAD'S SOS NOTE: The previous proposition is very useful when wanting to prove that a triangle is equilateral. It has made many appearances in competitions and other specialised university entrance exams. ♥

Exercise 7.14: (Napolean's Triangle) In an arbitrary triangle $\triangle ABC$ we construct the equilateral triangles $\triangle AFB$, $\triangle BGC$ and $\triangle CHA$ as shown on the diagram (all anticlockwise). If L, M, N are the centroids (barycenter) of these triangles prove that LMN is equilateral.

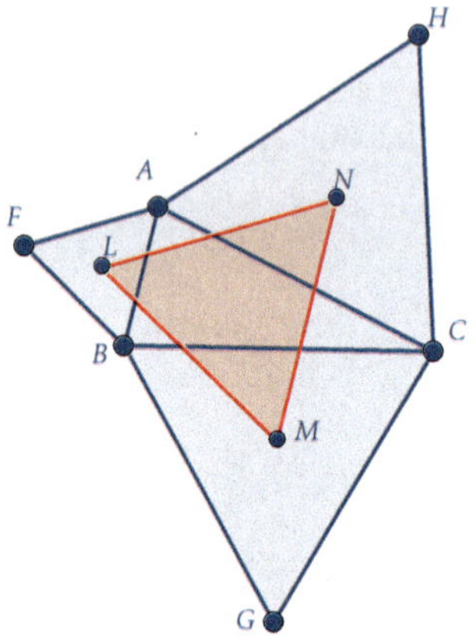

Ans: If we represent the complex numbers with small case letters, it is enough to prove that $A = l + m\omega + n\omega^2 = 0$. The point L being the centroid obeys $l = (a+b+f)/3$ and similarly $m = (b+c+g)/3$ and $n = (a+c+h)/3$. Therefore, we have

$$\begin{aligned}3A &= (a+b+f)+(b+c+g)\omega+(a+c+h)\omega^2\\ &= (a+b+f)+(c+h\omega)\omega+(g+c\omega)\omega+(b+a\omega)\omega\\ &= (a+b+f)-a\omega^3-b+(b+a\omega)\omega = f+(-f)=0\end{aligned}$$

Where, we have used the fact that for equilateral triangle $\triangle AFB$ we have $a + f\omega + b\omega^2 = 0$, for $\triangle BGC$ we have $b + g\omega + c\omega^2$ and for $\triangle CHA$ we have $c + h\omega + a\omega^2 = 0$. □

Exercise 7.15: Show that if $\omega^2 + \omega + 1 = 0$ then we can write the sum of two cubes as:

$$a^3 + b^3 = (a+b)(a\omega + b\omega^2)(a\omega^2 + b\omega)$$

Ans: The sum of two cubes is an identity that you should remember. In case you have forgotten it, $a^3+b^3=(a+b)(a^2-ab+b^2)$, all we need to prove is that that $(a\omega+b\omega^2)(a\omega^2+b\omega)$ is equal to (a^2-ab+b^2). By expanding we get

$$(a\omega+b\omega^2)(a\omega^2+b\omega) = a^2\omega^3+ab\omega^2+ab\omega^4+b^2\omega^3$$
$$\text{Since } \omega^3=1, \quad = a^2+ab(\omega^4+\omega^2)+b^2 = a^2-ab+b^2 \qquad \square$$

7.4 Questions on the Nth Root of Complex Numbers

Q 7.1 Find the roots of $z^3=8(1-z)^3$.

Q 7.2 Find the cube roots of $(\sqrt{3}+i)/2$, giving your answers in the form $\cos\theta+i\sin\theta$, where $0\le\theta<2\pi$. [4]

(OCR FP3 Jun2009)

Q 7.3 In this question, give all non-real numbers in the form $re^{i\theta}$ where $r>0$ and $0<\theta<2\pi$.

(i) Solve $z^5=1$. [2]

(ii) Hence, or otherwise, solve $z^5+32=0$. Sketch an Argand diagram showing the roots. [4]

(OCR FP3 Jun2016)

Q 7.4 (i) Solve the equation $z^6=1$, giving your answers in the form $re^{i\theta}$, and sketch an Argand diagram showing the positions of the roots. [4]

(ii) Show that $(1+i)^6=-8i$. [3]

(iii) Hence, or otherwise, solve the equation $z^6+8i=0$, giving your answers in the form $re^{i\theta}$. [3]

(OCR FP3 Jun2014)

Q 7.5 (a) Show that the roots of the equation $z^3=1$ are 1, ω and ω^2, where $\omega=-\frac{1}{2}+i\frac{\sqrt{3}}{2}$,
Express the complex number $5+7i$ in the form $A\omega+B\omega^2$, where A and B are real, and give the values of A and B in surd form.

(b) Given that $z = \cos\theta + i\sin\theta$, prove that

$$z^n + z^{-n} = 2\cos n\theta$$

Hence prove that $\cos 5\theta = 16\cos^5\theta - 20\cos^3\theta + 5\cos\theta$.

DAD's question!**(AEB 632/2 Nov1982)**

Q 7.6 (i) Solve the equation $z^4 = 2(1 + i\sqrt{3})$, giving the roots exactly in the form $r(\cos\theta + i\sin\theta)$, where $r > 0$ and $0 \le \theta < 2\pi$. [5]

(ii) Sketch an Argand diagram to show the lines from the origin to the point representing $2(1 + i\sqrt{3})$ and from the origin to the points which represent the roots of the equation in part (i). [3]

(OCR FP3 Jun2012)

Q 7.7 If $\omega^7 = 1$ find the value of the A expression

$$A = \frac{1}{\omega + \omega^6} + \frac{1}{\omega^2 + \omega^5} + \frac{1}{\omega^3 + \omega^4}$$

Q 7.8 In this question, w denotes the complex number $\cos\frac{2}{5}\pi + i\sin\frac{2}{5}\pi$.

(i) Express w^2, w^3 and w^* in polar form, with arguments in the interval $0 \le \theta < 2\pi$. [4]

(ii) The points in an Argand diagram which represent the numbers

$$1,\ 1 + w,\ 1 + w + w^2,\ 1 + w + w^2 + w^3,\ 1 + w + w^2 + w^3 + w^4$$

are denoted by A, B, C, D, E respectively. Sketch the Argand diagram to show these points and join them in the order stated. (Your diagram need not be exactly to scale, but it should show the important features.) [4]

(iii) Write down a polynomial equation of degree 5 which is satisfied by w. [1]**(OCR FP3 Jun2010)**

Q 7.9 Taking the roots of the equation $z^3 = 1$ as $1, \omega, \omega^2$ and given that $a, b \in \mathbb{R}$, show that a factorised form of the expression

$$x^3 - 3abx - (a^3 + b^3)$$

is

$$(x - a - b)(a - \omega a - \omega^2 b)(x - \omega^2 a - \omega b)$$

Hence, or otherwise, find in the form $p + iq$, where $p, q \in \mathbb{R}$, all the solutions to the equation $z^3 - 30z - 133 = 0$. **(AEB 632/2 Jun1988p)**

Q 7.10 You are given the complex number $\omega = \cos\frac{2\pi}{5} + i\sin\frac{2\pi}{5}$. Write down the value of ω^5 and prove that $1 + \omega + \omega^2 + \omega^3 + \omega^4 = 0$. Simplify $(\omega + \omega^4)(\omega^2 + \omega^3)$.

Form a quadratic equation with integer coefficients having roots $(\omega + \omega^4)$ and $(\omega^2 + \omega^3)$ and hence prove that

$$\cos\frac{2\pi}{5} = \frac{-1+\sqrt{5}}{4}$$

(AEB 632/2 Jun1989)

Q 7.11 Find all the solutions to $x^4 + x^3 + x^2 + x + 1 = 0$.

Q 7.12 Show that if $(z-1)^n = z^n$ then

$$z = \frac{1}{2}\left(1 + i\cot\frac{k\pi}{n}\right)$$

with $k \in \mathbb{Z}$. Show that all the roots of this equation have their real parts on the line $x = 1/2$ line.

Q 7.13 (i) Show that $(z - e^{i\phi})(z - e^{-i\phi}) \equiv z^2 - (2\cos\phi)z + 1$. [1]

(ii) Write down the seven roots of the equation $z^7 = 1$ in the form $e^{i\theta}$ and show their positions in an Argand diagram. [4]

(iii) Hence express $z^7 - 1$ as the product of one real linear factor and three real quadratic factors. [5]

(OCR FP3 Jun2007)

Q 7.14 By placing in Equation (7.5), the value $\alpha = 0$ show that, for even n we have

$$x^n - 1 = (x-1)(x+1)\prod_{k=1}^{k=\frac{n}{2}-1}\left(x^2 - 2x\cos\frac{2k\pi}{n} + 1\right)$$

Q 7.15 Two numbers z_1 and z_2 each have arguments between 0 and π. The product $z_1 z_2$ is $(i - \sqrt{3})$ and the quotient z_1/z_2 is $2i$. Find the values of z_1 and z_2 in polar form. **(AEB 132/2 Nov1973p)**

Q 7.16 Show that if $(x+iy)^{2024} = x - iy$ with $x + iy \neq 0$, then the complex number $z = x + iy$ is unimodular. Hence find the number of solutions of the equation $(x+iy)^{2024} = x - iy$.

Q 7.17 Two regular polygons inscribed on a circle have have 33 and 99 sides respectively. How many, if any, common vertices do they have?

Q 7.18 Calculate the sums

$$S_1 = 1 + \cos\frac{2\pi}{n} + \cos\frac{4\pi}{n} + \ldots + \cos\frac{2(n-1)\pi}{n}$$

and

$$S_2 = \sin\frac{2\pi}{n} + \sin\frac{4\pi}{n} + \ldots + \sin\frac{2(n-1)\pi}{n}$$

Q 7.19 The roots of the equation $z^3 - 1 = 0$ are denoted by 1, ω and ω^2.

(i) Sketch an Argand diagram to show these roots. [1]

(ii) Show that $1 + \omega + \omega^2 = 0$. [2]

(iii) Hence evaluate

(a) $(2+\omega)(2+\omega^2)$, [2]

(b) $\dfrac{1}{2+\omega} + \dfrac{1}{2+\omega^2}$. [2]

(iv) Hence find a cubic equation, with integer coefficients, which has roots $2, \dfrac{1}{2+\omega}$ and $\dfrac{1}{2+\omega^2}$. [4]

(OCR FP3 Jun2008)

Q 7.20 Prove by induction that $(\omega)^{2^{2n}} = \omega$ for all $n = 1, 2, \ldots$ if ω is a root of $\omega^2 + \omega + 1 = 0$

Q 7.21 If $\omega = \dfrac{-1}{2} + i\dfrac{\sqrt{3}}{2}$ show that

$$(1-\omega)(1-\omega^2)(1-\omega^4)(1-\omega^5) = 9$$

Hint: $\omega^3 = 1$.

Q 7.22 If $k = e^{2i\pi/7}$, form the quadratic with real coefficients whose roots are $k + k^2 + k^4$ and $k^3 + k^5 + k^6$ and deduce that

$$\sin\frac{2\pi}{7} + \sin\frac{4\pi}{7} + \sin\frac{8\pi}{7} = \frac{\sqrt{7}}{2}$$

Q 7.23 If $z = e^{2i\pi/11}$, form the quadratic with real coefficients, that has roots $z + z^3 + z^4 + z^5 + z^9$ and $z^2 + z^6 + z^7 + z^8 + z^{10}$. Deduce that

$$\sum_{k=1}^{5} \cos\frac{2k\pi}{11} = -\frac{1}{2}$$

Q 7.24 If ω is a cube root of unit different from 1 show that $\omega^2+\omega+1=0$. Show further

$$x^2+y^2+z^2=xy+yz+zx+(x+y\omega+z\omega^2)(x+y\omega^2+z\omega)$$

Q 7.25 Three complex numbers a, b and c obey the relation $\frac{a-c}{b-c}=e^{i\pi/3}$. Explain geometrically this relation for the points represented by a, b and c. Furthermore, prove that $a^2+b^2+c^2=ab+bc+ca$.

Q 7.26 If

$$z^4+z^3+z^2+z+1=0 \qquad (*)$$

and $u=z+z^{-1}$, find the possible values of u. Hence find the possible values of z. [Do not try to simplify your answers.]

Show that, if z satisfies $(*)$, then

$$z^5-1=0.$$

Hence write the solutions of $(*)$ in the form $z=r(\cos\theta+i\sin\theta)$ for suitable real r and θ. Deduce that

$$\sin\frac{2\pi}{5}=\frac{\sqrt{(10+2\sqrt{5})}}{4} \quad\text{and}\quad \cos\frac{2\pi}{5}=\frac{-1+\sqrt{5}}{4}.$$

(STEP II Jun1996)

Q 7.27 Let $\omega=e^{2\pi i/3}$. Show that $1+\omega+\omega^2=0$ and calculate the modulus and argument of $1+\omega^2$.

Let n be a positive integer. By evaluating $(1+\omega^r)^n$ in two ways, taking $r=1,2$ and 3, or otherwise, prove that

$$\binom{n}{0}+\binom{n}{3}+\binom{n}{6}+\cdots+\binom{n}{k}=\frac{1}{3}\left(2^n+2\cos\left(\frac{n\pi}{3}\right)\right),$$

where k is the largest multiple of 3 less than or equal to n. Without using a calculator, evaluate

$$\binom{25}{0}+\binom{25}{3}+\cdots+\binom{25}{24}$$

and

$$\binom{24}{2}+\binom{24}{5}+\cdots+\binom{24}{23}.$$

[$2^{25}=33554432$.] **(STEP I Jun1990)**

Q 7.28 Show by considering $(1+z)^n = \binom{n}{0} + \binom{n}{1}z + \binom{n}{2}z^2 + \ldots + \binom{n}{n}z^n$ that

$$\binom{n}{0} - \binom{n}{2} + \binom{n}{4} \ldots. = 2^{n/2}\cos\frac{n\pi}{4}$$

and

$$\binom{n}{1} - \binom{n}{3} + \binom{n}{5} \ldots. = 2^{n/2}\sin\frac{n\pi}{4}$$

8. Complex Logarithm and Exp

> The whole apparatus of the calculus takes on an entirely different form when developed for the complex numbers.
>
> Keith Devlin[5]

8.1 Matrix Representation of Complex Numbers

This is a very interesting section. It gives you a glimpse of the hidden interconnections between different and apparently disjoint concepts.

From the geometrical point of view (see Section (3.5)), a multiplication by a complex number is a rotation together with a scaling. From your matrix algebra you also know that rotations are represented by some very nice matrices. So there must be a connection between the two. For the moment forget about the scaling and consider complex numbers of unit modulus. An anticlockwise rotation of a point on a two dimensional plane about the origin by an angle θ is represented by the matrix

$$\begin{pmatrix} \cos\theta & -\sin\theta \\ \sin\theta & \cos\theta \end{pmatrix}$$

We can rewrite this matrix as

$$\cos\theta \begin{pmatrix} 1 & 0 \\ 0 & 1 \end{pmatrix} + \sin\theta \begin{pmatrix} 0 & -1 \\ 1 & 0 \end{pmatrix} \tag{8.1}$$

The above relation (8.1) looks awfully similar to the complex number $z = \cos\theta + i\sin\theta$. It suggests, that we can represent the 1 with the unit 2×2 matrix I:

$$1 \rightarrow \begin{pmatrix} 1 & 0 \\ 0 & 1 \end{pmatrix} = I$$

and the imaginary $i = \sqrt{-1}$, can be identified by

$$i \rightarrow \begin{pmatrix} 0 & -1 \\ 1 & 0 \end{pmatrix}$$

Now for the big prize. If we multiply

$$\begin{pmatrix} 0 & -1 \\ 1 & 0 \end{pmatrix}\begin{pmatrix} 0 & -1 \\ 1 & 0 \end{pmatrix} = \begin{pmatrix} -1 & 0 \\ 0 & -1 \end{pmatrix} = -I$$

which is minus the unit matrix I. This mimics exactly the behaviour of $i^2 = -1$.

We can therefore make the assumption that any complex number $z = a + ib$ can be represented by a 2×2 matrix $M(a,b)$ as follows

$$M(a,b) = a\begin{pmatrix} 1 & 0 \\ 0 & 1 \end{pmatrix} + b\begin{pmatrix} 0 & -1 \\ 1 & 0 \end{pmatrix} = \begin{pmatrix} a & -b \\ b & a \end{pmatrix}, \quad a,b \in \mathbb{R}$$

This is just an assumption. We need to show that the various complex operations are also valid in the matrix representation.

Addition of complex numbers We can verify that the sum and the product of two such matrices $M(a,b)$ and $M(c,d)$ obeys the rules of complex addition and multiplication.
The sum is

$$M(a,b) + M(c,d) = \begin{pmatrix} a & -b \\ b & a \end{pmatrix} + \begin{pmatrix} c & -d \\ d & c \end{pmatrix} = \begin{pmatrix} a+c & -b-d \\ b+d & a+c \end{pmatrix} = M(a+c, b+d)$$

And we also have that $M(a,b) + M(c,d) = M(c,d) + M(a,b)$, namely Commutativity.

Multiplication of complex numbers The product of two matrices is

$$M(a,b)M(c,d) = \begin{pmatrix} a & -b \\ b & a \end{pmatrix}\begin{pmatrix} c & -d \\ d & c \end{pmatrix} = \begin{pmatrix} ac-bd & -ad-bc \\ ad+bc & ac-bd \end{pmatrix} =$$
$$= M(ac-bd, ad+bc)$$

We can also verify that this matrix multiplication is commutative,

$$M(a,b)M(c,d) = M(c,d)M(a,b)$$

This means that the 2×2 matrices "mirror" exactly the operations of the complex numbers. We can also show that $M(a,0) + M(b,0) = M(a+b,0)$ and $M(a,0)M(b,0) = M(ab,0)$. This is just addition and multiplication of real numbers.

Conjugation How about the operation of conjugation? Well, since $z^* = a - ib$ the conjugate is the transpose of the matrix

$$z^* \rightarrow \begin{pmatrix} a & -b \\ b & a \end{pmatrix}^T = \begin{pmatrix} a & b \\ -b & a \end{pmatrix}$$

Modulus of complex number We can also verify that $zz^* = |z|^2$ since

$$\begin{pmatrix} a & -b \\ b & a \end{pmatrix}\begin{pmatrix} a & -b \\ b & a \end{pmatrix}^T = \begin{pmatrix} a & -b \\ b & a \end{pmatrix}\begin{pmatrix} a & b \\ -b & a \end{pmatrix}$$

$$= \begin{pmatrix} a^2+b^2 & 0 \\ 0 & a^2+b^2 \end{pmatrix} = (a^2+b^2)\begin{pmatrix} 1 & 0 \\ 0 & 1 \end{pmatrix} = (a^2+b^2)I$$

We can summarise what we described above in the following proposition.

Proposition 8.1: If $z = a + bi$ is a complex number, then it can be represented by the matrix

$$z = a + bi \longrightarrow \mathbf{C} = \begin{pmatrix} a & -b \\ b & a \end{pmatrix}$$

(i) Addition of complex numbers $z_1 + z_2$ is equivalent to addition of their matrix representations

(ii) Multiplication of two complex numbers $z_1 z_2$ is equivalent to multiplication of their matrix representations.

(iii) Complex conjugation of a complex number is equivalent to taking the transpose of its matrix representation.

(iv) The modulus square of the complex number $|z|^2 = a^2 + b^2$ is the determinant of its matrix representation

$$\det \mathbf{C} = \mathbf{C}\mathbf{C}^T = \begin{pmatrix} a^2+b^2 & 0 \\ 0 & a^2+b^2 \end{pmatrix} \longrightarrow |z|^2$$

(v) The inverse of a complex number z, is represented by the inverse of its matrix representation.

Proof: Addition and multiplication were shown earlier .
Similarly,

$$\mathbf{C}^T = \begin{pmatrix} a & b \\ -b & a \end{pmatrix}$$

which is the representation of z^*.
For the inverse of a complex number we have that the cofactor matrix of $\mathbf{C} = \begin{pmatrix} a & -b \\ b & a \end{pmatrix}$ is the same as $\mathbf{C}$. Hence, to find the inverse of the matrix

$$\mathbf{C}^{-1} = \frac{\mathbf{C}^T}{\det \mathbf{C}} = \frac{z^*}{|z|^2} = \frac{z^*}{zz^*} = \frac{1}{z} \qquad \square$$

Exercise 8.1: If $z_1 = 1+i$, $z_2 = 3+4i$ and $z_3 = 1-i$ write the z_1, z_2 and z_3 is matrix form. Furthermore, write in matrix form

(1) $z_1 + z_3$ (2) $z_2 - z_1$ (3) $z_1 z_2$

Ans: :

$$z_1 = \begin{pmatrix} 1 & -1 \\ 1 & 1 \end{pmatrix}, \quad z_2 = \begin{pmatrix} 3 & -4 \\ 4 & 3 \end{pmatrix}, \quad z_3 = \begin{pmatrix} 1 & 1 \\ -1 & 1 \end{pmatrix}$$

And we have

$$z_1 + z_3 = \begin{pmatrix} 1 & -1 \\ 1 & 1 \end{pmatrix} + \begin{pmatrix} 1 & 1 \\ -1 & 1 \end{pmatrix} = \begin{pmatrix} 2 & 0 \\ 0 & 2 \end{pmatrix},$$

$$z_2 - z_1 = \begin{pmatrix} 3 & -4 \\ 4 & 3 \end{pmatrix} - \begin{pmatrix} 1 & -1 \\ 1 & 1 \end{pmatrix} = \begin{pmatrix} 4 & -5 \\ 5 & 4 \end{pmatrix}$$

$$z_1 z_2 = \begin{pmatrix} 1 & -1 \\ 1 & 1 \end{pmatrix} \begin{pmatrix} 3 & -4 \\ 4 & 3 \end{pmatrix} = \begin{pmatrix} -1 & -7 \\ 7 & -1 \end{pmatrix}$$

Exercise 8.2: Show that

$$\begin{pmatrix} \cos\theta & -\sin\theta \\ \sin\theta & \cos\theta \end{pmatrix}^n = \begin{pmatrix} \cos n\theta & -\sin n\theta \\ \sin n\theta & \cos n\theta \end{pmatrix}$$

Ans: A complex number $z = \cos\theta + i\sin\theta$ is equivalent to the the matrix

$$z = \cos\theta + i\sin\theta \to \begin{pmatrix} \cos\theta & -\sin\theta \\ \sin\theta & \cos\theta \end{pmatrix}$$

By De Moivre (5.1) we also know that $z^n = (\cos\theta + i\sin\theta)^n = \cos n\theta + i\sin n\theta$. The last expression can also be written in the form

$$\cos n\theta + i\sin n\theta \to \begin{pmatrix} \cos n\theta & -\sin n\theta \\ \sin n\theta & \cos n\theta \end{pmatrix} \qquad \square$$

8.2 Functions of a Complex Variable

Up until now we dealt with complex numbers, defining addition, multiplication and integer or rational powers of it, like $(1+i)^n$. We also formed polynomials in the complex z and ratios of polynomials. But, if we have new numbers, we should be able to define more functions, like e^z or $\ln z$ and trigonometric functions like $\sin z$ or $\cos z$.

We need of course to define exactly what we mean by e^z or $\sin z$ if z is a complex number. For example, it is not clear what it means to have the sine of a complex number. In the case of real numbers the interpretation was the ratio of two lengths in a right-angled triangle. This cannot be the case with complex numbers. Hopefully, there is a way out. As we know how to deal with powers and polynomials of complex numbers, we would use the series expansions of these functions to define their complex extensions.

> DAD'S SOS NOTE: In order to define more functions of complex numbers like $\sin z$ or e^z, we are going to use the polynomial series expansions of these functions. This is because the usual interpretations of angles or ratios of lengths do not generalise. ♥

The complex e^z**:** We know that for real values $x \in \mathbb{R}$ we have $e^x = 1 + x + \frac{x^2}{2!} + ... + \frac{x^n}{n!}$. We would define e^z using the same form of the power series

$$e^z = 1 + z + \frac{z^2}{2!} + ... + \frac{z^n}{n!}, \quad z = x + iy$$

This definition is a natural extension of the exponential function since when $\text{Im}(z) = 0$ it falls back to our usual expansion of e^x. And we can further verify that for example $e^{z_1+z_2} = e^{z_1}e^{z_2}$ as expected.

> DAD'S SOS NOTE: Since we use a power series to define the exponential of a complex number, we should, if we want to be exact, investigate if this series is convergent. And if it is convergent, for what range of values it is. This is an advanced topic and we will not deal with it here. But for the record e^z is a convergent complex power series. ♥

The complex trigonometric functions: The real trigonometric functions like the sine and cosine where first defined and introduced as ratios of lengths on a right-angled triangle. Clearly, this is not easy to generalise in the case of complex numbers. But, what we can do, is to again define them using their power series expansion. We thus have

$$\sin z = z - \frac{z^3}{3!} + \frac{z^5}{5!} + \dots \tag{8.2}$$

and

$$\cos z = 1 - \frac{z^2}{2!} + \frac{z^4}{4!} + \dots \tag{8.3}$$

One can also show that both these two complex power series are convergent for all complex numbers z.

DAD'S SOS NOTE: One can verify that $\cos(-z) = \cos z$ and $\sin(-z) = -\sin z$. The cosine of a complex number is an even function and the sine an odd function, as it was the case for real numbers. ♥

The Euler relation: We can now generalise Euler's formula $\mathrm{e}^{ix} = \cos x + i\sin x$, $x \in \mathbb{R}$ to the complex numbers.

Proposition 8.2: If $z \in \mathbb{C}$ then

$$\mathrm{e}^{iz} = \cos z + i \sin z \tag{8.4}$$

Proof: If we consider the expression e^{iz} using the expansion we get

$$\begin{aligned} \mathrm{e}^{iz} &= 1 + iz + \frac{-z^2}{2!} + \frac{-iz^3}{3!} + \frac{z^4}{4!} + \frac{iz^5}{5!}\dots \\ &= \left(1 + z - \frac{z^2}{2!} + \frac{z^4}{4!}\right) + i\left(z - \frac{z^3}{3!} + \frac{z^5}{5!} + \dots\right) \\ &= \cos z + i \sin z \end{aligned} \tag{8.5}$$

We thus have a generalisation of Euler's Eq. (6.1). □

We can also back out the $\cos z$ and $\sin z$ as a function of $\mathrm{e}^{\pm iz}$ using Eq. (8.4)

Proposition 8.3: Using Eq. (8.4) The trigonometric sine and cosine in terms of $e^{\pm z}$ are:

$$\cos z = \frac{e^{iz} + e^{-iz}}{2} \tag{8.6}$$

$$\sin z = \frac{e^{iz} - e^{-iz}}{2i} \tag{8.7}$$

And by using these we can verify the $\cos^2 z + \sin^2 z = 1$ for complex numbers

Proposition 8.4: For $z \in \mathbb{C}$ we have

$$\cos^2 z + \sin^2 z = 1 \tag{8.8}$$

Proof: Squaring (8.6)-(8.7) we get

$$\cos^2 z + \sin^2 z = \frac{(e^z + e^{-z})^2}{4} + \frac{(e^z - e^{-z})^2}{-4} =$$

$$= \frac{\cancel{e^{2z}} + \cancel{e^{-2z}} + 2 - \cancel{e^{2z}} - \cancel{e^{-2z}} + 2}{4} = 1 \qquad \square$$

Dad's SOS Note: Be careful here. This is *no longer the traditional Pythagorean theorem* we have for real numbers. Equation (8.8) does *NOT mean* that $|\cos z| \le 1$ or that $|\sin z| \le 1$ as is the case in the real domain. In fact, $|\cos z|$ can be greater than 1 as the following exercise shows. ♥

Exercise 8.3: By computing $\cos(2i)$ show that the modulus $|\cos 2i|$ can be greater than 1.
Ans: Using the formula

$$\cos 2i = \frac{e^{2i^2} + e^{-2i^2}}{2} = \frac{e^{-2} + e^{2}}{2} \approx 3.76 > 1 \qquad \square$$

Using these as the definitions for the sine and cosine we can prove the following identities for the sum and difference

Proposition 8.5: The following identities are true

$$\sin(z \pm w) = \sin z \cos w \pm \sin w \cos z \qquad (8.9)$$
$$\cos(z \pm w) = \cos z \cos w \mp \sin w \sin z \qquad (8.10)$$
$$\tan(z \pm w) = \frac{\tan z \pm \tan w}{1 \mp \tan z \tan w} \qquad (8.11)$$

Proof: For example, starting from the RHS of Eq (8.9) we have

$$\begin{aligned}
\sin z \cos w + \sin w \cos z &= \frac{(e^{iz} - e^{-iz})(e^{iw} + e^{-iw})}{4i} + \\
&\quad + \frac{(e^{iw} - e^{-iw})(e^{iz} + e^{-iz})}{4i} \\
&= \frac{e^{i(z+w)} + e^{i(z-w)} - e^{i(w-z)} - e^{-i(z+w)}}{4i} + \\
&\quad + \frac{e^{i(w+z)} - e^{i(z-w)} + e^{i(w-z)} - e^{i(w+z)}}{4i} \\
&= \frac{e^{i(w+z)} - e^{-i(w+z)}}{2i} = \sin(w+z)
\end{aligned}$$

We can verify all the others in the same way. □

Dad's SOS Note: As I said earlier the $\cos z$ is an even function (from its expansion) and that $\sin z$ is an odd function. Moreover, $\sin(\pi/2 + z) = \cos z$ and $\sin(\pi - z) = \sin z$ and $\cos(\pi + z) = -\cos z$. So all the complementary and supplementary "complex angle" (there are no angles any more in the usual sense) relations work in the same way.
You can also prove that all the double angle identities carry over on the complex numbers. For example, by setting $z = w$ in (8.10) you get

$$\cos 2z = \cos^2 z - \sin^2 z = 2\cos^2 z - 1 = 1 - 2\sin^2 z$$

and

$$\sin 2z = 2 \sin z \cos z$$

Even the relation $\cos^2 z + \sin^2 z = 1$ carries over into complex numbers. ♥

The Hyperbolic functions: The Eqs. (8.6-8.7) should be familiar to you as the hyperbolic cosine and sine definitions, but this time in the complex domain. Thus,

$$\cosh z = \frac{e^z + e^{-z}}{2} \quad (8.12)$$

$$\sinh z = \frac{e^z - e^{-z}}{2} \quad (8.13)$$

Using these definitions for the hyperbolic functions we obtain

$$\cos iz = \cosh z \quad (8.14)$$

$$\sin iz = i \sinh z \quad (8.15)$$

$$\cosh iz = \cos z \quad (8.16)$$

$$\sinh iz = i \sin z \quad (8.17)$$

Proposition 8.6: The hyperbolic sine and cosine of a complex number $z \in \mathbb{C}$ obeys

$$\cosh^2 z - \sinh^2 z = 1 \quad (8.18)$$

Proof: Squaring (8.12-8.13) we get

$$\cosh^2 z - \sinh^2 z = \frac{e^{2z} + e^{-2z} + 2 - e^{2z} - e^{-2z} + 2}{4} = 1 \quad \square$$

Dad's SOS Note: There is a very good mnemonic, called Osborn's Rule on how to remember the hyperbolic equations if you remember the simple trigonometric versions of it. Osborn's Law is simple: *In any Trigonometrical formula for θ, 2θ, 3θ, or θ and ϕ, after changing* sin *to* sinh, cos *to* cosh, *etc., change the sign of any term that contains (or implies) a product of* sinh, *e.g.* $\tanh\theta\tanh\phi$ *implies a product of* sinh. See Osborn [10].
For example, $\cos^2\theta + \sin^2\theta = 1 \rightarrow \cosh^2\theta - \sinh^2\theta = 1$, or $\tan 2\theta = \frac{2\tan\theta}{1-\tan^2\theta} \rightarrow \tanh 2\theta = \frac{2\tanh\theta}{1+\tanh^2\theta}$, since $\tan^2$ has a $\sin^2$ hidden in it. ♥

Exercise 8.4: Show that

$$\cos(x + iy) = \cos x \cosh y - i \sin x \sinh y$$

Ans: Using Eq. (8.10) and the above relations we get

$$\cos(x + iy) = \cos x \cos iy - \sin x \sin iy = \cos x \cosh y - i \sin x \sinh y$$

We similarly get that

$$\sin(x+iy) = \sin x \cosh y + i \cos x \sinh y \qquad \square$$

The Logarithm of z: We usually define the logarithm of a real number as the inverse function of e^x for $x \in \mathbb{R}$. And in the case of real numbers this is well defined. For every real positive number we can define one and only one number that is its logarithm. We would carry over this definition to the complex domain. Thus, if $e^w = z$, we would call w the logarithm of z. So $\ln z = w$. However, there is a slight problem. This is because $e^w = e^{w+2k\pi i}$, with $k \in \mathbb{Z}$. Because of this, the logarithm is no longer singled-valued (a 1-1 function), but a multivalued function. So we need to be more careful.

Proposition 8.7: The logarithm of a complex number is given by

$$\ln z = \ln|z| + i\arg(z), \quad z \neq 0 \tag{8.19}$$

Proof: Let $e^w = z$ and $z = re^{i\theta}$. Taking the logarithm of z we get

$$\ln z = \ln r + i\theta = \ln|z| + i\arg(z) \qquad \square$$

Dad's SOS Note: The logarithm of a complex number is a multi-valued function since the argument of a complex number $\arg z = \operatorname{Arg} z + 2k\pi i$. In order to make this more clear we often use the symbol Ln for the logarithm that uses the principal argument $\operatorname{Arg}(z)$.

$$\operatorname{Ln} z = \ln|z| + i\operatorname{Arg}(z), \quad \ln z = \operatorname{Ln} z + 2k\pi i$$ ♥

We can now calculate the logarithm of negative number. Something that was not possible within the real numbers can now be done in the complex domain.

Proposition 8.8: Show that the logarithm ln and the principal logarithm Ln of a negative number $a < 0$ is

$$\ln a = \ln|a| + i(2k+1)\pi \tag{8.20}$$

$$\operatorname{Ln} a = \ln|a| + i\pi \tag{8.21}$$

Proof: The logarithm of a negative number $a < 0$ can be calculated if we write it as $|a|e^{i(2k+1)\pi}$. Applying Eq. (8.19) we get

$$\ln a = \ln(|a|e^{i(2k+1)\pi}) = \ln|a| + i(\pi + 2k\pi)$$

and the principal logarithm Ln is (with $k = 0$)

$$\mathrm{Ln}\, a = \ln|a| + i\pi$$

□

Exercise 8.5: Compute $\ln i$ and $\mathrm{Ln}\, i$.
Ans: Using (8.19) we have

$$\ln i = \ln 1 + i\left(\frac{\pi}{2} + 2k\pi\right) = i\left(\frac{\pi}{2} + 2k\pi\right)$$

whereas for $\mathrm{Ln}\, i = \ln 1 + i\frac{\pi}{2} = \frac{i\pi}{2}$. □

Exercise 8.6: Find the value of $\mathrm{Ln}(-3)$ and $\mathrm{Ln}(1+i)$.
Ans: For $\mathrm{Ln}(-3)$ we have

$$\mathrm{Ln}(-3) = \mathrm{Ln}(3e^{i\pi}) = \ln 3 + i\pi$$

and

$$\mathrm{Ln}(1+i) = \ln\sqrt{2} + i\frac{\pi}{4}$$

□

Dad's SOS Note: The logarithm of a complex number as we defined it is a tricky animal. When we dealt with the sine and the cosine we saw that most of the formulas carry over to the complex domain. This not true for the Principal logarithm Ln. For example, $\mathrm{Ln}(z_1 z_2) \neq \mathrm{Ln}\, z_1 + \mathrm{Ln}\, z_2$. ♥

Exercise 8.7: Show that the inverse sine function of a complex number z, $\arcsin z$ is given by

$$\arcsin z = -i\ln\left(iz + (1-z^2)^{1/2}\right) = -i\ln\left(iz + |1-z^2|^{1/2}e^{\frac{1}{2}\arg(1-z^2)}\right)$$

Ans: We need to find the complex number w such that $w = \arcsin z$, or $\sin w = z$. Using the definition of the complex sine Eq. (8.7) we have

$$\frac{e^{iw} - e^{-iw}}{2i} = z \Rightarrow e^{2iw} - 2ize^{iw} - 1 = 0$$

This is a quadratic in e^{iw} and the solutions are

$$e^{iw} = iz \pm \sqrt{1-z^2}$$

We can dispense with the minus sign since the square root is multivalued. Taking the logarithm

$$w = -i\ln\left(iz + \sqrt{1-z^2}\right)$$

Writing

$$\sqrt{1-z^2} = e^{\frac{1}{2}\ln(1-z^2)} = e^{\frac{1}{2}(|1-z^2|+\arg(1-z^2))} = |1-z^2|^{1/2}e^{\frac{1}{2}\arg(1-z^2)}$$

we obtain the second expression. □

8.3 Questions

Q 8.1 If $z_1 = 1+i$, $z_2 = 3+4i$ and $z_3 = 1-i$ write the z_1, z_2 and z_3 is matrix form. Furthermore, write in matrix form

(1) $z_1{}^*z_2$ (2) $z_2z_2{}^*$ (3) $z_2 + z_1{}^*$

(4) $|z_1|$ (5) $|z_1z_2|$ (6) $|z_1+z_2|$

Q 8.2 Find the numerical value of $\sin(3i)$ and $\cos(3i)$. Hence verify that $\cos^2(3i)+\sin^2(3i) = 1$.

Q 8.3 If $z \in \mathbb{C}$, show that $\cosh^2 z - \sinh^2 z = 1$.

Q 8.4 If $z \in \mathbb{C}$, show that $\cosh(-z) = \cosh(z)$ and $\sinh(-z) = -\sinh z$

Q 8.5 If $z \in \mathbb{C}$, show that $e^z = \cosh z + \sinh z$

Q 8.6 Show that if $z = x+iy$, $x, y \in \mathbb{R}$ then

$$|\cos z| = \sqrt{\cos^2 x + \sinh^2 y}$$

and

$$|\sin z| = \sqrt{\sin^2 x + \sinh^2 y}$$

Hence show that if $\sin z = 0$ then the zeros are located at $(k\pi, 0)$ (As is also in the case of the real sine). Show further that if $\cos z = 0$, then the zeros are located at $(k\pi + \pi/2, 0)$, for $k \in \mathbb{Z}$.

Q 8.7 Evaluate $\mathrm{Ln}(-5)$, $\mathrm{Ln}(1-i)$. (Remember that Ln is the principal value).

Q 8.8 Show that $\mathrm{Ln}(z_1 z_2) \neq \mathrm{Ln}\, z_1 + \mathrm{Ln}\, z_2$ using as an example $z_1 = -1$ and $z_2 = i$.

Q 8.9 Show that $\arccos z = -i \ln\left(z + i\sqrt{1-z^2}\right)$. Using the equivalent relation for $\arcsin z$ show that

$$\arccos z + \arcsin z = \frac{1}{2}\pi + 2k\pi, \quad k \in \mathbb{Z}$$

Q 8.10 Show that

(i) $\arctan z = \dfrac{1}{2i} \ln\left(\dfrac{i-z}{i+z}\right)$

(ii) $\operatorname{arccot} z = \dfrac{1}{2i} \ln\left(\dfrac{i+z}{z-i}\right)$

(iii) $\operatorname{arccot} z = \arctan \dfrac{1}{z}$

(iv) $\arctan z + \operatorname{arccot} z = \dfrac{\pi}{2}(2k+1)$, with $k \in \mathbb{Z}$

Q 8.11 Show that if $z \in \mathbb{C}$ then

$$\cosh(z + 2\pi i) = \cosh(z), \text{ AND } \sinh(z + 2\pi i) = \sinh z$$

and that

$$\cosh\left(z + i\frac{\pi}{2}\right) = i \sinh z, \text{ AND } \sinh\left(z + i\frac{\pi}{2}\right) = i \cosh z$$

9. Where is infinity? Riemann Sphere

Infinity is closer than you think.

Infinity is a very interesting concept. First of all, it is bigger than any real number $x \in \mathbb{R}$ and as such it does not belong to the set $\mathbb{R}$. So ∞ is not a number in the strict sense of real numbers, since it does not satisfy the usual laws of addition and multiplication that we have for the real number system. We are used to denote the real numbers as points on a horizontal line with $+\infty$ towards the far right and $-\infty$ towards the far left. So where exactly is infinity?

9.1 The Extended Real Line

There is a very neat way to actually bring infinity much closer than it is. Consider the following set up.

We have a circle of radius R sitting on the plane as in figure (9.1). The origin of our coordinate system is the "south" point S of the circle and the "north" point N is on the y-axis a distance $2R$ from S. The centre of the circle is $O(0,R)$.

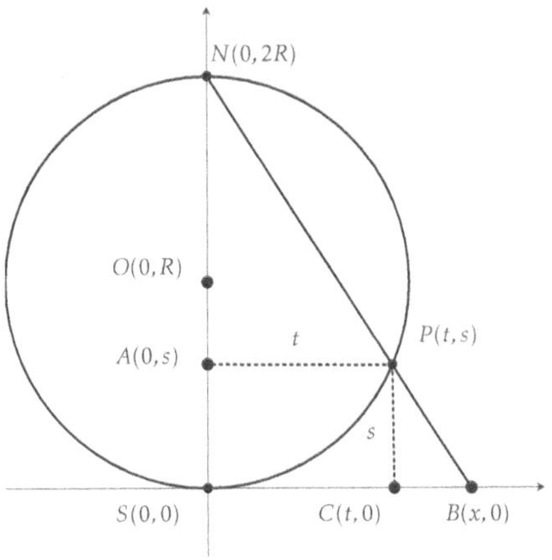

Figure 9.1: The real line including the infinity points can be represented by a circle.

From the point N ("north" pole) we draw a straight line crossing the x-axis at point $B(x,0)$. It crosses the circle at a point $P(t,s)$. Consider the two similar triangle $\triangle SNB \sim \triangle ANP$. We have

$$\frac{t}{x} = \frac{2R - s}{2R}$$

Since the point $P(t,s)$ is on the circle, we also have

$$t^2 + (s - R)^2 = R^2$$

Solving these two equations for t and s, after some algebra, we find that the point P has coordinates:

$$P\left(\frac{4R^2 x}{4R^2 + x^2}, \frac{2Rx^2}{4R^2 + x^2}\right)$$

We thus have that every point x on the real line has one and only one representative in the given circle. Notice that as we move further and further away in the positive axis the point P tend to approach the north pole $N(0, 2R)$. Thus the north pole could in principle represent the infinity of the real line. If we include this point in our construction we have that, the circle can represent all of $\mathbb{R}$ including the point at infinity, or $\mathbb{R} \cup \{\infty\}$. This is also known as the *Extended Real Line*. The North pole has joined both the $+\infty$ and $-\infty$ into a single point.

9.2 The Riemann Sphere

This is all very good when it comes to the real numbers but when we deal with complex numbers the infinity is not to the left or to the right but rather forms a circle of infinite radius around the centre of the Argand plane. We thus have infinite directions. But knowing how we got the Extended Real Plane we could do something similar to the Argand plane with a sphere. That sphere is known as the Riemann[1] Sphere, in honour to him, who used it, back in the 19th century.

Consider the following set up. A sphere of unit radius is centred at the point O. The horizontal plane through O is the complex Argand plane. The north pole of the sphere is $N(0,0,1)$. From the north pole we draw a line to a point $P'(X', Y', 0)$ on the horizontal plane. Thus the point P' is represented by the complex number $\zeta = X' + iY'$. See Figure (9.2). The

[1] Bernhard Riemann 1826-1866, German Mathematician. His ideas concerning geometry of space had a profound effect on the development of modern theoretical physics. He clarified the notion of integral by defining what we now call the Riemann integral. A student of Gauss.

line crosses the sphere at a point $P(x,y,z)$ and since it is a unit sphere we must have $x^2+y^2+z^2=1$. Also the point B is the projection of the point P on the horizontal plane and thus is represented by the complex number $x+iy$. We want to find the coordinate of the point $P(z,y,z)$ as functions of the complex number ζ of the point P'.

> Dad's SOS Note: This kind of mapping points of the sphere on plane is also known as the "Stereographic" projection and is how most maps of our planet are done. ♥

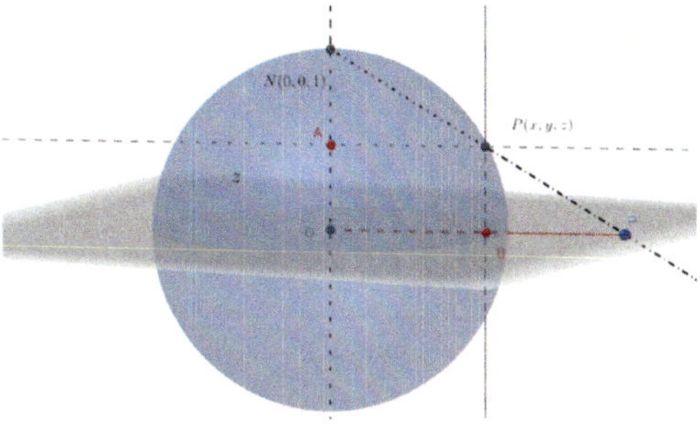

Figure 9.2: The Riemann sphere.

Using the similar triangles $\triangle ONP' \sim \triangle ANP$ and $\triangle OP'N \sim \triangle BP'P$ we find

$$\frac{1}{1-z}=\frac{PN'}{PN}, \qquad \frac{P'N}{PN}=\frac{\zeta}{x+iy}$$

Combining the above two relations we obtain that

$$\zeta=\frac{x+iy}{1-z}$$

In order to find z as a function of ζ we can take the modulus of $|\zeta|^2=\zeta\zeta^*$:

$$\zeta\zeta^*=\frac{x^2+y^2}{(1-z)^2}=\frac{1-z^2}{(1-z)^2}=\frac{1+z}{1-z}$$

and solving z we get

$$z=\frac{\zeta\zeta^*-1}{1+\zeta\zeta^*}$$

If we substitute this into $x+iy=\zeta(1-z)$ we get

$$x+iy=\frac{2\zeta}{1+\zeta\zeta^*}$$

We can now find x by adding the complex conjugate

$$x - iy = \frac{2\zeta^*}{1+\zeta\zeta^*} \Rightarrow x = \frac{\zeta+\zeta^*}{1+\zeta\zeta^*}$$

And if we subtract we find y

$$y = i\frac{\zeta^*-\zeta}{1+\zeta\zeta^*}$$

So, the coordinates of the point P are

$$x = \frac{\zeta+\zeta^*}{1+\zeta\zeta^*} = \frac{2X}{1+X^2+Y^2}, \tag{9.1}$$

$$y = i\frac{\zeta^*-\zeta}{1+\zeta\zeta^*} = \frac{2Y}{1+X^2+Y^2}, \tag{9.2}$$

$$z = \frac{\zeta\zeta^*-1}{1+\zeta\zeta^*} = \frac{X^2+Y^2-1}{1+X^2+Y^2} \tag{9.3}$$

Notice, that as we move to infinity $|\zeta| \to \infty$, the point P moves towards the North pole N. Thus, if we include this point in our construction we have represented the whole complex plane including the points at infinity with a unit sphere centred at the point O. This is the *Riemann Sphere*.

Proposition 9.1: The projection of a circle on the sphere onto the complex plane is a again a circle unless it goes through the North pole in which case it is a line (A circle of infinite radius).
Proof: A circle on the sphere can be defined as the cross-section of the sphere with a plane $\Pi : ax + by + cz + d = 0$. Plugging the values from Eq. (9.3) we get

$$\begin{aligned} a\frac{2X}{1+X^2+Y^2} + b\frac{2Y}{1+X^2+Y^2} + c\frac{X^2+Y^2-1}{1+X^2+Y^2} + d &= 0 \\ 2aX + 2bY + c(X^2+Y^2-1) + D(X^2+Y^2+1) &= 0 \\ (c+d)X^2 + (c+d)Y^2 + 2aX + 2bY - c + d &= 0 \end{aligned}$$

The last equation is the generalised equation of a circle, unless of course $c + d = 0$. In this case, the plane $ax + by + cz = c$ goes through the North pole $(0, 0, 1)$ and the circle on the Argand plane degenerates into the line $aX + bY = c$. See Figure (9.3). □

To see this with a geometric argument, consider a line that extends to infinity. Since, the infinity is mapped onto the North Pole it must be a closed curve through N. Now, lets follow the point P on the sphere as the point P' traces the line. It forms a plane (see figure (9.3)). And we know that the cross section of a plane with the sphere is a circle! Thus all lines on the plane map into circles on the Riemann sphere. And if two lines cross then the circles also cross on with the same angle on the sphere.
Thus the mapping preserves angles of intersection. This is also known as *Conformal* mapping.
The lines on the plane can thus be considered as circles on infinite radius!

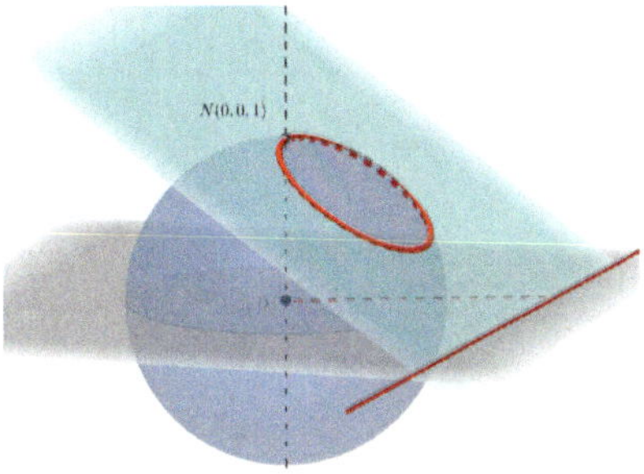

Figure 9.3: The mapping of a line on the complex plane is a circle through the North pole.

> **Proposition 9.2:** The stereographic projection preserves angles.

An angle between two curves is defined as the angle of the tangent vectors on the intersection point of the two curves. This is an amazing property of the stereographic projection. In fact this is exactly why it was used to make navigation maps. It is believed that Hipparchus[2] was the first to use it. We know of it indirectly through the work of Ptolemy[3] "The Planesphere" (meaning flat-sphere or flattening the sphere) that survives only in Arabic, see Sidoli [12]. In modern times it was popularised by the cartographer G.Mercator[4].

[2] Hipparchus 190BC-120BC, was a Greek mathematician who compiled an early example of trigonometric tables and gave methods for solving spherical triangles.

[3] Ptolemy 85AD-165AD, was the most influential of Greek astronomers and geographers of his time. He propounded the geocentric theory of the solar system that prevailed for 1400 years.

[4] Gerardus Mercator 1512-1594, was a Flemish map-maker and geographer who is best known for the map projection which bears his name.

DAD'S SOS NOTE: By adding the point of the North pole we can view the Riemann sphere $\mathbb{S} = \mathbb{R} \cup \{\infty\}$. We have thus attached infinity into a point. In doing so, we can make sense of operations like $z + \infty = \infty$ and thus do analysis on the complex plane. Stereographic projections maps circles on the sphere into circles on the plane. This mapping is very important as it preserves angles. This property is also known as "Conformal". ♥

Epilogue

The story of the Fantastic complex numbers is much much bigger. We only touched the very first chapter of a very big subject. The applications into modern Physics and Engineering are endless. For example, Quantum Mechanics would not exist without complex numbers and Electrical Engineering would have a hard time solving problems without it. Spinors and Twistors in General Theory of Relativity would not exist either if they did not exist. Complex numbers are not just Fantastic.

THEY ARE THE NUMBERS

Graph of complex function $f(z) = z + 1/z$. From the excellent website of Peter Francis https://peterefrancis.com/.

A. Hints and Answers to Questions

> Archimedes will be remembered when Aeschylus is forgotten, because languages die and mathematical ideas do not. "Immortality" may be a silly word, but probably a mathematician has the best chance of whatever it may mean.
>
> G.H. Hardy

Answers to Sec. 2.6,page 29

(Q2.1) Using $i^2 = -1$ etc, we get (1) 1,(2)0, (3) 0
(Q2.2) (1) $-3-1$, (2) $8+1$, (3) $21+i$, (4) i, (5) $1/2+i/2$, (6) $-3-4i$
(Q2.3) Setting $z = x+iy$ we get $2xi - 2y = 6i+4$. By comparing real and imaginary parts we get $z = 3-2i$. For (ii) we get $x^2+y^2+2xi = 4+2i$. So $x = 1$ and $x^2+y^2 = 4 \Rightarrow y^2 = 3 \Rightarrow y = \pm\sqrt{3}$
(Q2.4) (1) $\sqrt{13}$, (2)$\sqrt{13}$, (3) 1, (4) 2/5, (5) 1, (6) 1.
(Q2.5) (i) $z^3 = -11-2i$, (ii) $-2+3i$, (iii) -2, (iv) 4.
(Q2.6) Best to use determinant method. $z_1 = (-35+45i)/10$ and $z_2 = (34-28i)/10$.
(Q2.7) There is a reason why the question says $|z_1| \neq 0$. Notice that he question does not ask to determine either complex number, but the ratio. If we divide by this we get $|1+z_2/z_1| = 1 = |z_2/z_1|$. Now let $z_2/z_1 = x+iy$. This implies $1+x^2+2x+y^2 = 1 = x^2+y^2$. Hence $x = -1/2$ and $y = \pm\sqrt{3}2$. So $z_2 = (-1/2 \pm \sqrt{3}/2)z_1$ and $|z_1 - z_2| = |-3/2 \pm i\sqrt{3}/2|z_1 = \sqrt{3}|z_1|$.
(Q2.8) (1) $\pm(\sqrt{6}+i\sqrt{3})$, (2) $\pm(5-2i)$, (3) $\pm(5+6i)$, (4) $\pm(5+4i)$, (5) $\pm(3-4i)$, (6) $\pm(3-2i)$.
(Q2.9) In order to find A square the expression. $A^2 = 8+2\sqrt{(4+i\sqrt{20})(4-i\sqrt{20})} = 8 + 2\cdot 14 = 36$. Hence $A = \pm 6$. Alternatively you can write the $\sqrt{4+3i\sqrt{20}} = \pm(3+i\sqrt{5})$ and $\sqrt{4-3i\sqrt{20}} = \pm(3-i\sqrt{5})$.
(Q2.10) Suppose there was another element $1' \neq 1$ with the same properties. The $1\cdot 1' = 1$ if we treat the $1'$ as the unit. On the other hand, $1\cdot 1' = 1'$ if we treat the 1 as the unit. These two equations show that $1 = 1'$ contrary to the assumption that are different. Hence, there is only one unit element.
(Q2.11) Let $z_1 = x_1 + iy_1$ and $z_2 = x_2 + iy_2$, then $z_1 z_2 = (x_1x_2 - y_1y_2) + i(x_1y_2 + x_2y_1)$. We now have

$$\begin{aligned}
|z_1 z_2| &= \sqrt{(x_1x_2 - y_1y_2)^2 + (x_1y_2 + x_2y_1)^2} \\
&= \sqrt{x_1^2x_2^2 + y_1^2y_1^2 - 2x_1x_2y_1y_2 + x_1^2y_2^2 + x_2^2y_1^2 + 2x_1x_2y_1y_2} \\
&= \sqrt{x_1^2(x_2^2+y_2^2) + y_1^2(x_2^2+y_2^2)} = \sqrt{(x_2^2+y_2^2)(x_1^2+y_1^2)} = |z_1||z_2|
\end{aligned}$$

Alternatively, you can square to get $(z_1z_2)(z_1z_2)^* = z_1{z_1}^*z_2{z_2}^*$ which is true. For the triangle inequality after squaring we have $z_1z_2^* + z_2z_1^* \leq 2|z_1||z_2|$. But $z_1z_2^* + z_2z_1^* = 2\Re(z_1z_2^*)$ and by Proposition (2.9)(i), it is always less than $2|z_1z_2^*| = 2|z_1||z_2|$

(Q2.12) If we let $z_1 = x_1 + iy_1$ and $z_2 = x_2 + iy_2$ we get

$$\sqrt{(x_1+x_2)^2+(y_1+y_2)^2} = \sqrt{x_1^2+y_1^2} + \sqrt{x_2^2+y_2^2} \Rightarrow$$

$$\text{Squaring } 2x_1x_2 + 2y_1y_2 = 2\sqrt{(x_1^2+y_1^2)(x_2^2+y_2^2)} \Rightarrow$$

$$\text{Squaring again } 2x_1x_2y_1y_2 = x_1^2y_2^2 + y_1^2x_2^2 \Rightarrow (x_1y_2 - x_2y_1)^2 = 0$$

And the last equation implies $\dfrac{x_1}{x_2} = \dfrac{y_1}{y_2} = \lambda$ for some λ. And this means that $z_1 = \lambda z_2$.

(Q2.13) (i) $x = 5/49$, $y = -2\sqrt{6}/49$, (ii) $x = -2$, $y = 2$.

(Q2.14) The square root is $\pm(5+3i)$, and the solutions to the quadratic $6+3i$ and $-4-3i$.

(Q2.15) The square root is $\pm(5+4i)$. The roots are $9 \pm \sqrt{81-1681} = 9 \pm 40i$. Hence, $9+40i$ it is a root of the equation. Substituting $u^2 = 1/z$ we get $z^2 - 18z + 1681 = 0$. We already know the roots of this equation from the previous section. Hence $z = 9 \pm 40i$. The four solutions are $u = \pm\frac{\sqrt{9\mp 40i}}{41} = \pm\frac{5\mp 4i}{41}$.

(Q2.16) If we let $z = x+iy$, the relation to prove becomes $|x|+|y| \leq \sqrt{x^2+y^2}$. It is thus enough to show, (squaring) $x^2+y^2+2|x||y| \leq 2(x^2+y^2)$. This now can be written $0 \leq (|x|-|y|)^2$ which is true. Hence the original inequality holds.

(Q2.17) Since everything is positive, we can square the expression and write $(z_1 - z_2)(z_1^* - z_2^*) = (1 - z_1^* z_2)(1 - z_1 z_2^*)$. Expanding, simplifying and factorising we get $(1-|z_1|^2)(1-|z_2|^2) = 0$. Hence, either $|z_1| = 1$ or $|z_2| = 1$ or both.

(Q2.18) For A to be purely imaginary we have $A + A^* = 0 \Rightarrow \frac{z-i}{z+i} + \frac{z^*+i}{z^*-i} = 0$. Cross-multiplying and simplifying we get $2|z|^2 - 2 = 0 \Rightarrow |z| = 1$

(Q2.19) We would make use of the relation $z_1 = \lambda^2/z_1{}^*$ and $|z| = |z^*|$, etc. The LHS is

$$\left|\frac{\lambda^2 z_1}{z_2{}^*} + \frac{\lambda^2 z_2}{z_3{}^*} + \frac{\lambda^2 z_3}{z_1{}^*}\right| = \lambda^2 \left|\frac{z_1 z_1{}^* z_3{}^* + z_2 z_2{}^* z_1{}^* + z_3 z_3{}^* z_2{}^*}{z_1{}^* z_2{}^* z_3{}^*}\right| =$$

$$\lambda^2 \left|\frac{\lambda^2 z_3{}^* + \lambda^2 z_1{}^* + \lambda^2 z_2{}^*}{\lambda^3}\right| = \lambda |z_1 + z_2 + z_3|$$

(Q2.20) Squaring the expression (everything is positive) we get $(2z-1)(2z^*-1) = (z-2)(z^*-2)$. Expanding and simplifying we get $3|z|^2 = 3 \Rightarrow |z| = 1$.

(Q2.21) Induction is straightforward. For $n = 1$ holds by definition. Assume that it is true for $n = k$, $(z_1 + ... + z_k)^* = z_1^* + ... + z_k^*$. For $n = k+1$ we have $(z_1 + ... + z_{k+1})^* = (z_1 + ... z_k)^* + z_{k+1}^* = z_1{}^* + ... + z_{k+1}^*$. Hence it holds for any $n \in \mathbb{N}$. Similarly for the product.

(Q2.22) Multiplying S_n by i and subtracting from S_n we get $S_n(1-i) = 1 - i^{n+1}$, solving for $S_n = \frac{1-i^{n+1}}{1-i} = \frac{(1+i)(1-i^{n+1})}{(1-i)(1+i)} = \frac{1}{2}(1+i)(1-i^{n+1})$.

(Q2.23) Factorising $x^3 - 1 = (x-1)(x^2+x+1) = 0$. Roots are 1, $(-1 \pm \sqrt{3})/2$.

(Q2.24) Factorising $x^3 + 2^3 = (x+2)(x^2 - 2x + 4)$. Roots are -2, $1 \pm \sqrt{3}$.

(Q2.25) Using $|z|^2 = zz^*$ we get $(1 + z_1 z_2{}^*)(1 + z_1{}^* z_2) + (z_1 - z_2)(z_1{}^* - z_2{}^*)$ and after expanding, simplifying and factorising we get $(1 + |z_1|^2)(1 + |z_2|^2)$.

(Q2.26) $x = \pm\sqrt{3}/2$ and $y = \pm 1/2$.

(Q2.27) Squaring $z_1 + z_2 + z_3 = 0$ we get $z_1^2 + z_2^2 + z_3^2 + 2(z_1z_2 + z_2z_3 + z_3z_1) = 0$. It is enough to prove that $z_1z_2 + z_2z_3 + z_3z_1$ is zero. Since $|z_1| = 1$ we have $z_1 = 1/z_1{}^*$ etc. Substituting we get

$$\frac{z_1}{z_2{}^*} + \frac{z_2}{z_3{}^*} + \frac{z_3}{z_1{}^*} = \frac{|z_1|^2 z_3{}^* + |z_2|^2 z_1{}^* + |z_3|^2 z_2{}^*}{z_1{}^* z_2{}^* z_3{}^*} = \frac{z_1{}^* + z_2{}^* + z_3{}^*}{z_1{}^* z_2{}^* z_3{}^*} = 0$$

(Q2.28) Multiplying by z the relation $z^2 - z + 1 = 0$, ($z \neq 0$, since if it was, the relation would give 0=1), we get $z^3 = z^2 - z = -1$. We thus have $z^3 = -1$. For (i) we have that $2024 = 3 \cdot 674 + 2$ and $z_1^{3\cdot674+2} + z_2^{3\cdot674+2} = (-1)^{674} z_1^2 + (-1)^{674} z_2^2 = z_1^2 + z_2^2 = (z_1 + z_2)^2 - 2z_1 z_2$. The sum of the roots is $z_1 + z_2 = 1$ and the product is also $z_1 z_2 = 1$. Thus, $z_1^{2024} + z_2^{2024} = -1$. For (ii) we have $2022 = 3 \cdot 674$ and therefore $z_1^{3\cdot674} + z_2^{3\cdot674} = (-1)^{674} + (-1)^{674} = 2$. For the last part, we use the same reasoning. $z_1^{6k} + z_2^{6k} = 1 + 1 = 2$, $z_1^{6k+1} + z_2^{6k+1} = z_1 + z_2 = 1$, $z_1^{6k+2} + z_2^{6k+2} = z_1^2 + z_2^2 = -1$, $z_1^{6k+3} + z_2^{6k+3} = -1 - 1 = -2$, $z_1^{6k+4} + z_2^{6k+4} = -z_1 - z_2 = -1$ and $z_1^{6k+5} + z_2^{6k+5} = -z_1^2 - z_2^2 = 1$

(Q2.29) Let $z = a + ib$, then

$$z + 1/z = a + ib + \frac{a - ib}{a^2 + b^2} = a + \frac{a}{a^2 + b^2} + ib\left(1 - \frac{1}{a^2 + b^2}\right)$$

For this number to be real we must have either $b = 0$ in which case z is real or $a^2 + b^2 = 1$ in which case $|z| = 1$.

(Q2.30) Forming $1 + t^2 = 1 + \frac{(-x + iy)^2}{(x + iy)^2} = \frac{2(x^2 - y^2)}{(x + iy)^2}$. Dividing by $2t = 2\frac{-x + iy}{x + iy}$ we get $\frac{1 + t^2}{2t} = \frac{x^2 - y^2}{(x + iy)(-x + iy)} = \frac{y^2 - x^2}{x^2 + y^2}$.

(Q2.31) It is enough to prove that $E^* = E$. Since $z_1{}^* + z_2{}^* = \lambda^2 \frac{z_1 + z_2}{z_1 z_2}$. we have

$$E^* = \frac{(z_1{}^* + z_2{}^*)...(z_n{}^* + z_1{}^*)}{z_1{}^*...z_n{}^*} = \frac{(\lambda^2)^n \left(\frac{z_1+z_2}{z_1 z_2}\right)...\left(\frac{z_n+z_1}{z_n z_1}\right)}{z_1{}^*...z_n{}^*}$$
$$= \frac{\lambda^{2n}(z_1 + z_2)(z_2 + z_3)...(z_n + z_1)}{(z_1^2 z_2^2...z_n^2)(z_1{}^*...z_n{}^*)} = \frac{\lambda^{2n}(z_1 + z_2)(z_2 + z_3)...(z_n + z_1)}{(|z_1|^2|z_2|^2...|z_n|^2)(z_1 z_2...z_n)} = E$$

(Q2.32) Since all the c_i are inside the disc or radius l we must have $|c_i| < l$. Taking the modulus of the expression we have $0 < k = |c_1 z + c_2 z^2 + ... + c_n z^n| = k$. Using the triangular inequality for n-terms we get

$$0 < k = |c_1 z + c_2 z^2 + ... + c_n z^n| \leq |c_1 z| + |c_2 z^2| + ... + |c_n z^n| < l(|z| + |z|^2 + ...|z|^n) = l|z|\frac{1 - |z|^n}{1 - |z|}$$

This implies that $k - k|z| < l|z| - l|z|^{n+1} \Rightarrow l|z|^{n+1} < (l + k)|z| - k$ and since both l and $|z|^{n+1}$ are positive we must have $|z| > k/(l + k)$.

(Q2.33) Polynomials with real coefficients have complex conjugate roots. Hence the other root is $2 + 3i$. From Vieta, the sum of the roots is $-p = 4$ and the product $q = 2^2 + 3^2 = 13$. Thus the equation is $x^2 - 4x + 13 = 0$.

(Q2.34) Since we know one complex root $3 + i$, and the cubic has real coefficients the other root is $3 - i$. As we know the coefficient of z in the cubic we can use the Vieta, to find the third root r. So $40 = r(3 + i) + (3 - i)(3 + i) + r(3 - i) \Rightarrow r = 5$. We now have all the roots and we can find $-q = 5 \cdot 10 = 50$. Also $-p = 11$. So the equation is $z^3 - 11z^2 + 40z - 50 = 0$.

(Q2.35) You can substitute the given root or do the polynomial division. $c = 20 + 35i$ and the other root is $-5/2 + 5i$.

(Q2.36) $(-1 \pm \sqrt{2})/2$ and $(1 \pm i\sqrt{2})/2$

(Q2.37) $\pm 2i$

(Q2.38) Enough to show that expression plus its conjugate is zero. Namely, $\frac{z - |z|}{z + |z|} + \frac{z^* - |z|}{z^* + |z|} = 0$. The numerator becomes $zz^* + z|z| - z^*|z| - |z|^2 + zz^* - z|z| + |z|z^* - |z|^2 = 0$. Hence it is real.

(Q2.39) The other root is the conjugate $3 - i$. Using the Vieta, the sum of the roots is $8 = -a$.

The product of the roots is $20 = -c$. Plugging $x = 2$ we get that $b = 2$.
(Q2.40) The other root is $16+30i$, and $a = -32, b = 1156$. We have that the roots must be given by $y^2 = 16 \pm 30i$. The answer is $y = \pm(5 \pm 3i)$.
(Q2.41) (i) Roots are $3+i$ and $1+2i$. (ii) Since one root x is real then we get $x^3 - 5x^2 - 3ix^2 + 5x + 10ix = 1 + 7i$. Comparing real an imaginary we have $3x^2 - 10x + 7 = 0$ and $x^3 - 5x^2 + 5x - 1 = 0$. The only common solution of these is $x = 1$ (we discard all others). So $(z-1)$ is a factor and we can perform the polynomial division to get $(z-1)(z^2 - (4+3i)z + (1+7i)) = 0$. Hence the other two roots are the results of part (i).
(Q2.42) $-1, i$.
(Q2.43) The inequality becomes

$$(z_1 + z_2)(z_1{}^* + z_2{}^*) \le z_1 z_1{}^* + \lambda z_1 z_1{}^* + \frac{1}{\lambda} z_2 z_2{}^* + z_2{}^* z_2$$

Taking everything on the RHS we get $0 \le \frac{1}{\lambda}|z_2 - \lambda z_1|^2$ which is true.
(Q2.44) $2-i, 1+2i$.
(Q2.45) Roots are $2i, -2i, 2, -2$. $w = z/(1+z)$ and hence $w = \{2, 2/3, (4 \pm 2i)/5\}$.
(Q2.46) This is the Pythagorean theorem. For the expression to be purely imaginary we must have $\frac{b-c}{a-c} + \frac{b^* - c^*}{a^* - c^*} = 0$. The numerator of this is exactly the given relation when you expand it.
(Q2.47) Let x be the real root. Then we must have $x^3 + 10x^2 - 4ix^2 - 8x - 46ix + 108i - 32 = 0$. Since $x \in \mathbb{R}$ we can split the real and imaginary parts. For the imaginary part we obtain $4x^2 + 46x - 108 = 0$ which has roots $x = 2$ and $x = -27/3$. The real part is $x^3 + 10x^2 - 8x - 32 = 0$ and we can verify that $x = 2$ is also a root but not $x = -27/3$. Hence $z = 2$ is the real solution. Performing the polynomial division with $z - 2$ we now get $z^2 + (12 - 4i)z + 16 - 54 = 0$. The roots of this equation are $2i - 6 \pm \sqrt{16+30i}$. But $\sqrt{16+30i} = 5+3i$. Hence the other two roots are $5i - 1$ and $-(11+i)$.

Answers to Sec. 3.4, page 41

(Q3.1) The distance from the origin is the the modulus

$$|z| = \left|\frac{-1+i\sqrt{63}}{8}\right|^{2024} = \left(\frac{|-1+i\sqrt{63}|}{8}\right)^{2024} = \left(\frac{8}{8}\right)^{2024} = 1$$

(Q3.2) $|z| = 3\sqrt{5}$, $\text{Arg}(z) = 0.46$ radians. $\arctan\frac{8}{\mu+6} = \pi/4 \Rightarrow 8 = \mu + 6$. hence $\mu = 2$.
(Q3.3) We have, (1) $4(\cos\pi/3 + i\sin\pi/3)$, (2) $\sqrt{8}(\cos(-\pi/6) + i\sin(-\pi/6))$, (3) $\sqrt{2}(\cos(3\pi/4) + i\sin(3\pi/4))$, (4) $\sqrt{2}(\cos(-\pi/4) + i\sin(-\pi/4))$, (5) $\sqrt{8}(\cos 105^o + i\sin 105^o)$, (6) $\cos(-\pi/3) + i\sin(-\pi/3)$.
(Q3.4) Starting from z we have

$$z = \frac{(1+it)^2}{(1+it)(1-it)} = \frac{1-t^2+2it}{1+t^2} = \frac{1-t^2}{1+t^2} + i\frac{2t}{1+t^2} = \cos\theta + i\sin\theta$$

(Q3.5) Let $z = x + iy$, then $\text{Arg}(z + z^*) = \text{Arg}(2x)$. The argument of a real number would be zero only if it is positive $\Re(x) > 0$, whereas if $x < 0$ it would be π.

(Q3.6) Since $|z| = 1$ we can let $z = \cos\theta + i\sin\theta$. Then

$$\begin{aligned}\frac{1}{1-z} &= \frac{1}{1-\cos\theta - i\sin\theta} = \frac{1-\cos\theta + i\sin\theta}{(1-\cos\theta)^2 + \sin^2\theta} = \frac{1-\cos\theta + i\sin\theta}{2-2\cos\theta}\\ &= \frac{1}{2} + i\frac{\sin\theta}{2(1-\cos\theta)} = \frac{1}{2} + \frac{i}{2}\cot\frac{\theta}{2}\end{aligned}$$

Hence $\mathfrak{Re}\,\frac{1}{1-z} = \frac{1}{2}$.
(Q3.7) $|z_1 - 2z_2| = 13$, $\text{Arg}(z_1 - 2z_2) = 67.3^o$.
(Q3.8) $a = 2\sqrt{2}$, $b = -\sqrt{5}$, $|z_1 - z_2| = 5$.
(Q3.9) Roots are $2, -1 \pm \sqrt{3}$. They are the vertices of an equilateral triangle.

Answers to Sec. 3.12, page 72

(Q3.10) $(5+i)^2 = 24 + 10i$. And the argument of $\arg(5+i)^2 = 2\arg(5+i) = 2\arctan\frac{1}{5}$. On the other hand $\arg(24+10i) = \arctan\frac{10}{24} = \arctan\frac{5}{12}$. Thus $\arctan\frac{1}{5} = \frac{1}{2}\arctan\frac{5}{12}$.
(Q3.11) The slope of a lines with equation $A_1 z + {A_1}^* z^* + B_1 = 0$ and $A_2 z + {A_2}^* z^* + B_2 = 0$ are $m_1 = i\frac{A_1 + {A_1}^*}{A_1 - {A_1}^*}$ and $m_2 = i\frac{A_2 + {A_2}^*}{A_2 - {A_2}^*}$ respectively. Using $m_1 m_2 = -1$ we get the required relation.
(Q3.12) We can replace x_1 with $(z_1 + {z_1}^*)/2$ and y_1 with $(z_1 - {z_1}^*)/(2i)$ etc in the determinant to get

$$A = \frac{1}{2}\begin{vmatrix} \frac{z_1 + {z_1}^*}{2} & \frac{z_1 - {z_1}^*}{2i} & 1 \\ \frac{z_2 + {z_2}^*}{2} & \frac{z_2 - {z_2}^*}{2i} & 1 \\ \frac{z_3 + {z_3}^*}{2} & \frac{z_3 - {z_3}^*}{2i} & 1 \end{vmatrix} = \frac{1}{8i}\begin{vmatrix} z_1 + {z_1}^* & z_1 - {z_1}^* & 1 \\ z_2 + {z_2}^* & z_2 - {z_1}^* & 1 \\ z_3 + {z_3}^* & z_3 - {z_3}^* & 1 \end{vmatrix} = \frac{1}{8i}\begin{vmatrix} 2z_1 & z_1 - {z_1}^* & 1 \\ 2z_2 & z_2 - {z_1}^* & 1 \\ 2z_3 & z_3 - {z_3}^* & 1 \end{vmatrix} =$$

$$\frac{1}{4i}\begin{vmatrix} z_1 & z_1 - {z_1}^* & 1 \\ z_2 & z_2 - {z_1}^* & 1 \\ z_3 & z_3 - {z_3}^* & 1 \end{vmatrix} = \frac{1}{4i}\begin{vmatrix} z_1 & z_1 & 1 \\ z_2 & z_2 & 1 \\ z_3 & z_3 & 1 \end{vmatrix} + \frac{1}{4i}\begin{vmatrix} z_1 & -{z_1}^* & 1 \\ z_2 & -{z_1}^* & 1 \\ z_3 & -{z_3}^* & 1 \end{vmatrix} = \frac{i}{4}\begin{vmatrix} z_1 & {z_1}^* & 1 \\ z_2 & {z_1}^* & 1 \\ z_3 & {z_3}^* & 1 \end{vmatrix}$$

where we used the properties of the determinants to factor out common numbers per column, to add one column into another column and to split determinants.
(Q3.13) Let the centre of our unit circle be the origin of the Argand plane. We know that the tangents to the points A and B are perpendicular to radii. Hence, for the point A we have $\frac{p-a}{a} + \frac{p^*-a^*}{a^*} = 0$ and for the point B, $\frac{p-b}{b} + \frac{p^*-b^*}{b^*} = 0$. Since it is a unit circle we also have $aa^* = 1 = bb^*$. Using these, the equations simplify to $pa^* + p^*a = 2$ and $pb^* + p^*b = 2$. Solving for p we get $p = 2ab/(a+b)$.
(Q3.14) The first part is done in Exercise (3.12). For the second part we need to solve the system $a + b - abp^* = p = c + d - cdp^*$. If $ab = cd$ the two chords are parallel.
(Q3.15) If we multiply the given relation by z_1 (or z_2) we get $z_1^3 + z_1 z_2^2 = z_1^2 z_2 = (z_1 z_2 - z_2^2)z_2 \Rightarrow z_1^3 = -z_2^3$. Taking modulus of the last equation we have $|z_1| = |z_2|$. To prove that the triangle is equilateral it is enough to prove that $|z_1 - z_2| = |z_1| = |z_2|$. Let $|z_1| = |z_2| = \lambda$. We then have $|z_1 - z_2|^2 = |z_1|^2 + |z_2|^2 - {z_1}^* z_2 - {z_2}^* z_1 = 2\lambda^2 - \lambda^2\frac{z_1}{z_2} - \lambda^2\frac{z_2}{z_1} = 2\lambda^2 - \lambda^2\frac{z_1^2 + z_2^2}{z_1 z_2} = 2\lambda^2 - \lambda^2 = \lambda^2$. Therefore $|z_1 - z_2| = \lambda$ and the triangle is equilateral.

(Q3.16) Let the vertices of the quadrilateral be represented by the complex numbers a, b, c and d. Then the point M is represented by $(a+b)/2$ and N has $(b+c)/2$. Hence $MN = (b+c)/2 - (a+b)/2 = (c-a)/2$. Similarly, P is represented by $(c+d)/2$ and Q by $(a+d)/2$ and QP by $c+d-a-d)/2 = (c-a)/2$. Since $MN = QP$, $MNPQ$ is a parallelogram.
(Q3.17) This is another example of a question that is easy to do with complex numbers. We need to move around the diagram and find the complex coordinates of the points K, N and M. If we pick is our origin the point A then in order to go to the point N we need to go half way to the side AC and then turn anticlockwise by 90 degrees and travel again half AC. Doing the same for the other points we get

$$\text{Point N: } \frac{c}{2} + i\frac{c}{2}$$

$$\text{Point K: } \frac{b}{2} - i\frac{c}{2}$$

$$\text{Point M: } \frac{c+b}{2}$$

We therefore have that $KM = \frac{c+b}{2} - \frac{b}{2} + i\frac{b}{2} = \frac{c+ib}{2}$ and $NM = \frac{c+b}{2} - \frac{c}{2} - i\frac{c}{2}$ and the ratio

$$\frac{KM}{NM} = \frac{c+bi}{b-ic} = i$$

Hence the two line are perpendicular as the ratio is purely imaginary number.
(Q3.18) Since the three triangles are similar we must have

$$\frac{a-p_1}{b-p_1} = \frac{b-p_2}{c-p_2} = \frac{a-p_3}{c-p_3}$$

We need to show that $P_1P_3 = BP_2$ or $p_3 - p_1 = p_2 - b$. Solving the first and the third for

$$p_1 = \frac{a(b-c) + p_3(a-b)}{a-c} \qquad \Rightarrow p_3 - p_1 = \frac{(c-b)(a-p_3)}{a-c}$$

Solving now the second and third for

$$p_2 = \frac{(b-a)c + p_3(c-b)}{c-a} \qquad \Rightarrow p_2 - b = \frac{(c-b)(a-p_3)}{a-c} = p_3 - p_1$$

Hence $P_1BP_2P_3$ is a parallelogram.
(Q3.19) The angle between the sides Z_2Z_3 and Z_1Z_2 is the argument of the complex number $1/2 + i\sqrt{3}2$ which is $\pi/3$. Since the modulus is also 1 we have that $|z_3 - z_2| = |z_1 - z_2|$ and so the triangle is equilateral as two sides are equal and the in-between angle is 60 degrees.
(Q3.20) Forming the determinant (or using any other condition),

$$\begin{vmatrix} 1 & 1+i & 1 \\ 3+3i & 7-3i & 1 \\ 4+4i & 9-5i & 1 \end{vmatrix} = 0$$

(Q3.21) For the first part you need to show that $AB = DC \Rightarrow b-a = c-d$ then $ABCD$ is a parallelogram. The diagonals are always perpendicular and equal in a square. Hence we must have $\frac{d-b}{c-a} = i$. Conversely, if the condition holds then by taking the modulus we find that the diagonal are equal and hence a square. For the next part, the midpoint of PQ is $(p+q)/2$ and from that point to reach the centre of the square we need to move anticlockwise by 90 degrees (namely i) by $(p-q)/2$. So finally point X is represented by $(p+q)/2 + i(p-q)2$. For the next part, using what we have from the first part to be a square must be a parallelogram, so $x+z = y+t$ and also $i(x-z) = y-t$. The condition $x+z = y+t \Rightarrow p-q = s-r$ and this implies it is a parallelogram. Substituting $y = (r+q)/2 + i(q-r)/2$, $z = (s+r)/2 + i(r-s)/2$

and $t = (s+p)/2 + i(s-p)/2$ into $i(x-z) = y-t$, we find that it is satisfied. Hence, if $PQRS$ is a parallelogram, $XYZT$ is a square.
(Q3.22) Since the triangle is isosceles and right-angled at z_2 we must have that $z_1 - z_2 = i(z_3 - z_2)$ (the two sides are equal and perpendicular). Squaring, $z_1^2 + z_2^2 - 2z_1z_2 = -(z_2^2 + z_3^2 - 2z_3z_2) \Rightarrow z_1^2 + 2z_2^2 + z_3^2 = 2z_2(z_1 + z_3)$.
(Q3.23) The point Q can be reached from O by adding OP to PQ. But PQ is just $OP = 2$ rotated anticlockwise by $\pi/6$. Hence $q = 2 + 2(\cos\pi/6 + i\sin\pi/6) = 2 + \sqrt{3} + i$. We can repeat the process to find the point R which is PQ rotated by $\pi/6$ plus the point Q. $r = 2 + \sqrt{3} + i + (\sqrt{3} + i)(\sqrt{3}/2 + i/2) = 3 + \sqrt{3} + i(1 + \sqrt{3}$. Now the point S is RQ rotated again by $\pi/6$ plus r. Hence $s = 3 + \sqrt{3} + i(1 + \sqrt{3}) + (1 + i\sqrt{3})(\sqrt{3}/2 + i/2) = (3 + \sqrt{3})(1 + i)$. From the geometry of the regular polygon we see that for C to reach the real axis. it must be rotated by 105 degrees or $7\pi/12$. So, the new point S has $s' = (3 + \sqrt{3})(1 + i)e^{i7\pi/12}$. To get to the answer we need to convert $1 + i = \sqrt{2}e^{i\pi/4}$. So $s' = (3 + \sqrt{3})\sqrt{2}e^{i(\pi/4 + 7\pi/12)} = (3\sqrt{2} + \sqrt{6})e^{i5\pi/6} = (3\sqrt{2} + \sqrt{6})(-\sqrt{3}/2 + i/2)$.

(Q3.24) Using any of the conditions for concyclic points we can verify this. For example $\angle CBA$ has argument $\arg\frac{z+1}{2}$ and angle $\angle CDA$ has argument $\arg(z+1)$ The two are equal since $\arg(z+)/2 = \arg(1/2) + \arg(z+1) = \arg(z+1)$ as the argument of a positive real number is zero.
(Q3.25) Using Prop (3.16) with $\theta = \pi/2$, we can write the points as

$$z_2 = a + (z_1 - a)i, \quad z_3 = b + (z_2 - b)i, \quad z_4 = c + (z_3 - c)i, \quad z_5 = d + (z_4 - d)i$$

After some algebra and equating $z_5 = z_1$ you will get $(c + d - b - a) + i(c - d - a + b) = 0 \Rightarrow (c-a)(1+i) + (b-d)(i-i) = 0$. So finally $a - c = -(b-d)\frac{1-i}{1+i} = (b-d)i$. For the next part, lets represent the points A, B, C that are on a circle by $e^{i\alpha}$, $e^{i\beta}$ and $e^{i\gamma}$ and repeating the same procedure but this time by an angle θ, namely $e^{i\theta}$ you will find

$$z_4 = z_1e^{3i\theta} + (1 - e^{i\theta})\left[e^{i\gamma} + e^{i(\alpha+2\theta} + e^{\beta+\theta}\right]$$

For z_4 to coincide with z_1 we must have either the trivial solution $\theta = 2k\pi$ or $\theta = 2k\pi/3$ and $\left[e^{i\gamma} + e^{i(\alpha+2k\pi/3} + e^{\beta+2k\pi/3}\right] = 0$.
(Q3.26) Multiplying out we get $(k + l + i)(k^2 + kl + 1 + il) = k(k^2 + 2kl + l^2 + 1) + i(k^2 + 2kl + l^2 + 1)$. Taking the argument we have the required result. Let $k = 1$ and $l = 4$ for the last part.

Answers to Sec. 4.6, page 86

(Q4.1) The equation of the circle is $|z - z_0|^2 = R^2 \Rightarrow (z - z_0)(z^* - z_0^*) = |z|^2 + |z_0|^2 - (z_0z^* + zz_0^*) = R^2$. But $\Re(z^*z_0) = \dfrac{1}{2}(z^*z_0 + zz_0^*)$.
(Q4.2) Circle with centre $(0,1)$ and radius $\sqrt{2}$.
(Q4.3) letting $z = x + iy$ in $z^2 + (z^*)^2 = 2$ we get $x^2 - y^2 + 2ixy + x^2 - y^2 - 2ixy = 2 \Rightarrow x^2 - y^2 = 1$.
(Q4.4) Circle with center $z_0 = \sqrt{3} + i$ and radius 2. Ray line through zero at an angle $\pi/6$ with respect to real axis.
(Q4.5) Circle with center $z_0 = 2i$ and radius 2. Perpendicular bisector to the segment joining -1 and -i. Equation $y = x$. Points of intersection $(0,0)$, $(1,1)$.
(Q4.6) Circle with center zero and radius 2. Ray line with slope $\tan\pi/3 = \sqrt{3}$, $y = \sqrt{3}x$. Points of intersection $x = 1, y = \sqrt{3}$. The other points of intersection are not on the ray line.
(Q4.7) The equation of the point z is $|z - a| = R$. Letting $w = 1/z$ we get $|1/w - a| = R \Rightarrow$

$|1-wa| = R|w|$. If we factor $|a|$ out we get $|a||1/a - w| = R|w|$. Hence $|1/a - w| = \frac{R}{|a|}|w|$. But this is the Apollonian circle if $\frac{R}{|a|} \neq 1$ and a line if $\frac{R}{|a|} = 1$ that is the perpendicular bisector of the segment joining $1/a$ and the origin.

(Q4.8) The locus is a circle of radius 3. $|z+a| \leq |z| + |a| = 3 + \sqrt{26}$ whereas the minimum is $-3+\sqrt{26}$.

(Q4.9) We can re-write the condition as $\arg \frac{z_1 - z_2}{z_1 + z_2} = \pi/2$. This means that is purely imaginary and therefore $\frac{z_1-z_2}{z_1+z_2} + \frac{z_1{}^* - z_2{}^*}{z_1{}^* + z_2{}^*} = 0$. Cross multiplying we find that $|z_1| = |z_2|$. This is the condition for a rhombus.

(Q4.10) Apollonian circle $4x^2 + 4y^2 + 9y + x + 4 = 0$, $x = 1/4, y = -3/4$ and $x = -1/2, y = -3/2$.

(Q4.11) Locus is a circle with centre $1-i$ and radius $\sqrt{2}$. The shaded region is a circular ring between radii of 1 and $\sqrt{2}$.

(Q4.12) C_1 is a circle centred at $z = 3$ and radius 3. C_2 is a ray line starting at $z = 1$ at an angle of 45 degrees and heading north-east. The shaded region is the cross-section of the circle with the ray-line and the real axis (boundary included).

(Q4.13) Let $z = x + iy$ and $A = a + bi$ with $x, y, a, b \in \mathbb{R}$. If $\lambda \neq 0$ the given equation after completing the square becomes $(x + a/\lambda)^2 + (y - b/\lambda)^2 = (a^2 + b^2 - \mu\lambda)/\lambda^2$. This is a circle only if the radius is positive, namely $|A| = a^2 + b^2 > \mu\lambda$. When $\lambda = 0$ then it degenerates into a line $2ax + 2by + \mu = 0$.

(Q4.14) C_1 is the perpendicular bisector of the segment between the origin and $y = 4$. Hence the equation of the line is $y = 2$. C_2 is the ray-line emanating from the origin, at an angle of $\pi/6$ and heading north-east. $y = x/\sqrt{3}$. The intersection is at $2\sqrt{3} + 2i$.

(Q4.15) (i) $|a| = 5$ and $\arg z = \arctan 4/3 = 71.5^o$, (ii) locus is a circle, centred at $3+4i$ with radius 5, (iii) locus is a ray line starting from $z = 3$ and heading north-east at an angle of 71.5^o.

(Q4.16) Let $z = x+iy$. For the expression to be purely imaginary the real part must be zero. Hence, $x^2 + x + y^2 - y = 0 \Rightarrow (x+1/2)^2 + (y-1/2)^2 = 1/2$. This is a circle, centred at $(1/2, -1/2)$ with radius $1/\sqrt{2}$.

(Q4.17) The roots are $\pm(\sqrt{5/2} + i/\sqrt{2})$. The four roots of the quartic are $\pm(\sqrt{5/2} + i/\sqrt{2})$ and $\pm(\sqrt{5/2} - i/\sqrt{2})$. For part(iv), it is the perpendicular bisector of the segment between the origin and $a = \sqrt{5/2} + i/\sqrt{2}$.

(Q4.18) (1a) The locus is the perpendicular bisector to the segment with endpoints 0 and 8. Thus the locus is the line $x = 4$. (1b) The locus is the ray-line emanating from $-2i$ in the North-East direction at an angle of $\pi/4$. (ii) Shaded area is the triangle bounded by the $x = 4$, the ray-line and the $y = -2$ horizontal line.

(Q4.19) (i) $|a| = 2$, $\arg a = \pi/3$, (ii) $|z-a| = |a| = 2$ is a circle with centre $a = 1 + i\sqrt{3}$ and radius 2. The locus of $\arg(z-a) = \pi/2 \Rightarrow \frac{y-\sqrt{3}}{x-1} = \infty \Rightarrow x = 1$ is the perpendicular ray-line at $x = 1$ emanating from $1 + i\sqrt{3}$ and heading North.

(Q4.20) C_1 is a circle centred at $3+4i$ and radius 4. It is just touching the x-axis at $x = 3$. C_2 is the perpendicular bisector of the segment with end-points 0 and $8i$. Thus, it is the horizontal line $y = 4$. Intersection is at $y = 4, x = -1$ and $y = 4, x = 7$. The shaded region is bounded by the $y \geq 4$ and circle (including boundaries). It is thus the top-semicircle.

(Q4.21) $z = 2$ is the perpendicular line at $x = 2$. $\arg(z - (3+i)) = \pi$ is the ray-line starting from $3+i$ and heading West. It is just the horizontal semi-line from $3+i$. The shaded region is bounded by the $x \leq 2$ (left side of $x = 2$) and $y \geq 1$.

(Q4.22) C_1 is a ray-line starting at $2+2i$ and heading North-East at an angle of $\pi/4$. C_2 is the line $x = 5$ which is the perpendicular bisector of the segment with endpoints 0 and 10. The shaded region is bounded by the lower part of the ray-line, the right of the $x = 5$ line and the horizontal ray-line starting at $y = 2, x = 2$.

(Q4.23) C_1 is a circle, centred at $x=-2$ and radius 2, touching the imaginary axis. C_2 is the ray-line emanating from $x=-2$ and heading North-West at an angle of $5\pi/6$ to the horizontal positive axis. The equation of the ray-line is $y=-(x+2)/\sqrt{3}$. Substituting we find two solutions. Only one is North-West, $-2-\sqrt{3}+i$. The shaded region is the pie bounded by the circle and the two ray-lines emanating from $x=-2$ and with angles π and $5\pi/6$.
(Q4.24) The centre of the circle is the mid-point of the given points, hence $3+3i$. The radius is half the distance $r=|AB|/2=\sqrt{20}/2=\sqrt{5}$. The equation of the circle is $|z-(3+3i)|=\sqrt{5}$. The equation of l is $y=9-2x$ and the points of intersection are $2+5i$ and $4+i$.
(Q4.25) (ia) is a circle centred at $1+i$ and radius 2. (ib) Since $\Re z=1$, we have $z=1+iy$. The locus is the line segment on the line $x=1$ between the points $1+i$ and $1-\sqrt{3}$ which represent the cross section of the $\tan(-\pi/3)\le \arctan z\le \pi/4$. The maximum z for (ia) is $|z|=|z-(1+i)+(1+i)|\le|z-(1+i)|+|1+i|=2+\sqrt{2}$. Maximum for (ib) is $|z|=\sqrt{1+y^2}=\sqrt{1+3}=2$.
(ii) $w=u+iv$. Hence $z=w^2\Rightarrow x=u^2-v^2, y=2uv$. If the point z moves on a circle with $x^2+y^2=16$ then $u^4+v^4-2u^2v^2+4u^2v^2=16\Rightarrow(u^2+v^2)^2=16\Rightarrow u^2+v^2=4$. Hence, Q lies on a circle with radius 2.
(Q4.26) The imaginary part of $\mathrm{Im}(z/(1+z^2))=-y(x^2+y^2-1)$ and it is zero on a circle $x^2+y^2=1$. For the second part look at Prop. (3.14).
(Q4.27) $z=4+e^{2ki\pi/3}$, $k=0,1,2$. The three roots are $z_1=6$, $z_2=3+i\sqrt{3}$, $z_2=3-i\sqrt{3}$ and the modulus is 6,12 and 12. For $k=1$ the equation is $x=4$, and for $k=3$ the equation is $x^2+y^2-9x+18=0$. The equation is $(k^2-1)x^2+(k^2-1)y^2+16k^2-8k^2x=0$, the $z=3$ is on $k=3$ and the other two are on $k=\sqrt{3}$.
(Q4.28) $|z_1-z_2|=|z_2-z_3|=|z_1-z_3|=4\sqrt{3}$ hence the triangle is equilateral. $z_1^2=-16=z_2z_3$.
(iii) the equation is $x^2+(y-4)^2=16$. Since you know the points you can find the cross-point of the two perpendicular bisectors which the centre of the circle. Another way is to use the 4×4 determinant

$$\begin{vmatrix} x^2+y^2 & x & y & 1\\ x_1^2+y_1^2 & x_1 & y_1 & 1\\ x_2^2+y_2^2 & x_2 & y_2 & 1\\ x_3^2+y_3^2 & x_3 & y_3 & 1\end{vmatrix}=0$$

Yet another is to use the condition that the sum of opposite angles in a cyclic quadrilateral with complex vertices z, z_1, z_2, z_3 is π, namely Corollary (3.3). Finally (iv) the locus is the is the semicircle with diamter the points z_1 and z_2. See Theorem (4.4).
(Q4.29) See Theorem (4.4).
(Q4.30) This is a smart question. You can replace $z=x+iy$ and do the messy algebra. However, there is a fast way. Just complete the square

$$0=|z-2|^2+|z-2|-2=|z-2|^2+2\frac{1}{2}|z-2|+\frac{1}{4}-\frac{1}{4}\Rightarrow$$

$$\left(|z-2|+\frac{1}{2}\right)^2=\frac{9}{4}\Rightarrow|z-2|+\frac{1}{2}=\frac{3}{2}\Rightarrow|z-2|=1$$

And this is a circle center 2 and radius 1. For the next part $|z|=|z-2+2|\le|z-2|+2=3$. The last part is the tricky one. Obviously, you need to use the fact that $|a|,|b|,|c|$ are less than 3. If we solve for w^3 and take the absolute value we get $|w|^3=|aw^2+bw+c|\le|a||w|^2+|b||w|+|c|\le 3(|w|^2+|w|+1)$. We can re-write the last part as $|w|^3\le 3\frac{|w|^3-1}{|w|-1}$. We now can distinguish two cases, either $|w|\le1$ or $|w|>1$. If $|w|\le1$ there is nothing more to do as this is less than 4. If on the other hand $|w|>1$ then $|w|^3\le3\frac{|w|^3-1}{|w|-1}<3\frac{|w|^3}{|w|-1}\Rightarrow|w|^3(|w|-4)<0$ and the last condition implies that $|w|<4$.

(Q4.31) Letting $z = x+iy$ we get $x+y = 1/a$ and $x-y = a$. Multiplying them we get $x^2-y^2 = 1$ which is the equation of a hyperbola.
(Q4.32) (i) Apollonian circle $4x^2 + 4y^2 + 9x - y + 4 = 0$, (ii) Since it is real, it is equal to its complex conjugate $\frac{z+i}{z+1} = \frac{z^*-i}{z^*+1}$. Setting $z = x+iy$ we find the equation of the line $x+y+1 = 0$.

Answers to Sec. 5.3, page 106

(Q5.1) See Prop (5.1)
(Q5.2) We have

$$
\begin{aligned}
z^{-1} &= \frac{1}{1-(\cos\theta + i\sin\theta)} = \frac{1}{1-(1-2\sin^2\theta/2 + 2i\sin\theta/2\cos\theta/2)} \\
&= \frac{1}{2\sin\theta/2(\sin\theta/2 - i\cos\theta/2)} = \frac{\sin\theta/2 + i\cos\theta/2}{2\sin\theta/2} = \frac{1}{2} + i\cot\theta/2
\end{aligned}
$$

For the second part we have that

$$z^n = (2\sin^2\theta/2 - 2\sin\theta/2\cos\theta/2)^n = 2^n\sin^n\theta/2(\sin\theta/2 - i\cos\theta/2)^n$$

If we factor $(-i)$ from the brackets we get

$$z^n = 2^n(-i)^n\sin^n\theta/2(\cos\theta/2 + i\sin\theta/2)^n = 2^n(-i)^n\sin^n\theta/2(\cos n\theta/2 + i\sin n\theta/2)$$

(Q5.3) Writing $\tan\theta = \frac{\sin\theta}{\cos\theta}$ we get

$$\left(\frac{\cos\theta + i\sin\theta}{\cos\theta - i\sin\theta}\right)^n = \frac{\cos n\theta + i\sin n\theta}{\cos(-n\theta) + i\sin(-n\theta)} = \frac{1+i\tan n\theta}{1-i\tan n\theta}.$$

(Q5.4) Since $|z| = 1$ we can write $z = \cos\theta + i\sin\theta$ and $z - z^{-1} = 2i\sin\theta \Rightarrow (z-z^{-1})^2 = -4\sin^2\theta = -3$. We thus have $\theta = \pi/3, 2\pi/3$ or $\theta = -\pi/3, 4\pi/3$ and $z^3 + z^{-3} = 2\cos 3\theta = \pm 2$.
(Q5.5) The roots are $z_{1,2} = 3(1 \pm i\sqrt{3})$ or $z_{1,2} = 6(\cos\pi/3 \pm i\sin\pi/3)$. Hence, $z^{-3} = -6^{-3}$.
(Q5.6) We can re-write the given relation as $1+xz+(xz)^2+...+(xz)^{n-1}$ where $z = \cos\theta + i\sin\theta$. This is a geometric series and the sum is equal to

$$
\begin{aligned}
1 + xz + (xz)^2 + ... + (xz)^{n-1} &= \frac{1-(xz)^n}{1-xz} = \frac{1-x^n(\cos n\theta + i\sin n\theta)}{(1-x\cos\theta + ix\sin\theta} \\
&= \frac{[1-x^n\cos n\theta - ix^n\sin n\theta][(1-x\cos\theta) - i\sin\theta]}{(1-x\cos\theta)^2 + x^2\sin^2\theta}
\end{aligned}
$$

Comparing the real and imaginary parts we get the required result. For the last part, as $|x| < 1$ when taking the limit as $\lim_{n\to\infty} x^n = 0$. Hence the required results.
(Q5.7) $(\cos\theta + i\sin\theta)^5 = \cos 5\theta + i\sin 5\theta$ we have

$$
\begin{aligned}
&\cos^5\theta + 5\cos^4\theta(i\sin\theta) + 10\cos^3\theta(i\sin\theta)^2 + \\
&10\cos^2\theta(i\sin\theta)^3 + 5\cos\theta(i\sin\theta)^4 + (i\sin\theta)^5 = \cos 5\theta + i\sin 5\theta
\end{aligned}
$$

and comparing imaginary parts we get, $\sin 5\theta = \sin\theta(5\cos^4\theta - 10\cos^2\theta\sin^2\theta + \sin^4\theta)$, which becomes the required result after substituting for $\sin^2\theta = 1-\cos^2\theta$. If we let $\theta = \pi/5$, then $\sin 5\pi/5 = 0$ and therefore $\cos^2\pi/5$ is the root of the equation $16\cos^4\pi/5 - 12\cos^2\pi/5 + 1 = 0$. This is a quadratic in $\cos^2\pi/5$ and the roots are $\cos^2\pi/5 = \frac{6\pm\sqrt{20}}{16}$. We can discard the negative root since $\cos\pi/6 > \cos\pi/3 = 1/2 \Rightarrow \cos^2\pi/5 > 1/4$
(Q5.8) The first parts are theory. Look at Theorem (5.1). For the next part, note that

$(5-i)^2(1+i) = 34-14i$ and therefore $\arg\left[(5-i)^2(1+i)\right] = \arg(34-14i) \Rightarrow 2\arg(5-i) + \arg(1+i) = \arg(34+14i)$ and this becomes

$$2\arctan(-1/5) + \arctan(1) = \arctan(14/34) \Rightarrow -2\arctan(1/5) + \pi/4 = \arctan(7/17)$$

For the last part, it is enough to prove that $\arg\left[(4+i)^3(20+i)(1985+i)\right] = \pi/4$. Multiplying out, we find $\arg(1970113 + i1970113) = \arctan(1) = \pi/4$.
(Q5.9) Plugging $\theta = \pi/8$ we get $\sin 3\pi/4 = \sin \pi/4$ but $\sin(\pi-\alpha) = \sin(\alpha)$ as supplementary angles have the same sine (and opposite cosine). Hence $\sin(3\pi/4) = \sin(\pi - 3\pi/4) = \sin \pi/4$. The other solution is at $3\pi/8$. Expanding $(\cos\theta + i\sin\theta)^6 = \cos 6\theta + i\sin 6\theta$ using Pascal's triangle and comparing imaginary parts we get $\sin 6\theta = 6\cos^5\theta\sin\theta - 20\cos^3\theta\sin^3\theta + 6\cos\theta\sin^2\theta$. Factorizing $2\sin\theta\cos\theta = \sin 2\theta$ we have

$$\sin 6\theta = \sin 2\theta(3\cos^4\theta - 10\cos^2\theta\sin^2\theta + 3\sin^4\theta)$$

and after using $\sin^2\theta = 1-\cos^2\theta$ we get the result. For the last part, since $\sin 6\theta = \sin 2\theta$ the equation becomes $1 = 16\cos^4\theta - 16\cos^2\theta + 3$. Solving this bi-quadratic we get that $\cos^2\theta = (2\pm\sqrt{2})/4$. The plus solution corresponds to the smaller angle as the cosine is decreasing in the first quadrant.
(Q5.10) Multiplying top and bottom by the complex conjugate of the denominator we get

$$\frac{(1+\sin\theta+i\cos\theta)^2}{(1+\sin\theta)^2+\cos^2\theta} = \frac{1+\sin^2\theta-\cos^2\theta+2\sin\theta+2i\cos\theta(1+\sin\theta)}{2(1+\sin\theta)} = \sin\theta + i\cos\theta$$

For the next part, setting $\theta = \pi/5$ and raising to the 5th power we get

$$\begin{aligned}(1+\sin\pi/5+i\sin\pi/5)^5 &= i^5(\cos(-\pi/5)+i\sin(-\pi/5))^5(1+\sin\pi/5-i\sin\pi/5)\\ &= -i(\cos(-\pi)+i\sin(-\pi))(1+\sin\pi/5-i\sin\pi/5)\end{aligned}$$

Hence the result.
(Q5.11) Using $(\cos\theta+i\sin\theta)^6 = \cos 6\theta + i\sin 6\theta$ and Pascal's triangle we get after comparing imaginary parts that

$$\begin{aligned}\sin 6\theta &= 6\cos^5\theta\sin\theta - 20\cos^3\theta\sin^2\theta + 6\cos\theta\sin^5\theta\\ &= \cos\theta\left[6(1-\sin^2\theta)^2\sin\theta - 20(1-\sin^2\theta)\sin^2\theta + 6\sin^5\theta\right]\\ &= \cos\theta\left(32\sin^5\theta - 32\sin^3\theta + 6\sin\theta\right)\end{aligned}$$

For the next part if we factor out a $2\sin\theta$ we get $\sin 6\theta = \sin 2\theta(16\sin^4\theta - 16\sin^2\theta + 3) \Rightarrow \frac{\sin 6\theta}{\sin 2\theta} = 16\sin^4\theta - 16\sin^2\theta + 3$. The bi-quadratic has a minimum at $\sin^2\theta = 1/2$ of -1. Hence the lower bound is -1. The upper bound is when $\sin^2\theta = 1$ and it is 3. Alternatively, you can complete the square $16\sin^4\theta - 16\sin^2\theta + 3 = 16(\sin^2\theta - 1/2)^2 - 1$ and again we read off that the minimum is -1 and the maximum when $\sin^2\theta = 1$.
(Q5.12) Using $(\cos\theta+i\sin\theta)^6 = \cos 6\theta + i\sin 6\theta$ and Pascal's triangle we get after comparing real parts that $\cos 6\theta = C^6 - 15C^4S^2 + 15C^2S^4 - S^6 = C^6 - 15(1-C^2)C^4 + 15C^2(1-C^2)^2 + (1-C^2)^3$ where $C = \cos\theta$ and $S = \sin\theta$. After expanding and collecting terms we obtain $\cos 6\theta = 32C^6 - 48C^4 + 18C^2 - 1$. For the next part, notice that the given equation is $2\cos 6\theta - 1 = 0$ and the roots of these are $6\theta = 2k\pi \pm \pi/3$. The largest value corresponds to the minimum positive root. Namely $k = 0$, so $\theta = \pi/18$.
(Q5.13) Let $z = \cos\pi/11 + i\sin\pi/11$ then we can write the given expression as the real part of $\Re(A)$ where $A = z + z^3 + z^5 + z^7 + z^9$. This is a geometric progression with z^2 as the step.

Hence, $A = \frac{z-z^{11}}{1-z^2}$. But $z^{11} = \cos\pi + i\sin\pi = -1$. So,

$$A = \frac{z+1}{1-z^2} = \frac{1}{1-z} = \frac{1}{1-\cos\pi/11 - i\sin\pi/11}$$
$$= \frac{1-\cos\pi/11 + i\sin\pi/11}{2(1-\cos\pi/11)} = \frac{1}{2} + i\frac{\sin\pi/11}{2(1-\cos\pi/11)}$$

And the real part of $\Re(A) = 1/2$.

(Q5.14) Expanding $(C+iS)^4 = \cos 4\theta + i\sin 4\theta$ and comparing real part we get $\cos 4\theta = C^4 - 6C^2S^2 + S^4 = C^4 - 6C^2(1-C^2) + (1-C^2)^2 = 8C^4 - 8C^2 + 1$, where $C = \cos\theta$ and $S = \sin\theta$. For the next part, $\cos 6\theta\cos 2\theta = \cos 6\theta(2C^2-1) = (8C^4 - 8C^2 + 1)(2C^2-1) = 16C^6 - 24C^4 + 10C^2 - 1$. Next, we have $16C^6 - 24C^4 + 10C^2 - 2 = 0$. By inspection we see that $C^2 = 1$ is a root and if we do the polynomial division we get that it is equal to $(C^2-1)(16C^4 - 8C^2 + 2) = 0$. The only roots are $\cos^2\theta = 1$ as the bi-quadratic has negative discriminant and hence no real roots. Hence the roots are $\theta = n\pi$, $n \in \mathbb{Z}$. If $\cos 2\theta\cos 6\theta = -1$ then $16C^6 - 24C^4 + 10C^2 = 0 \Rightarrow C^2(8C^4 - 12C^2 + 5) = 0$. Again the bi-quadratic has no real roots as the discriminant is -16. Hence, the only allowed roots are $\cos^2\theta = 0$.

(Q5.15) For the first part look at Exercise (5.10). The solution to the trig equation is $\tan 5\theta = \tan\pi/4 \Rightarrow 5\theta = \pi/4 + k\pi$, with $k \in \mathbb{Z}$. The solutions less than π are with $k = 0,1,2,3,4$. Thus, the solution set is $\theta = \{\pi/20, 5\pi/20, 9\pi/20, 13\pi/20, 17\pi/20\}$. Setting $t = \tan\theta$ we get for the $\tan 5\theta = 1 \Rightarrow t^5 - 5t^4 - 10t^3 + 10t^2 + 5t - 1 = 0$. The last equation has the obvious root $t = 1 \Rightarrow \alpha = \pi/4$. Dividing the polynomial by $t-1$ we obtain $t^4 - 4t^3 - 14t^2 - 4t + 1 = 0$. And the set of solutions for the quartic is the previous set apart from $\pi/4$. Thus the solutions of the quartic are $\alpha = \{\pi/20, 9\pi/20, 13\pi/20, 17\pi/20\}$.

(Q5.16) Multiplying out the RHS we can verify the identity. Letting $x = \cos a + i\sin a$, $y = \cos b + i\sin b$ and $z = \cos c + i\sin c$ we have that $x^3 + y^3 + z^3 = 3xyz$ since $x + y + z = 0$ by the assumption given. But $3xyz = 3\cos(a+b+c) + i\sin(a+b+c)$.

(Q5.17) Writing $1+i$ and $1-i$ in polar form we have

$$\left[\sqrt{2}(\cos\pi/4 + i\sin\pi/4)\right]^n + \left[\sqrt{2}(\cos(-\pi/4) + i\sin(-\pi/4))\right]^n =$$
$$2^{n/2}(\cos n\pi/4 + i\sin n\pi/4) + 2^{n/2}(\cos(n\pi/4) - i\sin n\pi/4)$$
$$= 2^{n/2}2\cos n\pi/4 = 2^{(n+2)/2}\cos n\pi/4$$

Similarly for part (ii).

(Q5.18) Expanding $(\cos\theta + i\sin\theta)^5 = \cos 5\theta + i\sin 5\theta$ using Pascal's triangle and comparing real part we get $\cos 5\theta = C^5 - 10C^3S^2 + 5CS^4 = C^5 - 10C^3(1-C^2) + 5C(1-C^2)^2 = 16C^5 - 20C^3 + 5C$, where $C = \cos\theta$ and $S = \sin\theta$. So $\cos 5\theta = C(16C^4 - 20C^2 + 5)$ and if this is equal to zero we must have $\cos 5\theta = 0 \Rightarrow 5\theta = \pm\pi/2 + 2k\pi$. Thus the root that are less than π are $\alpha = \{\pi/10, \pi/2, 3\pi/10, 7\pi/10, 9\pi/10\}$. Clearly, the solution $\pi/2$ is not a solution of the quartic. So the only solutions of the quartic are $\tan\alpha$, where $\alpha = \{\pi/10, 3\pi/10, 7\pi/10, 9\pi/10\}$. Setting $\theta = \pi/10$ and solving the bi-quadratic we get $\cos^2\pi/10 = (20 \pm \sqrt{80})/32$. But we know all the solutions in terms of angles and the smallest angle is $\pi/10$ which means that the cosine must be the greatest value. Hence $\cos\pi/10 = \sqrt{(20+\sqrt{80})/32}$.

(Q5.19) Using $(\cos\theta + i\sin\theta)^6 = \cos 6\theta + i\sin 6\theta$ and Pascal's triangle we get after comparing real parts that $\cos 6\theta = C^6 - 15C^4S^2 + 15C^2S^4 - S^6 = C^6 - 15(1-C^2)C^4 + 15C^2(1-C^2)^2 + (1-C^2)^3$ where $C = \cos\theta$ and $S = \sin\theta$. After expanding and collecting terms we obtain $\cos 6\theta = 32C^6 - 48C^4 + 18C^2 - 1$. We need to factorise this expression. Fortunately the result is guiding us on how to do it. $32C^6 - 48C^4 + 18C^2 - 1 = 32C^6 - 48C^4 + 16C^2 + (2C^2-1) = 32C^6 - 32C^4 + 16C^2 - 16C^4 + (2C^2-1) = 16C^4(2C^2-1) - 16C^2(2C^2-1) + (2C^2-1) =$

$(2C^2-1)(16C^4-16C^2+1)$. Letting $\cos 6\theta = 0$ we get $6\theta = \pm\pi/2 + 2k\pi \Rightarrow \theta = \pm\pi/12 + k\pi/6$, and the solution set is $\theta = \{\pi/12, 3\pi/12, 5\pi/12, 7\pi/12, 9\pi/12, 11\pi/12\}$. Two of these solution, namely $3\pi/12$ and $9\pi/12$ are the zeros of $2C^2-1$. Hence the other roots are the zeros of the bi-quadratic. The product of these roots via the Vieta relations is $1/16$.

(Q5.20) $A = \frac{\sqrt{2}}{2}(1+i)(-1)^k\left(\sec \frac{4k+1}{4n}\pi\right)^n$.

(Q5.21) The roots of the quadratic are $\cos\theta \pm \sqrt{\cos^2\theta - 1} = \cos\theta \pm i\sin\theta$. Plugging this in the equation we get

$$\begin{aligned}
&(\cos\theta \pm i\sin\theta)^n - (\cos\theta \pm i\sin\theta)\sin n\theta + \sin(n-1)\theta\\
&= (\cos n\theta \pm i\sin n\theta)\sin n\theta - (\cos\theta \pm i\sin\theta)\sin n\theta + \sin(n-1)\theta\\
&= \cos n\theta \sin\theta - \cos\theta\sin n\theta + \sin(n-1)\theta = 0
\end{aligned}$$

Hence, both roots are roots of the given equation and therefore the quadratic is a factor.

(Q5.22) We can re-write the relation as

$$z + \frac{1}{2}z^2 + \frac{1}{4}z^3 + \ldots = z\left(1 + \frac{1}{2}z + \frac{1}{4}z^2 + \ldots \frac{1}{2^{n-1}}z^{n-1}\right) = z\frac{1-(z/2)^n}{1-z/2}$$

After the algebra we compare the real part to get the answer.

(Q5.23) Using $z^7+z^{-7} = 2i\sin 7\theta$ and the identity $a^n - b^n = (a-b)(a^{n-1}+a^{n-2}b+\ldots+b^{n-1})$ with $a = z$ and $b = z^{-1}$ we get $z^7 - z^{-7} = (z-z^{-1})(z^6+z^4+z^2+1+z^{-4}+z^{-2}+z^{-6}) = 2i\sin\theta(2\cos 6\theta + 2\cos 4\theta + 2\cos 2\theta + 1) \Rightarrow \frac{\sin 7\theta}{\sin\theta} = 2\cos 6\theta + 2\cos 4\theta + 2\cos 2\theta + 1$. But $\cos 6\theta = \cos 4\theta\cos 2\theta - \sin 4\theta \sin 2\theta = 4\cos^3 2\theta - 3\cos 2\theta$. Hence, $\frac{\sin 7\theta}{\sin\theta} = 8\cos^3 3\theta + 4\cos^2 2\theta - 4\cos 2\theta - 1 = x^3 + x^2 - 2x - 1$, where $x = 2\cos 2\theta$.

Answers to Sec. 6.4, page 119

(Q6.1) We can write

$$\left|1 - e^{i\theta}\right|^2 = \left|e^{i\theta/2}\left(e^{-i\theta/2} - e^{i\theta/2}\right)\right|^2 = \left|e^{i\theta/2}\right|^2 |-2i\sin\theta/2|^2 = 4\sin^2\theta/2$$

Since $|e^{i\alpha}| = 1$ for any α and $e^{i\theta/2} - e^{-i\theta/2} = 2i\sin\theta/2$.

(Q6.2) Writing $\cos\theta = (e^{i\theta} + e^{-i\theta})/2$, $\cos n\theta = (e^{in\theta} + e^{-in\theta})/2$ we have $\cos^5\theta = 1/32(e^{i\theta} + e^{-i\theta})^5$. Expanding using Pascal's triangle,

$$\begin{aligned}
\cos^5\theta &= 1/32\left(e^{5i\theta} + e^{-5i\theta} + 5(e^{3i\theta} + e^{-3i\theta}) + 10(e^{i\theta} + e^{-i\theta})\right)\\
&= 1/16(\cos 5\theta + 5\cos 3\theta + 10\cos\theta)
\end{aligned}$$

For part (ii) we have $16\cos^5\theta - \cos\theta = \cos 5\theta + 5\cos 3\theta + 9\cos\theta = 0$. Thus, the solutions are $\cos\theta = 0$ or $\cos^4\theta = 1/16 \Rightarrow \cos\theta = \pm 1/2$. The first gives $\theta = \pm\pi/2 + 2k\pi$ and the second has $\theta = \pm\pi/3 + 2k\pi$ or $\theta = \pm 2\pi/3 + 2k\pi$ for $k \in \mathbb{Z}$. The solutions must be in the range $0 \le \theta \le \pi$ and are $\{\pi/2, \pi/3, 2\pi/3\}$.

(Q6.3) The first part is simple. Just multiply out and use $2\cos\theta = e^{i\theta} + e^{-i\theta}$. For the next part use $n = 2$ we get using (i)

$$\left(z^2 - e^{i\pi/3}\right)\left(z^2 - e^{-i\pi/3}\right) = \left(z - e^{i\pi/6}\right)\left(z + e^{i\pi/6}\right)\left(z - e^{-i\pi/6}\right)\left(z + e^{-i\pi/6}\right)$$

Notice however that the question asks to place this in the form $z - e^{i\alpha}$, with $0 \le \alpha < 2\pi$, which means that we must get rid of the plus in two of the terms. Remember that $-1 = e^{i\pi}$

and write $z+e^{i\pi/6} = z-e^{i\pi+i\pi/6} = z-e^{i7\pi/6}$ and similarly $z+e^{-i\pi/6} = z-e^{i\pi-i\pi/6} = z-e^{i5\pi/6}$. The last bit is to convert the $z-e^{-i\pi/6} = z-e^{2i\pi-i\pi/6} = z-e^{i11\pi/6}$. The answer is

$$\left(z-e^{i\pi/6}\right)\left(z-e^{i7\pi/6}\right)\left(z-e^{i11\pi/6}\right)\left(z-e^{i5\pi/6}\right)$$

This question was not hard but you had to read it very carefully to get what was asked to do.

(Q6.4) We have $\sin n\theta = (e^{in0} - e^{-in\theta})/2i$. Raising to the 6th power and expanding we get

$$\sin^6\theta = \frac{-1}{64}\left(e^{6i\theta} - 6e^{5i\theta}e^{-i\theta} + 15e^{4i\theta}e^{-2i\theta} - 20e^{3i\theta}e^{-3i\theta} + 15e^{2i\theta}e^{-2i\theta}\right.$$
$$\left.-6e^{i\theta}e^{-5i\theta} + e^{-6i\theta}\right)$$
$$= \frac{-1}{64}\left[\left(e^{6i\theta}+e^{-6i\theta}\right) - 6\left(e^{4i\theta}+e^{-4i\theta}\right) + 15\left(e^{2i\theta}+e^{-2i\theta}\right) - 20\right]$$
$$= \frac{-1}{32}(\cos 6\theta - 6\cos 4\theta + 15\cos 2\theta - 10)$$

Replacing $\theta \to \pi/2-\theta$ and using the fact that for complementary angles we have $\sin(\pi/2-\theta) = \cos\theta$ and for supplementary angles $\cos(\pi-\theta) = -\cos\theta$ we get

$$\cos^6\theta = \frac{-1}{32}(-\cos 6\theta - 6\cos 4\theta - 15\cos 2\theta - 10)$$

The integral is now easy to evaluate as

$$\frac{-1}{16}\int_0^{\pi/4}(\cos 6\theta + 15\cos 2\theta)\,d\theta = \frac{-1}{16}\left[\frac{1}{6}\sin 6\theta + \frac{15}{2}\sin 2\theta\right]_0^{\pi/4} = \frac{-1}{16}\left[-\frac{1}{6}+\frac{15}{2}\right] = -\frac{11}{24}$$

(Q6.5) We can re-write the expression with complex numbers $x = e^{ia}$ and $z = e^{i\theta}$ as

$$\sum_{k=1}^{k=n} e^{i(a+k\theta)} = e^{ia}\sum_{k=1}^{k=n} e^{k\theta} = e^{ia}\frac{e^{i\theta} - e^{(n+1)\theta}}{1-e^{i\theta}}$$
$$= e^{ia}e^{i\theta}\frac{e^{in/2\theta}\left(e^{-in\theta/2} - e^{in\theta/2}\right)}{e^{i\theta/2}(e^{-i\theta/2} - e^{i\theta/2})} = e^{i(a+(n+1)\theta/2)}\frac{\sin n\theta/2}{\sin\theta/2}$$

The real part of this expression is the cosine series and the imaginary part

$$\sin(a+\theta) + \sin(a+2\theta) + \ldots + \sin(a+n\theta) = \sin\left(a + \frac{n+1}{2}\theta\right)\frac{\sin n\theta/2}{\sin\theta/2}$$

(Q6.6) The given complex number is $\frac{\sqrt{3}+i}{\sqrt{3}-i} = \frac{(\sqrt{3}+i)^2}{4} = \frac{1}{2} + i\frac{\sqrt{3}}{2} = e^{i\pi/3}$. For $e^{in\pi/3}$ to be real the argument must be 2π. Thus $n\pi/3 = 2\pi \Rightarrow n = 6$.

(Q6.7) The triangle is isosceles as the $|z| = |ze^{i\pi/3}| = |z||e^{i\pi/3}| = |z|$ since $|e^{i\theta}| = 1$ for any angle θ. The angle $\angle OAB = \pi/3$. For the second part the point E is rotated by $\pm\pi/3$ (the $\pm$ is because the question did not specify orientation) and of the same length as $CD = (5+2i)-(1+i) = 4+i$. Hence the point E is the vector to the point C plus $(4+i)e^{\pm\pi/3}$. So $w = 1+i+(4+i)e^{\pm\pi/6} = 1+i+(4+i)(\sqrt{3}/2 \pm i/2)$.

(Q6.8) We can re-write the relation

$$\frac{e^{i\theta}+e^{-i\theta}}{2} + \frac{e^{i(\theta+2\pi/3)}+e^{-i(\theta+2\pi/3)}}{2}e^{2\pi/3i} + \frac{e^{i(\theta-2\pi/3)}+e^{-i(\theta-2\pi/3)}}{2}e^{-2\pi/3i} =$$
$$\frac{e^{i\theta}+e^{-i\theta}}{2} + \frac{e^{i(\theta+4\pi/3)}+e^{-i\theta}}{2} + \frac{e^{i(\theta42\pi/3)}+e^{-i\theta}}{2} = \frac{e^{i\theta}}{2} + \frac{3}{2}e^{-i\theta} + e^{i\theta}\cos\frac{4\pi}{3} = \frac{3}{2}e^{-i\theta}$$

As $\cos 4\pi/3 = -1/2$.

(Q6.9) Using $\left(e^{i\theta} - e^{-i\theta}\right)^5 = 32i\sin^5\theta$ and expanding we get

$$e^{5i\theta} - 5e^{3i\theta} + 10e^{i\theta} - 10e^{-i\theta} + 5e^{-3i\theta} - e^{-5i\theta} =$$
$$\left(e^{5i\theta} - e^{-5i\theta}\right) - 5\left(e^{3i\theta} - e^{-3i\theta}\right) + 10\left(e^{i\theta} - e^{-i\theta}\right) =$$
$$2i\sin 5\theta - 10i\sin 3\theta + 20\sin\theta = 32i\sin^5\theta$$

And after simplifying we get the required relation. For part(ii) using the result from (i) we can re-write the equation to be solved as $16\sin^5\theta = 6\sin\theta$. The roots are a) $\sin\theta = 0 \Rightarrow \theta = 0$ or b) $\sin\theta = \pm\sqrt[4]{3/8} \Rightarrow \theta = \pm 51.5^o$. These are the only solutions in the range $-\pi/2 \le \theta \le \pi/2$.

(Q6.10) Using $\cos x = (e^{ix} + e^{-ix})/2$ we get $e^x\cos x = (e^{x(1+i)} + e^{1-i)})/2$. The expansion of $e^x = 1 + x + x^2/2! + ... + x^n/n!$, and the nth-term is $x^n/n!$. So the nth-term of $e^x\cos x$ is

$$\frac{1}{2}\left(\frac{x^n(1+i)^n}{n!} + \frac{x^n(1-i)^n}{n!}\right) = \frac{1}{2}\frac{x^n}{n!}\left[(1+i)^n + (1-i)^n\right]$$

The expression inside the brackets was computed in Question (5.17) as $2^{(n+2)/2}\cos n\pi/4$. So the nth-term is $\frac{x^n}{n!}2^{n/2}\cos n\pi/4$.

(Q6.11) Writing $z = e^{i\theta} = \cos\theta + i\sin\theta$ the expression $C + iS = 1 + \frac{1}{2}e^{i\theta} + \frac{1}{2^2}e^{2i\theta} + ...$ An infinite geometric series with $e^{i\theta}/2$ as the ratio of successive terms. The sum is $C + iS = \frac{1}{1-1/2e^{i\theta}} = \frac{2}{2-e^{i\theta}}$. To find C we need to take the real part of this expression. Hence

$$C + iS = \frac{2(2-e^{-i\theta})}{(2-e^{i\theta})(2-e^{-i\theta})} = \frac{4 - 2\cos\theta + 2i\sin\theta}{5 - 2(e^{i\theta} + e^{-i\theta})} = \frac{4 - 2\cos\theta + 2i\sin\theta}{5 - 4\cos\theta}$$

And the real part is $C = \frac{4-2\cos\theta}{5-4\cos\theta}$.

(Q6.12) Expanding $\left(e^{i\theta} - e^{-i\theta}\right)^4 = (2i\sin\theta)^4 = 16\sin^4\theta$ and collecting terms we get

$$16\sin^4\theta = e^{4i\theta} - 4e^{3i\theta}e^{-i\theta} + 6 + 4e^{i\theta}e^{-3i\theta} + e^{-4i\theta} = 2\cos 4\theta - 8\cos\theta + 6$$

The integral now becomes

$$\frac{1}{8}\int_0^{\pi/6}(\cos 4\theta - 4\cos 2\theta + 3)\,d\theta = \frac{1}{8}\left[\frac{\sin 4\theta}{4} - 2\sin 2\theta + 3\theta\right]_0^{\pi/6} = \frac{1}{64}(-7\sqrt{3} + 4\pi)$$

(Q6.13) There are more than one ways to prove the result. For example,

$$w = \frac{e^{i\theta/2}(e^{-i\theta/2} + e^{i\theta/2})}{e^{i\theta/2}(e^{-i\theta/2} - e^{i\theta/2})} = \frac{2\cos\theta/2}{-2i\sin\theta/2} = i\cot\theta/2$$

or you could write it as

$$w = \frac{1+e^{i\theta}}{1-e^{i\theta}} = \frac{(1+e^{i\theta})(1-e^{-i\theta})}{(1-e^{i\theta})(1-e^{-i\theta})} = \frac{1 + e^{i\theta} - e^{-i\theta} - 1}{2 - (e^{i\theta} + e^{-i\theta})} = \frac{2i\sin\theta}{2(1-\cos\theta)}$$
$$= \frac{4i\sin\theta/2\cos\theta/2}{2(1-(1-2\sin^2\theta/2))} = \frac{i\cos\theta/2}{\sin\theta/2} = i\cot\frac{\theta}{2}$$

The z locus is the unit circle and the direction is anti-clockwise. The w locus is the imaginary line and the direction is downward as θ increases from 0 to 2π.

(Q6.14) The expression

$$\cos^2\theta\sin^3\theta = \left(\frac{e^{i\theta}+e^{-i\theta}}{2}\right)^2\left(\frac{e^{i\theta}-e^{-i\theta}}{2i}\right)^3$$
$$= \frac{i}{32}\left(e^{2i\theta}+e^{-2i\theta}+2\right)\left(e^{3i\theta}-3(e^{i\theta}-e^{-i\theta})-e^{-3i\theta}\right)$$
$$= \frac{i}{32}\left[e^{5i\theta}-e^{-5i\theta}+e^{-3i\theta}-e^{3i\theta}-2(e^{i\theta}-e^{-i\theta})\right]$$
$$= \frac{i}{32}\left[2i\sin 5\theta-2i\sin 3\theta-4i\sin\theta\right] = \frac{-1}{16}(\sin 5\theta-\sin 3\theta-2\sin\theta)$$

The solutions to the equation are $\sin^3\theta\cos^2\theta = 0$. This means that either θ is an odd multiple of $\pi/2$, $\cos\theta = 0 \Rightarrow \theta = (2n+1)\pi/2$ or $\sin\theta = 0 \Rightarrow \theta = n\pi$. Combining the two we have $\theta = n\pi/2$ for any $n \in \mathbb{Z}$.
(Q6.15) If we write $e^x\cos x$ as the real part. $\mathfrak{Re}\left(e^x e^{ix}\right)$. Now it is easy to differentiate $e^{(1+i)x}$. For every derivative we bring a factor $(1+i)$. Hence, the nth derivative is

$$\frac{d^n}{dx^n}e^{(1+i)x} = (1+i)^n e^{x(1+i)} = (\sqrt{2})^n\left(e^{i\pi/4}\right)^n e^x e^{ix} = 2^{n/2}e^x e^{i(x+n\pi/4)}$$

the real part of this expression is $2^{n/2}e^x\cos(x+n\pi/4)$. The imaginary part would give

$$\frac{d^n}{dx^n}e^x\sin x = 2^{n/2}e^x\sin\left(x+\frac{n\pi}{4}\right)$$

Answers to Sec. 7.4, page 137

(Q7.1) Setting $\omega = \frac{z}{1-z}$ the equation transforms into $\omega^3 = 8 = 8e^{2ik\pi} \Rightarrow \omega = 2e^{2ik\pi/3}$ and the three solutions are $k = 0, 1, 2$. The obvious solution for $k = 0$ is $z_0 = 2$. For $k = 1$ we have $z_1 = 1 + i\sqrt{3}/3$ and for $k = 2$, $z_2 = 1 - i\sqrt{3}/3$.
(Q7.2) The complex number is $\cos\pi/6 + i\sin\pi/6$ and the cube roots are $(\cos(\pi/6+2k\pi) + i\sin(\pi/6+2k\pi))^{1/3} = \cos(\pi/18+2k\pi/3) + i\sin(\pi/18+2k\pi/3)$, for $k = 0, 1, 2$. Namely, $e^{\pi/18}$, $e^{13\pi/18}$ and $e^{25\pi/18}$.
(Q7.3) The five roots are $z_k = e^{2ik\pi/5}$, $k = 0, 1, 2, 3, 4$. For $z^5 = -32 = 32e^{i\pi}$ the roots are $z_k = e^{i(2k+1)\pi/5}$, $k = 0, 1, 2, 3, 4$. The shape is a regular pentagon with one vertex at the real axis $z = -2$.
(Q7.4) The solutions are $e^{2k\pi/6}$ for $k = 0, 1, ..., 5$ and it is a regular hexagon. For (ii) you can write $(1+i) = \sqrt{2}e^{i\pi/4}$ and raising to the 6th power you get $-8i$ or you can $(1+i)^2 = 2i$ and cubing it you get $-8i$. For (iii) the roots are $\sqrt{2}e^{i\pi(3+4k)/12}$ for $k = 0, 1, ..., 5$
(Q7.5) $A = -5+7\frac{\sqrt{3}}{3}$ and $B = -5-7\frac{\sqrt{3}}{3}$. Doing Pascal's triangle for $n = 5$ on $(\cos\theta + i\sin\theta)^5 = \cos 5\theta + i\sin 5\theta$ you get $C^5 + i5C^4 - 10C^3S^2 - 10iC^2S^3 + 5CS^4 + iS^5$ and comparing real parts $\cos 5\theta = C^5 - 10C^3(1-C^2) + 5C(1-C^2)^2 = 16C^5 - 20C^3 + 5C$, where $C = \cos\theta$.
(Q7.6) $z^4 = 4(\cos\pi/3 + i\sin\pi/3)$. The 4 roots are $z_k = \sqrt{2}(\cos(6k+1)\pi/12 + i\sin(6k+1)\pi/12)$, with $k = 0, 1, 2, 3$. Thus the arguments are $\pi/12, 7\pi/12, 13\pi/12$ and $19\pi/12$ and $r = \sqrt{2}$. The 4 roots make up a square. The lines are the diagonals of the square.
(Q7.7) Ans:0, Write as $\frac{\omega^7}{\omega+\omega^6} + \frac{\omega^7}{\omega^2+\omega^5} + \frac{\omega^7}{\omega^3+\omega^4}$ which becomes $\frac{\omega^6}{1+\omega^5} + \frac{\omega^5}{1+\omega^3} + \frac{\omega^4}{1+\omega}$. The numerator then becomes $2\omega^6 + 2\omega^5 + ... + 1 = 0$.
(Q7.8) w is the 5th root of unity, hence $w^5 - 1 = 0$. $w^2 = e^{4i\pi/5}$, $w^3 = e^{6i\pi/5}$ and $w^* = e^{-2i\pi/5} = e^{8i\pi/5}$. The points are the vertices of a regular pentagon with point A on the $z = 1$

(real axis) and point E at the origin of our Argand diagram. The polynomial is $1+z+z^2+z^3+z^4=0$.

(Q7.9) Expanding the RHS and using $\omega^3=1$ we get the identity. By inspection $a=2$ and $b=5$. Hence the roots are 7 and $r_1=2\omega+5\omega^2=2(\omega+\omega^2)+3\omega^2=-2+3(\cos 4i\pi/3+i\sin 4i\pi/3)=-(7+i3\sqrt{3})/2$ and $r_2=-(7-i3\sqrt{3})/2$.

(Q7.10) ω is the 5th root of unity and therefore $\omega^5-1=0 \Rightarrow (\omega-1)(1+\omega+\omega^2+\omega^3+\omega^4)$. Expanding $(\omega+\omega^4)(\omega^2+\omega^3)=\omega^3+\omega^4+\omega+\omega^2=-1$. The quadratic has thus the sum of the roots $\omega+\omega^2+\omega^3+\omega^4=-1$ and product also -1. By the Vieta relations, $z^2+z-1=0$. The roots are $(-1\pm\sqrt{5})/2$. However, the root $\omega+\omega^4=e^{2i\pi/5}+e^{8i\pi/5}=e^{2i\pi/5}+e^{-2i\pi/5}=2\cos 2\pi/5$ and since $2\pi/5$ is in the first quadrant the cosine is positive and equal to $(-1+\sqrt{5})/2$. Hence $\cos 2\pi/5=(-1+\sqrt{5})/4$. The other root is $\cos 4\pi/5=(-1-\sqrt{5})/4$.

(Q7.11) The solutions are the roots of $x^5-1=0$ apart from $z=1$. Hence, $x=e^{2k\pi/5}$, with $k=1,2,3,4$.

(Q7.12) Solving for z we get

$$\left(\frac{z-1}{z}\right)^n=1=e^{2k\pi} \Rightarrow \frac{z-1}{z}=e^{2k\pi/n} \Rightarrow z=\frac{1}{1-e^{2k\pi/n}}=\frac{-e^{-k\pi/n}}{e^{k\pi/n}-e^{-k\pi/n}}$$
$$=\frac{-(\cos k\pi/n-i\sin k\pi/n)}{2i\sin k\pi/n}=\frac{i\cos k\pi/n+\sin k\pi/n}{2\sin k\pi/n}=\frac{1}{2}\left(1+i\cot\frac{k\pi}{n}\right)$$

And the real part $\Re(z)=1/2$.

(Q7.13) Expanding, $(z-e^{i\phi})(z-e^{-i\phi})=z^2-(e^{i\phi}+e^{-i\phi})+1=z^2-2\cos\phi+1$. The solutions to $z^7=1$ form the vertices of a regular heptagon with the first vertex at $z=1$. The solutions are $z=e^{2k\pi/7}$ with $k=0,1,2,\ldots,6$. The equation can thus be written as

$$z^n-1=(z-1)(z-e^{2\pi/7})(z-e^{4\pi/7})(z-e^{6\pi/7})(z-e^{8\pi/7})(z-e^{10\pi/7})(z-e^{12\pi/7})$$

We can pair $(z-e^{2\pi/7})$ with $(z-e^{12\pi/7})=(z-e^{12\pi/7-14\pi/7})=(z-e^{-2\pi/7})$ and use the result of the first part to write it as $z^2-2z\cos 2\pi/7+1$. Similarly, we can pair $(z-e^{4\pi/7})(z-e^{10\pi/7})=z^2-2z\cos 4\pi/7+1$ and $(z-e^{6\pi/7})(z-e^{8\pi/7})=z^2-2\cos 6\pi/7+1$. Thus the result is

$$z^7-1=(z-1)(z^2-2z\cos\frac{2\pi}{7}+1)(z^2-2z\cos\frac{4\pi}{7}+1)(z^2-2z\cos\frac{6\pi}{7}+1)$$

(Q7.14) Placing $\alpha=0$ we get $(x^n-1)^2=\prod_{k=0}^{n-1}(x^2-2x\cos 2k\pi/n+1)$. Since, n is even the product for $k=0$ and $k=n/2$ would be $(x-1)^2$ and $(x+1)^2$ respectively. All the other terms in the product would also pair. For example, for $k=n-1$ we get $x^2-2x\cos(2(n-1)\pi/n)+1=x^2-2x\cos 2\pi/n+1$. Therefore on taking the square root we get the result.

(Q7.15) If we multiply the two given relations we eliminate z_2. We thus have $z_1z_2\frac{z_1}{z_2}=z_1^2=(i-\sqrt{3})(2i)=-2-2i\sqrt{3}=4e^{4\pi/3}$. Hence, the two roots are $2e^{4\pi/6+k\pi}$ for $k=0,1$, or $2e^{2\pi/3}$ and $2e^{5\pi/3}$ However, for $k=1$ the argument becomes $5\pi/3$ which is outside the range that was given in the question. Hence we reject this solution and we leave only the $k=0$ solution.

Now in order to find the z_2 we can plug z_1 into $z_1/z_2=2i$ to get $z_2=\frac{1}{2i}z_1=-ie^{2\pi/3}=e^{-i\pi/2}e^{2\pi/3}=e^{\pi/6}=\sqrt{3}/2+i/2$.

(Q7.16) If we multiply by $x+iy$ we get that $(x+iy)^{2025}=x^2+y^2$. Taking the modulus of this equation we get $|z|^{2025}=|z|^2$ where $z=x+iy$. Hence either $|z|=0$ or $|z|=1$. Since $z\neq 0$ we have $|z|=1$. This however, means that $(x+iy)^{2025}=1$ and this equation has 2025 roots.

(Q7.17) The common vertices are the Greatest Common divider of 99 and 33 which is 33. So there are 33 common vertices.

(Q7.18) We can write the $S_1 + iS_2 = 1 + e^{2\pi/n} + e^{4\pi/n} + ... + e^{2(n-1)\pi/n}$. This is a geometric series and the sum is $S_1 + iS_2 = \frac{1-(e^{2\pi/n})^n}{1-e^{2\pi/n}} = \frac{1-e^{2\pi}}{1-e^{2\pi/n}} = 0$. Hence, $S_1 = S_2 = 0$.
(Q7.19) The solutions are the vertices of an equilateral triangle with one vertex at $z = 1$. Since $z^3-1 = (z-1)(z^2+z+1) = 0$, setting $z = \omega \neq 1$ we get that $\omega^2+\omega+1 = 0$. The expression $(2+\omega)(2+\omega^2) = 4 + 2(\omega+\omega^2) + \omega^3 = 5 - 2 = 3$. The expression, $\frac{1}{2+\omega} + \frac{1}{2+\omega^2} = 1$. Using the Vieta relations (B.5), for the cubic we have the product of the roots is -2/3, the sum of the roots is -3 and the sum of the pairs is 7/3. Hence the cubic is $3x^3 - 9x^2 + 7x - 2 = 0$.
(Q7.20) Since $\omega^2+\omega+1 = 0$ we have $\omega^3 = 1$. Using induction we have, that for $n = 1$ $(\omega)^{2^2} = \omega^4 = \omega$. So it is true for $n = 1$. Assuming that it is true for $n = k$ we have that $(\omega)^{2^{2k}} = \omega$. To prove that it is also true for $n = k+1$ we have $(\omega)^{2^{2k+2}} = (\omega)^{2^{2k}2^2} = \left((\omega)^{2^{2k}}\right)^4 = \omega^4 = \omega$. So it is true for all $n \in \mathbb{N}$.
(Q7.21) We have that $\omega = e^{2i\pi/3} \Rightarrow \omega^3 = 1$. Using this repeatedly we get the value of 9 for the expression.
(Q7.22) The sum of the roots are $B = k + k^2 + k^3 + k^4 + k^5 + k^6 = -1$, since $k^7 = 1$ and the product is $C = (k+k^2+k^4)(k^3+k^5+k^6) = k^4+k^6+1+k^5+1+k+1+k^2+k^3 = 2$. Hence the quadratic is $k^2+k+2 = 0$. The roots of this quadratic are $k = -1/2 \pm i\sqrt{7}/2$. So one of the roots is with the plus and the other with the minus. Drawing a quick diagram we see that the $k+k^2+k^4 = -1/2 + i\sqrt{7}/2$ and hence $\sin 2\pi/7 + \sin 4\pi/7 + \sin 8\pi/7 = \sqrt{7}/2$.
(Q7.23) Use the same method as in the previous Question **(Q7.22)**.
(Q7.24) We have $\omega^3 = 1$ and expanding the RHS we have

$$\begin{aligned}
&xy + yz + zx + (x + y\omega + z\omega^2)(x + y\omega^2 + z\omega) \\
&= xy + yz + zx + x^2 + y^2 + z^2 + xy(\omega+\omega^2) + yz(\omega+\omega^2) + xz(\omega+\omega^2) \\
&= xy + yz + zx + x^2 + y^2 + z^2 - xy - yz - zx = x^2 + y^2 + z^2
\end{aligned}$$

since $\omega + \omega^2 = -1$.
(Q7.25) The three points are the vertices of an equilateral triangle since turning $|b-c| = |a-c|$ and the angle in between angle is 60 degrees. Since the triangle is equilateral we can also write $\frac{c-b}{a-b} = e^{i\pi/3}$. Equating the two relations we have $\frac{a-c}{b-c} = \frac{c-b}{a-b} \Rightarrow a^2+b^2+c^2 = ab+bc+ca$.
(Q7.26) If we divide the equation by z^2 ($z \neq 0$ since if it was we would have $1 = 0$) then we get

$$z^2 + \frac{1}{z^2} + z + \frac{1}{z} = 0 = \left(z + \frac{1}{z}\right)^2 - 2 + z + \frac{1}{z} + 1 = u^2 + u - 1 = 0$$

Hence $u = (-1 \pm \sqrt{5})/2$. And if we substitute this back we get the quadratic $2z^2 + (1 - \mp\sqrt{5})z + 2 = 0$. The solutions are $(-1 \pm \sqrt{5} \pm i\sqrt{10 \mp 2\sqrt{5}})/4$, a rather horrible looking expression. Multiplying by z the $z^4 + z^3 + z^2 + z + 1 = 0$ we get $z^5 + z^4 + z^3 + z^2 + z = 0 \Rightarrow z^5 - 1 = 0$. The roots of this equation are $e^{2i\pi/5}$, with $k = 0, 1, 2, 3, 4$. Excluding the obvious $z = 1$ the $z = e^{2i\pi/5}$ is in the first quadrant. Hence the cosine must be the greatest positive value and the sine the greatest positive. Thus $\cos 2\pi/5 = (-1 + \sqrt{5})/2$ and $\sin 2\pi/5 = (\sqrt{10 + 2\sqrt{5}})/4$.
(Q7.27) This is the cube root of 1. so $\omega^3 - 1 = 0 = (\omega-1)(\omega^2+\omega+1)$ hence $\omega^2+\omega+1 = 0$. The modulus of $|1+\omega^2| = |-\omega| = 1$ and the argument $\arg(1+\omega^2) = \arg(-\omega) = \arg e^{i\pi+2\pi/3} = 5\pi/3$ or $-\pi/3$ if we subtract 2π. By considering $(1+\omega^r)^n$ for $r = 0, 1, 2$ we get from the binomial

expansion

$$(1+1)^n = \binom{n}{0} + \binom{n}{1} + \binom{n}{2} + \ldots + \binom{n}{n} = 2^n \qquad (*)$$

$$(1+\omega)^n = \binom{n}{0} + \binom{n}{1}\omega + \binom{n}{2}\omega^2 + \ldots \binom{n}{n}\omega^n = (-1)^n \omega^{2n}$$

$$(1+\omega^2)^n = \binom{n}{0} + \binom{n}{1}\omega^2 + \binom{n}{2}\omega^4 + \ldots \binom{n}{n}\omega^{2n} = (-1)^n \omega^n$$

If we add these three equations notice that since $1+\omega+\omega^2 = 0$ all terms apart from those with n a multiple of 3 cancel out. So

$$2^n + (-1)^n(\omega^n + \omega^{2n}) = 3\binom{n}{0} + 3\binom{n}{3} + 3\binom{6}{6} + \ldots + 3\binom{n}{k}$$

with k the largest multiple of 3 less than or equal to n. Now $(-1)^n(\omega+\omega^2) = e^{in\pi}(e^{2in\pi/3} + e^{4in\pi/3}) = e^{5in\pi/3} + e^{7in\pi/3} = e^{-in\pi/3} + e^{in\pi/3} = 2\cos n\pi/3$. We thus have the result

$$\binom{n}{0} + 3\binom{n}{3} + \binom{6}{6} + \ldots + \binom{n}{k} = \frac{1}{3}\left(2^n + 2\cos\frac{n\pi}{3}\right) \qquad (**)$$

Placing $n = 25$ we get $\frac{1}{3}(2^25 + 2\cos 25\pi/3) = \frac{1}{3}(33554432 + 1) = 11,184,811$. For the final part, if we set $n = 24$ in (*) we get

$$\binom{24}{0} + \binom{24}{1} + \binom{24}{2} + \ldots + \binom{24}{24} = 2^{24}$$

Letting $n = 24$ in (**) and subtracting from (*) we get

$$\binom{24}{1} + \binom{24}{2} + \binom{24}{4} + \binom{24}{5} + \ldots + \binom{24}{23} = 2^{24} - \frac{1}{3}\left(2^{24} + 2\right)$$

and since $\binom{24}{1} = \binom{24}{23}$, $\binom{24}{2} = \binom{24}{22}$ etc, we arrive at

$$\binom{24}{2} + \binom{24}{5} + \cdots + \binom{24}{23} = \frac{1}{2}\left[2^{24} - \frac{1}{3}\left(2^{24} + 2\right)\right] = 5,592,405$$

(Q7.28) Using $z = i$ we have $(1+i)^n = (\sqrt{2})^n(\cos n\pi/4 + i\sin \pi/4) = 2^{n/2}(\cos n\pi/4 + i\sin n\pi/4)$. Looking at the expansion now we have the powers of i that are $\{i, -i, -i, 1\}$ and by comparing real and imaginary parts we get the required formulae.

Answers to Sec. 8.3, page 154

(Q8.1) we have $z_1 = \begin{pmatrix}1 & -1\\ 1 & 1\end{pmatrix}$, $z_2 = \begin{pmatrix}3 & -4\\ 4 & 3\end{pmatrix}$, $z_3 = \begin{pmatrix}1 & 1\\ -1 & 1\end{pmatrix}$. And

$$z_1{}^* z_2 = \begin{pmatrix}1 & -1\\ 1 & 1\end{pmatrix}^T \begin{pmatrix}3 & -4\\ 4 & 3\end{pmatrix} = \begin{pmatrix}7 & -1\\ 1 & 7\end{pmatrix} \qquad (1)$$

$$z_2 z_2{}^* = \begin{pmatrix}3 & -4\\ 4 & 3\end{pmatrix}\begin{pmatrix}3 & -4\\ 4 & 3\end{pmatrix}^T = \begin{pmatrix}25 & 0\\ 0 & 25\end{pmatrix} = 25I \qquad (2)$$

$$z_2 + z_1{}^* = \begin{pmatrix}3 & -4\\ 4 & 3\end{pmatrix} + \begin{pmatrix}1 & -1\\ 1 & 1\end{pmatrix}^T = \begin{pmatrix}4 & -3\\ 3 & 4\end{pmatrix} \qquad (3)$$

To get (4) $|z_1|$ we know that $|z_1|^2 = \begin{pmatrix}1 & -1\\1 & 1\end{pmatrix}\begin{pmatrix}1 & -1\\1 & 1\end{pmatrix}^T = \begin{pmatrix}2 & 0\\0 & 2\end{pmatrix} = 2I = (\sqrt{2}I)^2$ So $|z| = \sqrt{2}I$.
For (5) we have $z_1 z_2 = \begin{pmatrix}1 & -1\\1 & 1\end{pmatrix}\begin{pmatrix}3 & -4\\4 & 3\end{pmatrix} = \begin{pmatrix}-1 & 7\\7 & -1\end{pmatrix}$ and $|z_1 z_2|^2 = \begin{pmatrix}-1 & 7\\7 & -1\end{pmatrix}\begin{pmatrix}-1 & 7\\7 & -1\end{pmatrix}^T = 50I$. Hence $|z_1 z_2| = \sqrt{50}I$.
For (6) we have $z_1 + z_2 = \begin{pmatrix}1 & -1\\1 & 1\end{pmatrix} + \begin{pmatrix}3 & -4\\4 & 3\end{pmatrix} = \begin{pmatrix}4 & -5\\5 & 4\end{pmatrix}$ and

$$|z_1 + z_2|^2 = \begin{pmatrix}4 & -5\\5 & 4\end{pmatrix}\begin{pmatrix}4 & -5\\5 & 4\end{pmatrix}^T = 41I$$

Hence $|z_1 + z_2| = \sqrt{41}I$.
(Q8.2) $\sin 3i = \frac{e^{-3i^2} - e^{3i^2}}{2i} = i10.01787$ and $\cos 3i = \frac{e^{-3i^2} + e^{-3i^2}}{2} = 10.0676$. So $\sin^2 3i + \cos^2 3i = 0.9988 \approx 1$.
(Q8.3) See Proposition (8.6).
(Q8.4) Using the definition of $\cosh z = \frac{e^z + e^{-z}}{2}$ we have that $\cosh(-z) = \frac{e^{-z} + e^z}{2} = \cosh z$ and similalry for $\sinh(-z) = \frac{e^{-z} - e^z}{2} = -\sinh z$.
(Q8.5) Using the definitions of $\cosh z = \frac{e^z + e^{-z}}{2}$ and $\sinh z = \frac{e^z - e^{-z}}{2}$, the result follows.
(Q8.6) Letting $z = x + iy$ we get $\cos z = \cos(x + iy) = \cos x \cos iy - \sin x \sin iy = \cos x \cosh y - \sinh y \sin x$. Taking the modulus of

$$\begin{aligned}|\cos z|^2 &= \cos^2 x \cosh^2 y + \sinh^2 \sin^2 x = \cos^2 \cosh^2 y + \sinh^2 y(1 - \sin^2 x)\\ &= \cos^2 x(\cosh^2 y - \sinh^2 y) + \sinh^2 y = \cos^2 x + \sinh^2 y \Rightarrow |\cos z| = \sqrt{\cos^2 x + \sinh^2 y}\end{aligned}$$

and similarly for $|\sin z|$. For $\sin z = 0$ we also have $|\sin z| = 0 \Rightarrow (\sin x = 0 \wedge \sinh y = 0)$. $\sinh y = 0 \Rightarrow y = 0$ and $\sin x = 0 \Rightarrow x = k\pi$ for $k \in \mathbb{Z}$. These are the same zeros as the real sine. For $\cos z = 0$ we also have $|\cos z| = 0 \Rightarrow (\cos x = 0 \wedge \sinh y = 0)$. These are the the same zeros as the real cosine.
(Q8.7) $\mathrm{Ln}(-5) = \ln|5| + i\pi$ and $\mathrm{Ln}(1 - i) = \ln|1 - i| + i\pi = \ln\sqrt{2} + i\pi$.
(Q8.8) $\mathrm{Ln}(-i) = \ln|-i| + i\,\mathrm{Arg}(-i) = 0 + i(-\pi/2) = -\pi/2$. If instead we use $\mathrm{Ln}(-i) = \mathrm{Ln}(-1) + \mathrm{Ln}(i) = i\pi + \mathrm{Ln}(i) = i\pi + i\pi/2 = 3/2i\pi$. And this clearly means that $\mathrm{Ln}(z_1 z_2) \neq \mathrm{Ln}\, z_1 + \mathrm{Ln}\, z_2$. This is a consequence of the multivariate nature of the complex logarithm.
(Q8.9) Let $w = \arccos z$ then $\cos w = \frac{e^{iw} + e^{-iw}}{2} = z \Rightarrow e^{2iw} - 2ze^{iw} + 1 = 0$. This is a quadratic in e^{iw} and the roots are $e^{iw} = z + i\sqrt{1 - z^2}$. We do not need the $\pm$ as the square root is a multivalued anyway. So, $iw = \ln(z + i\sqrt{1 - z^2}) \Rightarrow w = -i\ln(z + i\sqrt{1 - z^2})$. Similarly, for $\arcsin z = -i\ln(iz + \sqrt{i - z^2})$. Adding them we get

$$\begin{aligned}\arccos z + \arcsin z &= -i\left[\ln(z + i\sqrt{1 - z^2} + \ln(iz + \sqrt{i - z^2})\right]\\ &= -i\ln\left[(z + i\sqrt{1 - z^2})(iz + \sqrt{i - z^2})\right]\\ &= -i\ln\left[iz^2 + z\sqrt{1 - z^2} - z\sqrt{1 - z^2} + i(1 - z^2)\right]\\ &= -i\ln i = -i(i\frac{\pi}{2} + 2ik\pi) = \frac{\pi}{2} + 2k\pi\end{aligned}$$

(Q8.10) Let $w = \arctan z \Rightarrow \tan w = z$. So $z = \frac{e^{iw} - e^{-iw}}{i(e^{iw} + e^{iw})}$. Solving for $e^{2iw} = \frac{i-z}{i+z}$, hence $w = \arctan z = \frac{1}{2i} \ln \frac{i-z}{i+z}$. Similarly for $w = \operatorname{arccot} z$. For (iii) we have

$$\arctan 1/z = \frac{1}{2i} \ln \frac{i - 1/z}{i + 1/z} = \frac{1}{2i} \ln \frac{iz - 1}{iz + 1} = \frac{1}{2i} \ln \frac{(z+i)i}{(z-i)i} = \frac{1}{2i} \ln \frac{z+i}{z-i} = \operatorname{arccot} z$$

Finally, adding the first two we get

$$\arctan z + \operatorname{arccot} z = \frac{1}{2i} \left[\ln \frac{i-z}{i+z} + \ln \frac{i+z}{z-i} \right] = \frac{1}{2i} \left[\ln \frac{-(z^2+1)}{z^2+1} \right] = \frac{1}{2i} \ln(-1) =$$
$$\frac{1}{2i} \left[i(\pi + 2k\pi) \right] = (2k+1)\frac{\pi}{2}$$

(Q8.11) It is clear from the definition that

$$\cosh(z + 2ki\pi) = \frac{e^{z+2ik\pi} + e^{-(z+2ki\pi)}}{2} = \cosh z$$

as $e^{\pm 2ki\pi} = 1$. Similarly for $\sinh(z + 2ki\pi) = \sinh z$. Finally

$$\cosh = \frac{e^{z+i\pi/2} + e^{-(z+i\pi/2)}}{2} = \frac{ie^{z} - ie^{-z}}{2} = i \sinh z$$

since $e^{i\pi/2} = i$ and $e^{-i\pi/2} = -i$. Similarly for $\sinh\left(z + i\frac{\pi}{2}\right) = i \cosh z$.

B. Useful Identities

Quadratic Vieta: If $ax^2 + bx + c = 0$ with $a \neq 0$, then if the roots are α and β we have

$$\alpha + \beta = \frac{-b}{a} \tag{B.1}$$

$$\alpha\beta = \frac{c}{a} \tag{B.2}$$

Cubic Vieta: If $f(x) = ax^3 + bx^2 + cx + d = 0$ then if the roots are α, β and γ we have Vieta's relations for the cubic

$$\alpha + \beta + \gamma = -\frac{b}{a} \tag{B.3}$$

$$\alpha\beta + \beta\gamma + \gamma\alpha = \frac{c}{a} \tag{B.4}$$

$$\alpha\beta\gamma = -\frac{d}{a} \tag{B.5}$$

Binomial Expansion: I list the different forms that one uses the binomial expansion. Remember

$$\binom{n}{k} = {}^nC_k = \frac{n!}{k!(n-k)!} = \frac{n(n-1)(n-2)...(n-(r-1))}{r!}$$

$$(a+b)^n = \binom{n}{n}a^n + \binom{n}{1}a^{n-1}b + \binom{n}{2}a^{n-2}b^2 + ... + \binom{n}{n-1}ab^{n-1} + \binom{n}{n}b^n \tag{B.6}$$

$$(a+b)^n = {}^nC_na^n + {}^nC_1a^{n-1}b + ... + {}^nC_{n-1}ab^{n-1} + {}^nC_nb^n \tag{B.7}$$

$$(a+b)^n = a^n + na^{n-1}b + \frac{n(n-1)}{2!}a^{n-2}b^2 + ... + b^n \tag{B.8}$$

$$(1+x)^n = 1 + nx + \frac{n(n-1)}{2!}x^2 + ... + x^n \tag{B.9}$$

Cardano's-Tartaglia-Del Fero Cubic: For the depressed cubic $x^3 = px + q$, the solution was first given by Del-Ferro, who passed it on to Tartaglia who in turn confided it to Cardano. It was finally published in 1545 by Cardano in his famous Ars Magna [2].

$$x = \sqrt[3]{\frac{q}{2} + \sqrt[2]{\frac{q^2}{4} - \frac{p^3}{27}}} + \sqrt[3]{\frac{q}{2} - \sqrt[2]{\frac{q^2}{4} - \frac{p^3}{27}}} \tag{B.10}$$

Standard Trigonometric Values

θ-Deg	0°	30°	45°	60°	90°	Period
θ-Rad	0	$\frac{\pi}{6}$	$\frac{\pi}{4}$	$\frac{\pi}{3}$	$\frac{\pi}{2}$	
sin	0	$\frac{1}{2}$	$\frac{\sqrt{2}}{2}$	$\frac{\sqrt{3}}{2}$	1	2π
cos	1	$\frac{\sqrt{3}}{2}$	$\frac{\sqrt{2}}{2}$	$\frac{1}{2}$	0	2π
tan	0	$\frac{1}{\sqrt{3}}$	1	$\sqrt{3}$	Undefined	π
cot	Undefined	$\sqrt{3}$	1	$\frac{1}{\sqrt{3}}$	0	π

Pascal's Triangle

$n = 0$ 1

$n = 1$ 1 1

$n = 2$ 1 2 1

$n = 3$ 1 3 3 1

$n = 4$ 1 4 6 4 1

$n = 5$ 1 5 10 10 5 1

$n = 6$ 1 6 15 20 15 6 1

Alphabetical Index

Bibliography

For those who want to dig further on the fantastic complex numbers, I would recommend the book by Tristan & Needham [9]. A very concise but rather old book on complex numbers is by Ledermann [7]. For topics on geometry of complex numbers and advanced preparation for National mathematics competitions, I recommend the books of Andreescu and Andrica [1] and Hanhn [6]. Some older books that cover these topics but with an older mathematical language are Deaux [3] and Schwerdtfeger [11].

[1] Titu Andreescu and Dorin Andrica. *Complex Numbers from A to ...Z*. Birkhauser, 2006. ISBN: 10 0-8176-4326-5.

[2] Girolamo Cardano, T Richard Witmer, and Oystein Ore. *The rules of algebra: Ars Magna*. Vol. 685. Courier Corporation, 2007.

[3] Roland Deaux. *Introduction to the geometry of complex numbers*. Courier Corporation, 2013.

[4] René Descartes. *La géométrie de René Descartes*. Vol. 1. A. Hermann, 1886.

[5] Keith J Devlin. *Mathematics: The new golden age*. Columbia University Press, 1999.

[6] Liang-shin Hahn. *Complex numbers and geometry*. Vol. 1. Cambridge University Press, 1994.

[7] Walter Ledermann. *Complex Numbers*. Springer Science & Business Media, 2013.

[8] Paul J Nahin. *An imaginary tale*. Princeton University Press, 2010.

[9] Tristan Needham. *Visual Complex Analysis*. A wonderfull introduction to Complex numbers through geometry. Clarendon Press, Apr. 1998. ISBN: 978-01-9853-446-4.

[10] G Osborn. "109. [D. 6. d.] Mnemonic for hyperbolic formulae". In: *Math. Gaz.* 2 (1902), p. 189.

[11] Hans Schwerdtfeger. *Geometry of complex numbers: circle geometry, Moebius transformation, non-euclidean geometry*. Courier Corporation, 1979.

[12] Nathan Sidoli and J Lennart Berggren. "The Arabic version of Ptolemy's Planisphere or Flattening the Surface of the Sphere: text, translation, commentary". In: *Sciamvs* 8 (2007), p. 37.

[13] François Viète. *In artem analyticam isagoge*. 1591.